The Gathering of Vidyadharas

Text and Commentaries on the Rigdzin Düpa

Jigme Lingpa, Khenpo Chemchok,

Khangsar Tenpe Wangchuk,

Patrul Rinpoche, Jamgön Kongtrul Lödro Tayé

TRANSLATED BY
Gyurmé Avertin

SNOW LION
BOULDER
2017

Snow Lion
An imprint of Shambhala Publications, Inc.
4720 Walnut Street
Boulder, Colorado 80301
www.shambhala.com

9 8 7 6 5 4 3 2 1

First Edition
Printed in the United States of America

⊛ This edition is printed on acid-free paper that meets the American National Standards Institute z39.48 Standard.
♻ This book is printed on 30% postconsumer recycled paper.
For more information please visit www.shambhala.com.

Distributed in the United States by Penguin Random House LLC and in Canada by Random House of Canada Ltd

Library of Congress Cataloging-in-Publication Data
Names: 'Jigs-med-gling-pa Rang-byung-rdo-rje, 1729 or 1730–1798. |
O-rgyan-'jigs-med-chos-kyi-dbang-po, Dpal-sprul, 1808–1887.
Title: The gathering of vidyadharas: text and commentaries on the Rigdzin Düpa / Jigme Lingpa, Patrul Rinpoche, Khenpo Chemchok; Khangsar Tenpe Wangchuk, Jamgön Kongtrul Lödro Tayé Translated by Gyurmé Avertin.
Description: First edition. | Boulder: Snow Lion, 2017. | Includes bibliographical references and index. | Includes translations from Tibetan.
Identifiers: LCCN 2016030189 | ISBN 9781611803617 (paperback: alk. paper)
Subjects: LCSH: Spiritual life—Rnying-ma-pa (Sect) | Rnying-ma-pa (Sect)—Rituals. |
BISAC: RELIGION / Buddhism / Tibetan. | RELIGION / Buddhism / Rituals & Practice.
Classification: LCC BQ7662.6 .G38 2017 | DDC 294.3/444—dc23
LC record available at https://lccn.loc.gov/2016030189

CONTENTS

FOREWORD

This volume enshrines a number of sacred treatises on Rigdzin Düpa, the Gathering of Vidyadharas. They reveal the profound views, powerful meditations, sacred conduct, and ultimate goals of the Vajrayana teachings of Tibetan Buddhism.

The Rigdzin Düpa is one of the important tantric sadhanas—including both meditation and ritual manuals—that integrates the heart essences of both the inner yogas and Dzogchen. It is one of the three roots—the three main tantric sadhanas—of the Longchen Nyingtik tradition.

The Rigdzin Düpa was initially transmitted by Guru Padmasambhava to King Trisong Detsen, Khandro Yeshe Tsogyal, and Lochen Vairochana in Tibet at Samyé Monastery in the ninth century. Guru Rinpoche then concealed it as a *ter*[1]—a mystically concealed treasure—through his enlightened power. In 1760, Rigdzin Jigme Lingpa (1729–1798), an incarnation of King Trisong Detsen, and a most renowned author, ter revealer, and fully accomplished adept, discovered the Rigdzin Düpa as a ter teaching.

Jigme Lingpa writes[2] that this text is entitled Rigdzin Düpa, the Gathering of Vidyadharas, because all the deities of the six yogas and the vidyadharas—fully accomplished adepts—of India and Tibet are present in it as guests.

Two important commentaries on the Rigdzin Düpa are offered in this volume. (1) *The Words of the Vidyadhara*[3] is a detailed commentary of the Rigdzin Düpa written by Kyala Khenpo, Chemchok Thonduptsal (1893–1957). Since the Rigdzin Düpa was first discovered as a ter, its sacred instructions were passed down through an unbroken master-disciple oral-transmission lineage. *The Words of the Vidyadhara* became the first detailed instructions on the Rigdzin Düpa in written form.

Kyala Khenpo was one of the four main khenpos of the renowned Dodrupchen Monastery in Golok, eastern Tibet. From the ages of six through eighteen, I had the privilege of having him as my teacher and parent without separation. Although I haven't got a trace of his extraordinary qualities in me, the inspirations that I enjoyed from his amazing life and love still sustain me through the power of blessed memories. What I saw outwardly of him was an utmost humble and ascetic monk. He never ate food after lunch, was never seen sleeping lying down, never accepted any offerings of faith (*kor*) for his own use, was always as easy to be with as a child, and as fully caring for many as a parent. Despite being a brilliant scholar of both sutras and tantras and one of the four main khenpos of a renowned monastic institution, he never showed any ego. He remained in strict seclusion doing meditations on the Rigdzin Düpa and other liturgies for over nine years. Many witnessed his mystical attainments. But far from boasting about them, he kept his accomplishments strictly private. With smiles of true joy and eyes of heartfelt love, he kept sharing the teachings of what he enjoyed most until the last hours of his life—a true, living bodhisattva. *The Words of the Vidyadhara* was one of his Tibetan writings that escaped with me from Tibet and is now in your hands in its English incarnation.

(2) *The Light of the Sun and the Moon*[4] is a shorter and less dense commentary of the Rigdzin Düpa, written by Tulku Tenpe Wangchuk (1938–2014) of Khangsar Monastery in Golok. He was a learned author, a ter discoverer, and a great propagator of Dharma. Since the doors for teaching Dharma reopened in Tibet in the early 1980s, he became one of those dynamic teachers who dedicated his life to resurrecting the pure Dharma of learning and realization widely and deeply for over three decades.

The view and meditation of the Rigdzin Düpa are centered on training in the development (*kyerim*) and the perfection (*dzogrim*) stages integrated with the Great Perfection (Dzogchen). The steps are as follows:

After being introduced to the true nature of our own mind, we dissolve all our concepts into that great primordial nature that is the sky-like awareness (*rigpa*), free from fixation.

From this openness nature, like the sun and its rays, we let the mandala of Rigdzin Düpa arise as the natural radiance (*rang dang*) of the awareness—through the four fully awakening (*ngon chang*) meditations on (a) the emptiness essence, (b) the seed syllables of the deities, (c) the forms of the deities, and (d) the vajra syllables at the sacred centers of the deities.

We then meditate on approaching (*nyenpa*)[5] the deity by seeing, hearing, and feeling all as his or her divine forms, sounds, and dharmakaya. By offering blissful rays of light from the garland of mantras, we please all of the vidyadharas and accumulate merit. In return, we receive rays of light from them and enjoy their wisdom blessings. Then we send blessing lights to purify all beings and the world, transforming them into the vidyadhara mandala.

We next meditate on realizing the accomplishments (*drubpa*)[6] by focusing on the revolving chain of the mantra-garland of great bliss that merges all into wisdom—the union of bliss and emptiness.

Finally, we dissolve[7] the whole mandala of the Rigdzin Düpa into the great wisdom free from concepts, the state of indivisibility of awareness and emptiness. We remain in it, as it is.

There are different ways to classify the Rigdzin Düpa—whether as Anuyoga or as Anuyoga of Atiyoga. Jigme Lingpa says,[8] "[The Rigdzin Düpa] mandala is not developed through the three samadhis as in the case of the lower yoga (i.e., Mahayoga). Rather, it is taught that all are enlightened from their ultimate sphere, as taught in Anuyoga."

Tulku Tenpe Wangchuk also says,[9] "[In the Rigdzin Düpa] you focus on the ultimate nature—the indivisibility of the ultimate sphere and wisdom—as you do in Anuyoga."

Kyala Khenpo agrees that the Rigdzin Düpa is affiliated with Anuyoga, just as a similar liturgy, the Yumka Dechen Gyalmo, is. However, since his teacher Lushul Khenpo classified Yumka as an Anuyoga of Atiyoga practice, by dividing each of the three inner yogas into three, Kyala Khenpo also classified Rigdzin Düpa as an Anuyoga practice—but the Anuyoga division of Atiyoga.

As Lushul Khenpo writes[10] about Yumka, "The way of developing (the mandala) is similar to the arising of appearances-of-the-basis from the basis so, I think, it is proper to classify Yumka as an Anuyoga of Atiyoga."

Kyala Khenpo explains,[11] "In the Rigdzin Düpa, you develop the mandala through the four fully awakening (*ngon chang*) meditations, as is done in Anuyoga. That is why it is said that the Rigdzin Düpa belongs to Anuyoga. However, the way of developing the Rigdzin Düpa mandala is actually similar to Atiyoga, as it is in the case of Yumka."

Practicing Rigdzin Düpa according to the right class of tantra is important. However, just as important is practicing it according to our ability. When Khenpo Ngawang Palzang was a young student, his master Nyoshul Lungtok told him,[12] "[In the Rigdzin Düpa] you meditate on the appearances, i.e., the power (*tsal nang*), of the indivisibility of the ultimate sphere (*ying*) and wisdom (*yeshe*) as the deities." He added, "At this time, however, it is better for you to practice the Rigdzin Düpa through the three samadhis as taught in Mahayoga." Here, Master Lungtok saw[13] that Khenpo

Ngawang already had the realization of the true nature of his mind, a must for practicing Rigdzin Düpa as an Atiyoga practice. However, to make certain that Khenpo's realization would fully mature and that the pure transmission tradition would be preserved intact, he advised Khenpo to practice the Rigdzin Düpa according to Mahayoga for the time being.

Later, at the time of his Yumka transmission, the master told Khenpo again,[14] "As Yumka belongs to Atiyoga, you are supposed to develop the mandala through instant recollection (*kéchik drendzog*). But you can't do that yet, as you haven't received the actual instructions [of Atiyoga]." Here, Master Lungtok made it clear that the Rigdzin Düpa could be practiced as any of the three inner yogas, depending on one's level.

So how should readers practice the Rigdzin Düpa? Ideally, as Kyala Khenpo points out:[15] "We should first get the introduction to the luminous awareness. Then we recognize that our own awareness and the wisdom of the guru are indivisible. Then, contemplating in that awareness, we train on allowing the awareness itself to arise as the mandala of the Rigdzin Düpa."

As a whole, eminent Rigdzin Düpa masters agree that the ultimate key to this practice is to realize the awareness, the true nature of mind. We then train in the stages of the sadhana as the power, the radiance, of the awareness itself. That combination enables us to awaken the realization of the awareness, accomplish the two stages swiftly, and attain the union of Buddha wisdom and Buddha bodies as the result.

But what if we haven't had any glimpses of wisdom, let alone awakened our true nature? In this case, we should practice Rigdzin Düpa through devotion and trust[16] in the Gathering of Vidyadharas. Then the powers of (a) our own devotional mind, (b) the unconditional love, omniscient wisdom, and the boundless blessing power of the Gathering of Vidyadharas, and (c) the merit and wisdom accumulations of our meditation exercises will lead us to glimpse our true nature before long. Incidentally, until this happens, any empowerment that we receive of Rigdzin Düpa would simply be a blessing, rather than an awakening.

It is important to note that even if we have had some glimpses of realization, unless we have stabilized them through meditation, our experiences could fade away like beautiful rainbows into the atmosphere. That is why his teacher was extra careful about not even hinting to Khenpo Ngawang prematurely that his experiences were the real thing, even though he had already glimpsed the true nature of reality.[17] The teacher let Khenpo pursue more general meditations for awhile to safeguard the realizations that

Khenpo already had and to enable him to progress towards the goal naturally, without falling into any conceptual traps. Only after going through more trainings, did Khenpo formally receive the introduction to and affirmation of the true nature of mind, eventually becoming the famed Dzogchen master.[18]

The Gathering of Vidyadharas reveals the elaborate trainings of skillful means taught in Vajrayana, as they are. It awakens the profound innate nature of Dzogchen, as it is. Merely enshrining this sacred volume on our altar with respect will ensure its blessings for now and accomplishments for later.

The Gathering of Vidyadharas, the lineage masters, and the Dharma protectors, I beseech you with deep devotion to forgive all faults that have caused these sacred teachings to be brought before those who are not open to them. I pray that all devotees and meditators may enjoy your blessings and awaken their innate awareness, buddhahood.

Tulku Thondup, The Buddhayana Foundation

ACKNOWLEDGMENTS

The Casket of Siddhis was translated by Adam Pearcey with thanks to Ringu Tulku Rinpoche, Khentrul Lodrö Tayé, Lama Chökyi Nyima, and Patrick Gaffney. The other texts have been translated by Gyurmé Avertin with thanks to Gonpo Tulku, Tulku Thondup, Alak Zenkar Rinpoche, Khenpo Namdrol, Orgyen Tobgyal Rinpoche, and Khenpo Yeshe Dorje, who generously shared their knowledge of Vajrayana practice and rituals, as well as Özer Palzang, Dodrupchen Rinpoche's thangka master, for help with the section on the mandala. Thank you also to Ane Tsondu, Ane Sangye Chozom, Cécile Boquin, Aaron Coote, Pete Fry, Ian Ives, Jane Packham, Adam Pearcey, Sebastien Reggiany, Erric Solomon, Jeremy Tattersall, and many others for various forms of assistance.

INTRODUCTION

The great Buddhist masters of the past, who were experts at identifying and presenting clearly every practical aspect of the path, even the most obvious ones, advised authors before writing any text to reflect on four elements: the content of the intended book, the purpose of writing about it, its ultimate purpose, and the connection between these different elements. The "connection" means that the content must achieve the purpose, which in turn must lead toward the ultimate purpose. It seems fairly obvious, but when we apply these four principles to publications produced these days, we may find that some texts serve no purpose.

Let's be clear, the "ultimate purpose" of any Buddhist teaching is enlightenment. So if we are not interested in buddhahood, or if we think that it is a utopia that can never be attained, we might as well contentedly shelve this book, and all Dharma books as it were.

Concerning the "content" of this book, it presents explanations on how to do the inner lama practice of the Longchen Nyingtik cycle, a sadhana called the Gathering of Vidyadharas (Rigdzin Düpa in Tibetan). You'll find here translations of most of the existing written instructions on the Rigdzin Düpa.

The "purpose" of the book is to help people know how to practice the Rigdzin Düpa, and thereby derive the benefits that this practice was designed to provide. Practitioners who apply these instructions as best as they can will mature their minds, and will be able to have a direct experience of the ultimate nature and sustain this experience, and thereby reach awakening—the "connections."

The Nyingma school is best known in the West for its Dzogchen teachings. But its approach actually follows nine *yanas*, which are graduated steps toward the "summit of all yanas," the Great Perfection, or Dzogchen. Present day teachers of this tradition often marvel at seeing people trying to jump directly to the top without using the stairs of the *ngöndro*, the preliminary practices, and of Vajrayana in general. Khangsar Tenpe Wangchuk was the most renowned Dzogchen master in the Golok region of eastern Tibet toward the end of his life, and a great bodhisattva according to Khenpo Jigme Phüntsok; everyone with an interest in these teachings would go to him. But he would never give any Dzogchen teachings unless the person, whoever they were, had at least completed the "fivefold one hundred thousand ngöndro accumulations."

The Longchen Nyingtik cycle provides a complete path to enlightenment. People following it will first train their minds in the ngöndro or preliminary practices. These include the outer preliminaries—the four thoughts that turn the mind toward the Dharma—and then the inner preliminaries, which involve the "fivefold one hundred thousand accumulations": refuge, bodhichitta, Vajrasattva, mandala offering, and guru yoga. It is said that it is very beneficial to repeat these sets of accumulations several times in order to purify obscurations and accumulate merit, in other words, to mature one's mind to be able to *actually* practice Dzogchen.

Next the practitioner practices the three roots (*lama, yidam, dakini*) in closed retreat—the Rigdzin Düpa is the first of these three, the lama practice. After the practitioner engages in the *tsalung* practices (these include "inner heat" practices, or *tummo*, using one's body alone, and union practices, using both one's own and someone else's body together). Once these meditations have somewhat matured the practitioner's mind, he or she will engage with the Dzogchen practices of *trekchö* and *tögal*, which, if practiced properly, can lead to enlightenment in this life or in the *bardo*.

The three roots practices involve the practice of *kyerim* ("generation phase" or "creation meditation"). This practice is attuned to the way in which beings are born in samsara. It purifies the habitual tendencies associated with the four types of birth through meditation on ordinary appearances as deities, sounds as mantras, and thoughts as wisdom.

The three roots are the practices of the lama, the root of blessings; yidam, the root of accomplishments; and dakini, the root of activities. The first one invokes the lama who is the root or source of all blessings. Then, one must practice the yidam to gain accomplishments, the actual goal of practice. The understanding is that no realization will come without the blessings of the lama; our relation to the lama is the heart of Vajrayana practice. But having received blessings, we need to accomplish the purpose of practice, which is to attain the supreme accomplishment or enlightenment. For that we practice the yidam; it is also said that to see the yidam as indivisible from the lama makes the practice more powerful. Then once we have gained the accomplishments and are enlightened, we must perform the enlightened activities for sentient beings, which we do with the help of the dakinis and the Dharma protectors (*dharmapalas*).

The sequence can also be different. Within the oral tradition of the Longchen Nyingtik, it is advised to do the dakini practice right after the lama practice, and before the yidam. This is because the dakini Yeshe Tsogyal has a strong connection with the lama Guru Rinpoche, Padmasambhava, making this way of practicing very potent.

There are several lama and dakini practices in the Longchen Nyingtik.[1] Ideally the practitioners who follow this path would do all these sadhanas before receiving Dzogchen teachings, and continue doing them afterward to support his or her practice. Typically, in practice, practitioners are expected to have done lama Rigdzin Düpa, yidam Palchen Düpa, and dakini Yumka Dechen Gyalmo before receiving Dzogchen instructions. Then they would continue to accumulate the other sadhanas of the cycle while practicing the different stages of Dzogchen.

We need to accomplish all these sadhanas to support our Dzogchen meditation. "Doing the practice" or "accumulating the sadhana" means doing the number of recitations or spending the amount of time indicated in the retreat manuals for each practice, or practicing until there are signs of realization. To recite a given number of mantras might seem very goal oriented, an approach that does not marry very well with dharma practice. Indeed, ideally we would practice until signs of realization appear. But that is not always very realistic. As human beings we are naturally more or less goal oriented, so instructions on time and number of recitations have been given to help hurried practitioners.

Kyerim practice alone does not take practitioners all the way to enlightenment, as they must also rely also on *dzogrim*, whether tsalung practices of dzogrim, or the "great dzogrim," Dzogchen. The Longchen Nyingtik emphasizes the Dzogchen, as it is a powerful, swift path. However, in the Longchen Nyingtik, as in other *terma* cycles, some degree of tsalung practice is often advised to be an important preparation to practicing Dzogchen. Actually, as Tulku Thondup explains clearly in his foreword to this book, the Longchen Nyingtik sadhanas are practices that unite kyerim and dzogrim, which together can lead directly to enlightenment. This combination is referred to as the Maha-Ati or practices integrating Mahayoga and Dzogchen.[2] Mipham Rinpoche clarifies,

The *Tantra of the Secret Essence* is the ati of mahā, which is the same as the mahā of ati in terms of the three divisions of the great perfection. In this way, the secret great perfection can be explained in three ways: (1) by revealing indivisible development and completion as the self-displayed maṇḍala of mind and wisdom; (2) through pointing out how mind in essence is the nature of primordial enlightenment, independent of development and completion; and (3) by showing that wisdom is the nature of enlightenment as the essence of self-display. Here the explanation will be given in terms of the first of these three.[3]

Sadhanas such as the Rigdzin Düpa, which are practiced according to the teachings of the *Tantra of the Secret Essence* (*Guhyagarbha Tantra*), correspond to the first category that Mipham Rinpoche mentions, while the second category is trekchö, and the third is tögal.

As Khenpo Chemchok says (p. 69),

To awaken the wisdom of the path and develop it, it is essential to meditate according to the instructions given in *The Scroll of the Oral Lineage* [i.e. tsalung practices], and on tögal.

Masters of the Nyingma tradition explain that Dzogchen teachings certainly are extremely beneficial, yet they are also extremely difficult to practice genuinely. Why isn't Dzogchen easy? Because practitioners need "merit." In Dzogchen you are told, "Your mind is the Buddha." If you have enough merit, when you hear this statement, it is enough to liberate you— which is what happened when Shri Singha gave this instruction to Guru Rinpoche. He said, "Your mind is the Buddha!" And that was it! Guru Rinpoche was liberated. Dilgo Khyentse Rinpoche used to say that if you feed a baby adult food, the baby won't be able to digest it. Similarly, if you receive Dzogchen teachings but do not have enough merit, you will not be able to digest or retain them. That is why everyone who is genuine about following this path focuses on accumulating merit. Fortunately, the teachings provide many skillful methods for that. Training in relative bodhichitta is very important to accumulating merit through bringing both bodhichitta of aspiration and bodhichitta in action together. There is also the approach of the Secret Mantra Vajrayana, which involves "kyerim."

KYERIM PRINCIPLES

The principles of kyerim apply universally—they remain the same in most sadhana practices. Sadhanas are "guided contemplations." These practices involve recitations of sadhana texts and prayers. However, as we have just said, it is also important to meditate on the words that are being recited; just chanting the words is not useful. At the same time, we need to remember that the words are different for different practices: Rigdzin Düpa and a Vajrakilaya sadhana, for example, are different. So what you visualize will be different, yet the meaning underlying the words will always remain the same. So, if you consider that each and every word has a special significance and you focus intently upon each word as you practice while failing to apply the general principles of kyerim practice, then you will be, as the saying goes, like "a strutting crow who does not cover much ground." Generally speaking, once you have thoroughly understood a text such as the *Tantra of the Secret Essence*, you automatically come to know the crucial points of kyerim and dzogrim practice, and then it is no longer necessary to seek instruction on individual sadhanas.

As Tulku Thondup explained clearly in his foreword to this book, the Rigdzin Düpa sadhana can be practiced according to the level of the practitioner. Less experienced practitioners are generally advised to follow the Mahayoga approach of kyerim, which involves three aspects: the clarity of visualization, remembering the purity, and vajra confidence. First, the practitioner "sets the framework" of the three samadhis—the samadhi of suchness, the samadhi of universal manifestation, and the causal samadhi—to bring about the "clear visualization" of the deities. A clear visualization is said to be crucial to the practice. Even if beginners cannot visualize all the deities in the mandala, the palace, and so on, to visualize oneself as the main deity is an essential requirement. Having established a clear visualization, we must "remember the purity," bringing to mind the enlightened qualities that correspond to each feature of the visualization, or simply remembering the nature of mind. We also need to develop a feeling of "vajra confidence." As you practice, if you imagine that you and the deity are different, then you are not practicing Mahayoga. You cannot think, "At the moment we are different, but as I continue to practice, we will become the same." It won't work.

In addition, the Nyingma tradition includes specific instructions. One of the special Nyingma teachings about kyerim practice is the four nails that bind the life-force of the practice: the nail of all appearances as the deity, the nail of all sounds as mantra, the nail of emanation and reabsorption of rays of light to accomplish activities, and the nail of the unchanging wisdom-mind. Patrul Rinpoche gave an important explanation of the four nails in a text known as the *Melody of Brahma*. Khangsar Tenpe Wangchuk directly quotes most of the text in his Rigdzin Düpa commentary presented in this book.[4] These four nails should be brought to mind during each session of sadhana practice.

By perfecting the accumulation of merit, you purify obscurations. How you purify obscurations can be explained through the following example: Imagine you have a precious object that has been wrapped so well that you cannot see it. To be able to look at what is inside, you must first unwrap it. Finally, seeing the precious object is like seeing the mind. When you see the mind, you see the Buddha. When you see the Buddha, you automatically have all of the Buddha's qualities. This is what is called "seeing the nature of mind." As Orgyen Tobgyal says, "Once you've seen the nature of mind, there is nothing else to do. But until you've seen it, just talking about it won't bring it out." To see it, we need to do practices such as the Rigdzin Düpa, as Tulku Thondup illustrated with Khenpo Ngawang Palzang.

LONGCHEN NYINGTIK

The Longchen Nyingtik, "The Vast Expanse Heart Essence," is a "Heart Essence" (Nyingtik) cycle, the most profound Dzogchen teachings. Dzogchen teachings are divided into three categories: Mind, Expanse, and Pith-Instruction sections. The highest teachings, those of the Pith-Instruction section, are also divided into four categories: the outer, inner, secret, and innermost cycles. The innermost category is known as the "Heart Essence" section. As Tulku Thondup explains, "All these cycles are similar in being teachings on the primordially pure nature (*kadag*), which is called 'cutting through' (*trekchö*) all the grasping. However, the Innermost Esoteric Cycle focuses on the trainings of spontaneous perfection of appearances (*lhun-drup*), which is called the 'direct approach' (*tögal*)."[5] This means that the most important feature of the Longchen Nyingtik is tögal practice.

The Pith-Instruction teachings are composed of numerous tantras, of which nineteen constitute the root texts of this tradition. There are many instructional teachings (*mengak*), which are elucidated and condensed into two major Heart Essence teachings: the Vima Nyingtik brought to Tibet by Vimalamitra, and the Khandro Nyingtik brought to Tibet by Guru Padmsamabhava. In addition to the original tantras and pith-instructions translated into Tibetan, many other Nyingtik teachings were brought to Tibet through Vimalamitra, Guru Rinpoche, and Vairochana. The Longchen Nyingtik is the essence of the two great Nyingtik teachings, Vima Nyingtik and Khandro Nyingtik.

The Longchen Nyingtik is a mind terma cycle of teachings that was discovered by Jigme Lingpa. Dilgo Khyentse Rinpoche explained,

> Mind treasures arise in the following way: In many instances, after bestowing an empowerment or giving a teaching, Padmasambhava made the prayer, 'In the future, may this treasure arise in the mind of such and such tertön.' While doing so, he would focus his prayers and blessings on the tertön, usually an incarnation of one of his disciples. When, due to Guru Rinpoche's blessings, the time comes, both the words and the meaning of the treasure arise clearly in the tertön's mind. The tertön can then write these down without having to think.[6]

The Longchen Nyingtik contains a root tantra (*Tantra of the Root Expanse of Samantabhadra*), a subsequent tantra (*Subsequent Tantra of Dzogchen Instruction*), teachings (*Experiencing the Enlightened Mind of Samantabhadra*), and instructions (*Distinguishing the Three Essential Points of the Great Perfection* and *Vajra Verses on the Natural State*), as well as their commentaries (*Yeshe Lama*, with its supporting texts).[7] It also contains sadhanas: male vidyadhara practices, both peaceful (outer: Guru Yoga; inner: Rigdzin Düpa; secret: Duk-ngal Rangdrol; innermost secret: Ladrup Tiklé Gyachen) and wrathful (blue: Palchen Düpa; red: Takhyung Barwa); and female vidyadhara practices, both peaceful (root: Yumka Dechen Gyalmo) and wrathful (secret: Sengé Dongchen).

PADMASAMBHAVA

The Rigdzin Düpa is a lama practice; with this sadhana you become Guru Padmasambhava indivisible from your own root teacher. Guru Rinpoche, the "Precious Master" is the tantric master who brought the Buddha's teachings to Tibet. Invited by King Trisong Detsen, on the advice of the great Indian scholar Shantarakshita, Padmasambhava traveled the length and breadth of the country, teaching and practicing, taming the forces that were inhibiting the Buddhadharma, and infusing his blessing into the whole landscape of Tibet and the Himalayas. But he is not an ordinary person like us who came into existence as the result of our karma. Kyabje Dilgo Khyentse Rinpoche explains, "Guru Rinpoche is the union of all the buddhas and bodhisattvas who dwell in the countless buddha-fields throughout the ten directions. He is the gathering of all their excellent qualities, ability, and power to benefit beings. In this universe, he displayed an absolute and unchallengeable mastery of all the techniques and accomplishments of the Secret Mantrayāna."[8] As for Padmasambhava's life story, he says, "Guru Padmasambhava, glorious Master of Oddiyana and king of the Dharma, is the single embodiment of the activity of the victorious ones throughout the three times. According to the ways in which sentient beings perceive reality, there exists an inconceivable number of life stories of the three mysteries of his body, speech, and mind."[9]

JIGME LINGPA

Jigme Lingpa was born in 1729 in Yarlung in Central Tibet. He was still young when he went to Palri Monastery where he studied the Dharma. At twenty-eight he entered a three-year retreat at the monastery, and on a winter night of the first year he received the Longchen Nyingtik terma. Tulku Thondup writes,

> In the evening of the twenty-fifth day of the tenth month of the Fire Ox year of the thirteenth Rabjung cycle (1757), he went to bed with an unbearable devotion to Guru Rinpoche in his heart; a stream of tears of sadness continuously wet his face because he was not in Guru Rinpoche's presence, and unceasing words of prayers kept singing in his breath. He remained in the depth of that meditation experience of clear luminosity ('Od gSal Gyi sNang Ba) for a long time. While being absorbed in that luminous clarity, he experienced flying a long distance through the sky while riding a white lion. He finally reached a circular path, which he thought to be the circumambulation path of Charung Khashor, now known as Bodhnath Stūpa, an important Buddhist monument of giant structure in Nepal.[10]

In this vision, the wisdom dakini gave Jigme Lingpa a casket containing five yellow scrolls and seven crystal beads. One of the scrolls contained the prophetic guide to the Longchen Nyingtik. At the instruction of a dakini, he ate the yellow scrolls and crystal beads, and all the words and meaning of the Longchen Nyingtik terma were awakened in his mind. Jigme Lingpa kept this terma secret for years, and he did not even transcribe the terma until he entered another retreat in which he had a series of visions of Longchen Rabjam (also known as Longchenpa). Tulku Thondup explains,

> In the earth-hare year (1759) he started another three-year retreat, at Chim phu near Samyé monastery. During that retreat, because he was inspired by three successive pure visions of Kun khyen Long chen Rab jam (1308–1363), and was urged by repeated requests of dākinis, he transcribed his Terma as the cycle of Long chen nying thig. On the tenth day of the sixth month (monkey month) of the monkey year (1764) he made his Terma public for the first time by conferring the transmission of empowerment and the instructions upon fifteen disciples.[11]

After this second three-year retreat he settled at Tsering Jong, a hermitage he established in Chongye. He spent the remainder of his life practicing, teaching, and accomplishing other activities for the Dharma, such as restoring monasteries and publishing the *Collection of Nyingma Tantras* (*Nyingma Gyubum*) with the help of one of his main sponsors, the queen of Dergé. He passed away in 1798 at Tsering Jong. His main incarnations were Do Khyentse Yeshe Dorje, Jamyang Khyentse Wangpo, and Dza Patrul Rinpoche.

During his second three-year retreat Rigdzin Jigme Lingpa received the transmission of the Nyingtik teachings from Longchenpa. Longchenpa himself was a recipient of the lineage of both Vima Nyingtik and Khandro Nyingtik.[12] Longchenpa is the most influential Nyingma teacher of Dzogchen. He collected the Vima Nyingtik and Khandro Nyingtik instructions, together with his own clarifications, in the Nyingtik Yabshi collection. He also gave seminal teachings drawing chiefly from the Pith-Instruction tantras found in the collection called the "Seven Treasures."

LINEAGE

After Jigme Lingpa, the chief recipient of the Longchen Nyingtik cycle, the "custodian of the teaching" was the first Dodrupchen Rinpoche. A "chödak," or custodian of a terma cycle, is the master who is prophesied in the terma prophecy as the principal person who will uphold the tradition of the tertön by studying, teaching and practicing his or her terma teachings.[13] Tulku Thondup lists thirty-five chief disciples to whom Jigme Lingpa gave the Longchen Nyingtik.[14] This lineage of masters who practice these teachings ensures that they are faithfully transmitted from one generation to the next, in a way a book or a recording could not, as the teacher leads the student step-by-step through the practices based on his or her own experience.

Translated Texts

1. The first text is a prayer written by Jigme Lingpa invoking the great beings he has been in his past lives, and giving indication of his future life. At the beginning of a practice such as the Rigdzin Düpa, it is customary to invoke the blessings of the great masters in the lineage of this teaching to remove obstacles and to receive the blessings quickly.

2. Next is Jigme Lingpa's retreat instructions for the Longchen Nyingtik.[15] As is habitual for a retreat manual, the text is rather short (about ten pages): only the instructions specific to the particular practice are given, and there is hardly any mention of the more general points of practice that are expected to be known from the *Guhyagarbha Tantra* and other teachings.

3. It is followed by a short visualization instruction for the Rigdzin Düpa long-life practice, also written by Jigme Lingpa.

4. The fourth text contains a more detailed set of instructions that expands on the first retreat manual written by Jigme Lingpa. Khenpo Chemchok gathered the notes he took of teachings he received from his root teacher Lushul Khenpo Könchok Drönme on the Rigdzin Düpa, to give an exceptional presentation of the key points preserved in the oral lineage that make this practice so special. Khenpo Chemchok gives an explanation of the words of the practice, but he also explains how to actually practice the sadhana by presenting the general principles for this kind of practice.

He presents general points about retreat as well, which make it very useful for practitioners who stay on their first three roots retreat.

5. Khangsar Tenpe Wangchuk (also known as Tulku Tenpo) was a great master who passed away in 2014. This text is a transcript of oral teachings he gave on the Rigdzin Düpa. Rather than paraphrasing Khenpo Chemchok's commentary, Tulku Tenpo gives a presentation that borrows from Guru Rinpoche's *A Garland of Views*[16] and Patrul Rinpoche's *Melody of Brahma*[17] on the general principles that underlie the words of the text. Tulku Tenpo explains the words of the Rigdzin Düpa text like Khenpo Chemchok does, while adding a presentation of the way to practice each section of the sadhana from the Dzogchen perspective.

6. The sixth text presented in this book is Patrul Rinpoche's *drupchö* instructions. A drupchö is an elaborate Vajrayana practice that takes place over several days. As a result, the text gives clear instructions on the *chöpön* activities related to the Rigdzin Düpa.

7. The last text is Jamgön Kongtrul's empowerment text. In this short empowerment text, Jamgön Kongtrul expands on the original *Empowerment Conferring Majesty* and includes in one text all the prayers and practices that must be meditated upon to give the empowerment, making it easier for masters giving the empowerments.

This book also contains a translation of the Rigdzin Düpa sadhana itself, in Khangsar Tenpe Wangchuk's commentary, and a translation of the Melody of Brahma, interwoven within Khangsar Tenpe Wangchuk's commentary, that he quotes almost entirely.

AUTHORS

Patrul Rinpoche

Dza Patrul Rinpoche (1808–1887) was a direct incarnation of Jigme Lingpa, his speech emanation. Although he lived the life of a vagabond, he was one of the most illustrious spiritual teachers of the nineteenth century. His principal teacher was Jigme Gyalwe Nyugu, a great master who was one of the foremost students of Jigme Lingpa. Patrul Rinpoche received the teachings on the preliminary practices of the Longchen Nyingtik, as well as many other important transmissions, from Jigme Gyalwe Nyugu no less than twenty-five times. Occasionally, he would write a text of his own and these treatises were later collected into six volumes of his writings. Among them is the well-known *Words of My Perfect Teacher*.

Jamgön Kongtrul Lodrö Tayé

Jamgön Kongtrul the Great (1813–1899) was one of the most prominent teachers of the nineteenth century, who championed the Nonsectarian (Rimé) movement. He was a tertön, an accomplished master who spent years in retreat, and the author and compiler of more than a hundred volumes of teachings. In particular, he gathered in "The Five Great Treasures" the knowledge and experience of the many lineages of Buddhism in Tibet, a testimony to his deep respect for all the Buddhist teachings. He was recognized by all schools of Buddhism in Tibet as one of the greatest masters.

He was born in the hidden valley of Rong-gyap, in Kongpo, eastern Tibet. From his fifth year, he studied the basics of the alphabet and so on. Then, from the age of about ten, he began to study on an enormous scale and without sectarian bias, receiving teachings from many spiritual guides of various traditions, including Gyurmé Thutob Namgyal of Shechen Monastery, Tai Situ Pema Nyinche Wangpo, and Jamyang Khyentse Wangpo. He learned all the common sciences, such as Sanskrit grammar, logic and epistemology, arts and crafts, medicine and so on. He studied, reflected, and meditated upon all the unique Buddhist topics of learning, including the Madhyamika, Prajnaparamita, Vinaya, and Abhidharma of the Sutra Vehicle, as well as the teachings of the Tantrayana, from both the *kama* and terma, and from both the Old and New Translation schools. In addition, he dedicated his whole life to teaching and spreading the Dharma, by giving empowerments, instructions, advice, and reading transmissions for both sutra and mantra, kama and terma, Old and New Translation schools, without any sectarian bias. He passed away at the age of eighty-seven.

Khenpo Chemchok

Kyabje Kyala Khenpo Chemchok Thondrup (1893–1957) was a living bodhisattva and a master of Dharma. He was teacher and tutor of Tulku Thondup, who is the incarnation of his teacher, Khenpo Könme.

Khenpo was in born in 1893 in the Mar Valley of Golok. In his youth he spent most of his days as a shepherd. At the age of nineteen, he decided to go to Dodrupchen Monastery, and was ordained at age twenty. There he studied with Khenpo Könme, who became his main teacher. Khenpo was always busy with studies of deep religious and philosophical works, reciting prayers, and doing his meditation and sadhanas. He never rested, except for sleeping four hours or so at night. At the age of about thirty-five, he started to concentrate on the training of tantra and Dzogchen. All together he spent nine years in long retreat in total seclusion. One morning, when he was on retreat, he learned that Dodrupchen Rinpoche had passed away by hearing people talking outside. Since that day, for the remaining thirty years of his life, unless he was walking or riding, he always remained in the sitting meditative posture. He would say, "By sitting up I sleep for four hours, but if I lay down I would sleep longer, and then the time would be wasted instead of being used for meditation."

At the age of forty-two, after the death of his other teacher, Khenpo Könme, he reluctantly accepted appointment as one of the four major khenpos at Dodrupchen and at other monasteries to students who included the two young fourth Dodrupchen Rinpoches.

In 1957 he left Dodrupchen Monastery secretly for exile with Tulku Thondup. He never reached India; at Drak Yangdzong, he merged into the ultimate peace of death on the second month of the Fire Bird year (1957), after reading the third chapter of *Treasury of Dharmadhatu*.

Among his writings are this *Commentary on Rigdzin Düpa*, *A Brief Notation on Palchen Düpa*, *A Brief Notation on Vajrakila*, *A Brief Instruction on the Three Words That Hit the Heart*, and *The Commentary on Dagni Changchup Miche* (lost).[18]

Khangsar Tenpe Wangchuk

Khangsar Tenpe Wangchuk was born amid miraculous signs in Akyong Khangsar in Golok at dawn on January 1, 1938. He was soon recognized as the incarnation of Payak Önpo Rigdzin Dorje, who was an emanation of Yudra Nyingpo, one of Guru Rinpoche's twenty-five disciples.

He studied with Palyul Choktrul Jampal Gyepe Dorje, Akyong Tokden Rinpoche Lodrö Gyatso, and other masters, gaining profound levels of realization, so that he met deities in visions and received prophecies from them, and his understanding of the sutras and tantras expanded to become limitless. He revealed both earth and mind termas. Some of them he even unearthed in public, before crowds of people. Khenpo Jigme Phüntsok declared him to be a great bodhisattva who had reached the more advanced stages (*bhumis*). He established both Khangsar Taklung Monastery and Payak Monastery.

He passed away on April 13, 2014. His collected writings include commentaries on Gyalse Shenpen Tayé's *Thirty-Seven Practices of a Bodhisattva*, the Rigdzin Düpa sadhana presented here, Garab Dorje's *Hitting the Essence in Three Words*, Longchenpa's *Treasury of the Way of Abiding* and *Treasury of the Dharmadhatu*, or Shabkar's *Flight of the Garuda*.

TRANSLATIONS

The Casket of Siddhis was translated by Adam Pearcey with clarifications by Ringu Tulku Rinpoche, Khentrul Lodrö Tayé, Lama Chökyi Nyima (Richard Baron), and Patrick Gaffney.

A draft translation of Khenpo Chemchok's notations had been prepared by John Newnham in 1991. In 2003 I reviewed it with the help of Gonpo Tulku. Every morning for five weeks, I went to see Tulku Rinpoche in his room at Dodrupchen Monastery in Sikkim, and he would explain the text and clarify my questions. However, he declined to explain the palace section which he said he could not understand clearly, and instead sent me to Özer Palzang, an expert at building three-dimensional palace models. Then I went over the text a number of times, and clarified points further with Tulku Thondup via e-mail, and also with Alak Zenkar Rinpoche. Many of my friends at Lerab Ling read and edited the text, making invaluable suggestions.

Having translated Khenpo Chemchok's commentary to the Rigdzin Düpa, in 2006, Alak Zenkar Rinpoche suggested that it would also be good to have the commentary of Khenpo Kangshar, a master for whom Zenkar Rinpoche has the greatest respect, in English. I spent a month drafting a translation, and years checking it primarily with Zenkar Rinpoche, and have had many friends read it and suggest improvements. Thus, I reviewed and included the translation in this publication.

I had translated the chöpön instructions by Patrul Rinpoche in 2001 with the help of Khenpo Yeshe Dorje, Chokling Monastery's abbot in Bir, India, who is extremely learned in all of the aspects of elaborate ritual practices, such as *drupchens* and *drupchös*. Similarly, I reviewed and included the translation in this publication.

Adam Pearcey had translated the root empowerment by Rigdzin Jigme Lingpa. Some years later I added the other sections that Jamgön Kongtrul included in his empowerment text.

Despite the help and support of several very knowledgeable and accomplished people, there must still be some mistakes, which are all due to my own limitations.

Gyurmé Avertin
Written at the Charung Khashor Stupa, Boudhanath, June 2016.

PRAYER TO RIGDZIN JIGME LINGPA INVOKING HIS PREVIOUS INCARNATIONS

BY JIGME LINGPA

Protector, lord presiding over the whole of samsara and nirvana,
    Samantabhadra
Whose very essence is the "ground continuum," the *sugatagarbha*;
Avalokiteshvara, the manifestation of the union of emptiness and
    compassion;
And Garab Dorje—to you we pray!

You manifested as the son of King Krikri in the presence of Buddha
    Kashyapa,
As Nanda, the younger brother of the Kinsman of the Sun,[1]
As Akaramati emanated by King Songtsen Gampo,
And as King Trisong Detsen—to you we pray!

Mahasiddha Virupa and Princess Pemasal,
Vihardhara[2] in person, venerable Gyalse Lharje,
Drime Künden, Yarje Orgyen Lingpa,
Young Moon,[3] Jetsün Drakpa Gyaltsen, to you we pray!

Samyépa, the actual manifestation of Mahapandita Vimalamitra,[4]
Ngari Panchen, Chögyal Püntsok,
Tashi Tobgyal, Dzamling Dorje,
And Jigme Lingpa, to you we pray!

Later, manifesting as Yeshe Dorje,
You will uphold the tradition of the Vajra-Essence teachings,
And, once again display for abusers and calumniators
All manners of manifestations—to you we pray!

In brief, you generated bodhichitta in front of Buddha Kashyapa,
Then perfected the supreme training in the bodhisattvas' conduct,
And finally, completely victorious, you attained buddhahood—
May we be reborn among your foremost students!

May we see whatever you do with faith and devotion,
And repeatedly bringing your visage to mind,
May we never be separated from the supreme lama,
And attain complete enlightenment in one mandala!

This was written by Khyentse Lha at the request of a few devoted students, such as Jetsün Jnana,[5] while abiding in natural rest, leaving delusional appearances as they are, mere rising.

THE CASKET OF SIDDHIS

A Recitation Manual for the Rigdzin Düpa

BY JIGME LINGPA

I prostrate at the feet of Padma, the awakened one!

When performing the approach recitation of Rigdzin Düpa, in a place where you are unlikely to face obstacles or interruptions, begin by offering a *torma* to the local deities who control the land and entrusting them with activity. Before entering strict retreat, clean the place where you will stay. Then, upon a raised surface, arrange heaps of grain[1] and the offerings of "medicinal nectar" (*amrita*), *rakta*, and torma, together with the seven regular offerings. It is said that you should draw a crossed vajra beneath your seat, but since this might bring about the fault of disrespecting the attribute of a deity,[2] you can draw a swastika and put down some kusha grass instead.[3]

Sit comfortably. Refine your attitude by means of the common preliminaries. By focusing with special emphasis on receiving the four empowerments at the conclusion of the guru yoga practice, you will purify any impairments or breakages of *samaya* and ensure that the practice will be completed successfully. Then, as you go through the practice, beginning with refuge and bodhichitta, ensure that you connect the words of the text to their actual meaning.

In this context, the threefold generation of bodhichitta can be explained as follows: the bodhichitta of aspiration is the thought, "I will accomplish the practice of the guru for the sake of all sentient beings, each of whom has been my very own mother in the course of our past lives." Since bodhichitta in action means actually carrying out actions for others' sake, in this case giving away the obstructing forces torma (*gektor*), the offerings, and the feast (*tsok*) without any feeling of loss or stinginess, is generosity. Not forsaking your various pledges—to refrain from going outside or letting others in; to keep silent; never to leave your retreat under any circumstances, and so on regardless of the problems or setbacks you might face, is ethical discipline. Enduring hardship by keeping to your original pledge, whether it was to practice in four, six, or however many sessions a day, without giving in to the urge to do less, is patient endurance. Not slipping into indolence or laziness, even for a single instant, while carrying out any of your tasks during and between the sessions is diligence. Concentrating your five senses on the clear appearance of the supporting (palace) and its supported (deities), so that all ordinary thoughts and perceptions are overwhelmed, and, at the same time, not allowing yourself to fall prey to even the slightest distraction is meditative concentration. Not practicing the generation phase (*kyerim*) with an ordinary frame of mind, but instead allowing the visualization to unfold naturally and spontaneously in the clarity of the unaltered nature of reality, is wisdom. This is how to understand the six transcendent perfections in this context. Being sure to apply them serves as the bodhichitta in action. The term "absolute bodhichitta" can be applied whenever all this is embraced by an awareness of what is beyond the ordinary conceptual mind. Understanding this, you will also come to know the crucial point of how sutra and mantra are in harmony.

Here the seven-branched practice is related to absolute truth. Someone of the highest capacity who understands the Dzogchen practice of tögal will therefore apply the profound generation phase in which spontaneous perfection dawns as appearance and emptiness. It is rare, however, to find anyone capable of such practice, and so those whose practice is on an aspirational level should train their minds to gather the accumulations through applying the seven branches in the general way.

Next, carry the tormas outside. Visualize the boundary markers, together with the four kings and the seventy-five glorious protectors. As you recite, "Accept this offering torma . . . ," offer the torma and consider that it pleases the deities, who remain, guarding against any obstacles. Seal your door. Put a stop to all coming and going. Even if you are in an isolated place with no one else around, it is still a serious fault to break your retreat, so do not allow yourself to become too careless and relaxed, to wander outside for leisurely strolls, and so on. Should you ever find yourself doing this, return to your retreat.

To bring about the foremost "protective tent," recognize that your mind is beyond arising and ceasing, and understand that obstructing forces have no reality. If this is beyond the capacity of your conceptual mind, visualize vajras of various shapes and sizes, all forming a great tent, similar to a giant iron helmet that is tightly closed. The meaning of the root text here is that conceptual thoughts are the obstructing forces, which are temporary in character, while the indestructible "vajra sphere" is the actual nature of things, which has always been unchanging.

The descent of blessings and what follows it are easy to understand. When it comes to the actual practice of the generation phase, this is not a practice of generation through the three samadhis, as in some practices of the lower yogas. Instead this follows the vision of Anuyoga, according to which all phenomena are awakened out of basic space.[4] This means that the actual nature of things, pure awareness (*rigpa*), which is unaltered and unfabricated by thought, is empty by its very essence, and yet through its radiance, as the dynamic expression of clear insight (*vipashyana*), all that appears is visualized as the mandala (*kyil khor*, literally "center and periphery") of the great natural perfection of infinite purity. In this context, "center" refers to the supported deities, whereas "periphery" refers to the supporting palace. All the apparent forms of the visualization, including the four corners, four doors, steps of the palace, and so on, are related to the pure qualities of the factors of enlightenment, beginning with the four applications of mindfulness. You can learn more about symbolic images, their significance, and the supporting logic by consulting *The Great Chariot*[5] and other texts.

Then there is the way in which the supported deities are generated in the center of the supporting palace. Of the means of purifying habitual tendencies associated with the four modes of birth, the approach here is not connected with the two coarser modes. And of the two subtler modes, it is associated with birth through warmth and moisture. The sun-disk seat represents warmth; the moon-disk seat represents moisture; and the HUNG syllable represents the consciousness of beings in the intermediate state (*bardo*). (Note that if someone with advanced realization has to prepare for bestowing an empowerment, the method used is that of generating the visualization through the four fully awakening meditations.[6] The significance of this approach is explained in my detailed commentary on the generation phase, *A Staircase for Ascending to Akanishtha*.[7])

The deity that manifests fully through HUNG is the general embodiment, actual presence, and essential identity of all the buddhas: Guru Rinpoche, the Master Prevailing Over All That Appears and Exists. He is endowed with all the major signs and minor marks, and his form and attributes relate to pure phenomena in the following way:

· To symbolize that all phenomena are of a single taste in their true nature, he has one face.

· To signify the coexistence of skillful means and wisdom, he has two hands.

· To symbolize the inseparable unity of bliss and emptiness, his complexion is white tinged with red.

· To symbolize his perfection of the vehicles of the shravakas, bodhisattvas, and Secret Mantra, he wears a monastic robe, brocade cloak, and gown.

· As a sign that he has reached the level of a spontaneously accomplished vidyadhara, the very embodiment of the five *kayas*, which is buddhahood according to the Mantrayana and the culmination of elimination and realization, he holds in his right hand a five-spoked golden vajra. Threateningly, he points it toward the demonic forces of dualistic clinging and conceptual thought, and performs the enlightened activity of annihilating what is harmful.

· As a sign that he matures and liberates beings exclusively through the resultant vehicle and guides his followers with the great accomplishment of a vidyadhara who has power over life, he holds in his left hand a skull-cup containing a long-life vase.

· Since he is the embodiment of the three kayas, complete with their seven attributes, beyond the two extremes of samsara and nirvana, he cradles in his arm the beautiful Princess Mandarava.

· As a sign that he is empowered with the five buddha families, he wears the lotus hat.

· To signify that he has carried out actions for his own welfare and is always ready to benefit others, his two legs are in the graceful posture of royal poise.

· Since his followers are brought to nirvana through the pinnacle of all yanas, above his head preside the two teachers of the supreme of all vehicles [i.e., Garab Dorje and Samantabhadra].

· As a symbol of the purification of the eight types of consciousness, which characterize samsara, he is surrounded by the eight vidyadharas who are the embodiments of the eight bodhisattvas and the eight classes of accomplishment.[8]

In short, all deluded, dualistic experiences involving mind and phenomena are generated through the coarse and subtle essences (*tiklé*), which, in turn, are caused by the potential inherent within the six ordinary elements. When this potential is eliminated through the profound Mantrayana path of skillful means, it is replaced by the embodiment of the wisdom essence, the vajra master, the second Buddha, Padmasambhava. He is the one who causes the other deities of the mandala to appear through emanation and who also brings about their dissolution. In order to signify your identification with this master (and the other deities), all the various deities associated with the six classes of tantra—the three outer tantras of samaya, practice, and accomplishment (i.e., Kriya, Charya, and Yoga), as well as the yogas of the inner tantras associated with enlightened body, speech, and mind— together with the vidyadharas of India and Tibet who have reached accomplishment through these paths appear in the space above Guru Rinpoche like invited guests. This is in fact the very meaning of the title—*Rigdzin Düpa, the Inner Sadhana for the Longchen Nyingtik Cycle.* Then follows the invocation, offering praise, and so on. Since they are easy to understand, there is no need to elaborate upon them here.

A. Mantra Recitation for Approach and Accomplishment

B. Approach

Once you have actually brought to mind the points contained in the series of verses that begins, "At my heart, upon a lotus, sun, and moon..." and you begin the practice, you don't need to visualize the emanation and reabsorption of light rays until there is some clarity to the appearance of the deity. Practice so that the deluded perceptions, which arise through the radiance or clarity of the completely unfabricated nature of reality, dawn as the mandala of the palace and deities. This is known as "clear appearance." Whenever the visualization is unclear, practice remembering the purity, as it was explained earlier. This will help you to avoid the pitfall of clinging to the deity as an ordinary expression of self. To put it simply, seeing, hearing, or thinking in an ordinary way does not qualify as approach practice. So it is said:

> All sights and grasping at them are perfected as the *mudra* of deity's
> forms,
> All sounds are purified into the great bliss of mantra,
> All thoughts are matured into the clear light dharmakaya.[9]

In our tradition, these three principles of purifying, perfecting, and maturing are the central themes of approach practice. When you have arrived at a clear appearance of the deity, consider that rays of light emanate from the extremely fine mantra-garland. By making offerings to the buddhas and their bodhisattva heirs, you gather the accumulation of merit. When the rays of light reconverge and dissolve back into you, consider that you purify the four types of obscurations, receive the four empowerments, and realize the four kayas. Then, by settling in a genuine experience of *dharmata*, you will gather the accumulation of wisdom. This is how you "approach" and come closer to the deity through the two accumulations. Once you have been infused with blessings and accomplished your own welfare, visualize further rays of light, which shine out and strike all sentient beings. Through this, you purify all the karma and habitual tendencies of beings of the six classes or five types.[10] Any ordinary clinging to the environment and its inhabitants is purified, just as when frost is melted by the sun. Meditate on the pure perception of the environment as the palace and its inhabitants as deities who are vidyadharas. This will establish the interdependent circumstances for the activity of benefiting others, and lead you to the level at which your own and others' benefit is spontaneously accomplished.

Pledging never to let go of the practice until you have truly realized these points for yourself, and then training to bring this vow to fruition, is the real measure of approach practice. This means that reciting a particular number of mantras, such as 1,200,000 for the approach mantra, is aspirational practice, undertaken in the hope of establishing positive tendencies. And, therefore, regardless of whether or not you undertake a strict retreat, as long as you never neglect the three principles of purifying, perfecting, and maturing, you will undoubtedly be reborn on the Glorious Copper-Colored Mountain. As it is said:

> Everything is circumstantial
> And hinges on one's aspiration.

If reinforcing our deluded perceptions and negative attitudes will lead us to wander further in samsara and the lower realms, there can be no deceiving ourselves about the result of meditating on the three mandalas of the deity's appearance, sound, and awareness. So now that the final era is upon us, and only a small fraction of the teachings survives, let us develop enthusiastic diligence. It is said that of all the practices, that of the guru is supreme. In fact, the great master Padmasambhava himself, the embodiment of all the buddhas, said:

Seeing me, all the buddhas are seen;
Accomplishing my practice, the practice of all
The buddhas is accomplished;
For I am the embodiment of all the sugatas.

The reliability of this statement can be validated through direct
perception.

C. Accomplishment

The visualization of the *jnanasattva* at the heart and all other such details
about deity, mantra, and samadhi can be learned from the secret manual
called *The Dazzling Vision of Crucial Points*.[11] In addition, as the unique
result of this practice, in this very lifetime you will be fully awakened within
the absolute space of the five kayas by perfecting the stages of attainment—
the five paths mentioned in the sutras and the four levels of a vidyadhara
outlined in the tantras. There will be no need to depend on creating the
right karmic connections for journeying to a pure realm like the Glorious
Copper-Colored Mountain. Such details are to be understood from the
vajra master's instructions.

This was written by the master of this teaching [Jigme Lingpa] *in response
to persistent requests from the one called Kundrol, a student of this lineage.*[12]

THE CRUCIAL POINTS OF VISUALIZATION FOR THE RIGDZIN DÜPA LONG-LIFE PRACTICE

BY JIGME LINGPA

Homage to the vidyadhara deities of long life!

I will present the different stages of visualization for the verses of the Rigdzin Düpa long-life practice (*tsedrup*), called *Elixir from the Amrita Vase*. To do the practice, follow the text down to the dissolution, practicing and actualizing the instructions of the main text of Rigdzin Düpa. You do this by maintaining total confidence in Dzogchen yoga, realizing that you, the object of meditation, and the practice materials placed on the shrine are all indivisibly united.

After the offering praise section, recite the verses of *Elixir from the Amrita Vase,* starting with "HRIH! I am Padmakara, the vidyadhara with power over life..."[1] and visualize the jnanasattva as Amitayus. He is brilliant red in color, wears the *sambhogakaya* ornaments, and is in union with his consort, who is his own self-radiance. His two hands are in the mudra of equanimity and hold a long-life vase made of ruby. At the heart of the indivisibly united male and female deities is the core seed syllable HRIH, which is the subtle essence of the elements of the whole universe and all the beings within it. It is contained within a closed amulet made from a sun and a moon. Around the syllable HRIH the chain of the mantra-garland turns clockwise and emanates brilliant rays of light. Focus one-pointedly on perfecting skill in clarity and stability. Rays of brilliant white light emanate from the mantra-garland in an intertwined web, effervescently. All the essences of samsara and nirvana are gathered instantaneously into an elixir. Imagine that the qualities of the ever-revolving wheel of eternity, one of the five perfections of the Akanishtha pure field, the long-life elixir of the vidyadharas and rishis that enable them to live for as long as a *kalpa*, the essence of the elements, the radiance and splendor of the whole inanimate world and all the sentient beings it contains, all vitality, power, and merit are drawn into the elixir, just like iron filings attracted by a magnet. The elixir fills you and transforms into innumerable minute Amitayuses. They completely fill your whole body, even the pores of the skin, but do not leave the body. This is how you gain vajra vitality and your body becomes immutable.

The Amitayuses are like a pile of sesame seeds—they do not touch or obstruct each other, yet the space between them is neither too wide nor too narrow. From the mouth of each one of them comes the essence-mantra of long life. As it emerges, it transforms into the innermost essence mantra, the single syllable HRIH. This syllable is the quintessence of all life essences, and the heart of the wisdom that invokes the crucial point—the force of life. You can hear HRIH being murmured softly, like the sound of bees around a broken hive. Recite the mantra silently as you practice the gentle vase breath. Alternatively, simply practice the vajra recitation. For those of the highest capacity who practice the extremely unelaborate method, long-life practice is accomplished by uniting wind-energy (*prana*; *lung*) and mind. In general when practicing for others, or if you are a beginner whose samadhi and *lung* are weak and are practicing for yourself, focus mainly on the activity of emanating and reabsorbing rays of light as you actualize the accomplishment mantra at your heart and the Amitayuses who resound the syllable HRIH. When practicing for others, though, the essence of the life-force to actualize is the syllable NRI. Visualize it appearing in the same way as the core seed syllable HRIH. The elixir of long life concentrates in it. It would be very good to always end a session with this short vajra recitation.

At the end of sessions,[2] do the practice that brings the profound crucial point of summoning the *siddhis* associated with each vidyadhara. As you do so, maintain the awareness that brings together these three elements: view, kyerim, and powerful devotion. At the end of the practice, it is crucial to bury and seal your life in the vast expanse of spontaneously present basic space, where there is neither birth nor death.

The Words of the Vidyadhara That Bestow the Majesty of Great Bliss

*Notations on the Rigdzin Düpa, the Inner Sadhana for
the Longchen Nyingtik Cycle*

By Khenpo Chemchok

Namo Guru Padma Manjushriye
In the sky-like expanse of the dharmadhatu, free from the clouds of
    conceptual elaboration,
Shines the sun of the rupakaya, adorned with the major and minor marks,
Constantly emanating brilliant rays of compassion throughout the ten
    directions—
To my teacher, the only refuge who dispels the darkness of the ignorance of
    beings in this degenerate time, I pay homage!

A. Preliminaries

1. Preparation

Here I will expand briefly on some notes of my incomparable and precious
teacher's[1] oral instructions on the approach (*nyenpa*) and accomplishment
(*drubpa*) of the Lama Rigdzin Düpa.

Begin by using chalk or some white powder to draw a swastika on the
ground where your seat will be. Place some kusha grass on top of the swastika so that the heads of the stalks all face the direction in which you will
be sitting. Neatly place your sleeping mat on top of the grass.[2]

To practice the Lama Rigdzin Düpa from the Longchen Nyingtik cycle
authentically, it is first necessary to lay the foundations of the Dzogchen
Nyingtik teachings. As the various commentaries on the ngöndro explain,
we do this by purifying the mind through accumulating the ordinary or outer

preliminaries and the extraordinary or inner preliminaries. However, few practitioners actually accumulate these practices at this juncture. According to the oral tradition, we must spend at least seven days practicing the ngön-dro; as this is the custom, I will give a brief presentation on the ngöndro.

a) A Brief Presentation on the Ngöndro

(1) The Four Thoughts

When entering the extraordinary path of the Secret Mantrayana, it is essential as a preliminary to arouse bodhichitta, because it is the heart and source of the Mahayana teachings.

The authentic generation of bodhichitta is dependent upon arousing compassion with the intention of taking responsibility for the benefit and ultimate enlightenment of others. This profound, almost overwhelming feeling of compassion for all beings, who are without exception immersed in suffering, is the result of an unwavering revulsion for samsara.

True renunciation comes from realizing how you yourself are oppressed by suffering, and from recognizing the causes of suffering, such as negative actions. Therefore, it is essential to begin training by contemplating on the four thoughts that turn the mind away from samsara and by generating an unshakable longing to renounce samsara.

(2) How to Follow a Spiritual Friend

The teaching on how a student should follow a spiritual friend is, in the Hinayana, generally explained at the very outset of the path. However, here, in the teachings of the Mahayana, the Great Vehicle, this is not the case. The way to follow an extraordinary Mahayana teacher is presented after the explanation of the four thoughts. In this regard, it is important that we follow a qualified master properly, in both thought and deed.

(3) Taking Refuge

Taking refuge has many benefits: it blesses the mind and dispels unfavorable circumstances on the path. Refuge is just like a reliable armed escort who protects travelers from harm as they journey through wild and dangerous places.

Bodhichitta is the active direction of all our efforts toward the goal of complete enlightenment. It arises when the longing to attain the fruition of the path for ourselves and the desire to lead others to enlightenment have been born in our mind. The motivation of bodhichitta can only arise once we have identified the fruit of the path and understood its benefits through taking refuge. This is why we take refuge before we arouse bodhichitta.

We take refuge by gaining the total confidence and trust that results from knowing the essence of the Three Jewels, by knowing their nature, qualities, and different aspects of refuge, as well as the fact that the Three Jewels always express the truth in every situation,[3] and so on.

(4) Bodhichitta

First, acknowledge that without bodhichitta we cannot possibly attain the ultimate goal of complete enlightenment, and then generate bodhichitta. To begin with the path of Dzogchen, we have no choice but to arouse bodhichitta, because it is the only doorway to Dzogchen. Then we practice guru yoga as the special, powerful, skillful means for accomplishing this path and attaining the siddhis. However, before beginning with guru yoga, we need to remove any unfavorable circumstances that may hinder our progress and also gather favorable circumstances.

(5) Vajrasattva

We meditate on Vajrasattva and recite his mantra in order to purify all adverse circumstances, general faults and downfalls, as well as transgressions particular to the Mantrayana. It is good to have received the *Vajrasattva Practice of Purifying the Abhirati Buddha Field*[4] empowerment before beginning this practice.

(6) Mandala Offering

Of the many methods that exist for gathering favorable circumstances, it is mandala offering that is taught here. All the wealth and prosperity of the world—the entire universe and every being within it—is arranged as a mandala and manifests as pure buddha fields. This method of making offerings is the most powerful way of accumulating merit.

(7) Kusali Accumulation

The *kusali* accumulation[5] can either be connected with the practice of guru yoga, as it is in Longchenpa's *Finding Comfort and Ease in the Nature of Mind*,[6] or with the accumulation of merit, which is how it is presented here. While mandala offering is a general offering, the kusali accumulation of merit is a specific offering of the body. This practice reveals the source of our attachment to our body: the root of the three bases for grasping at the self. If we can learn to offer up our body, it becomes much easier for us to make sumptuous and abundant offerings of all other things, and to give up desire and attachment naturally. There can be no greater merit than to offer the very thing for which we have the most attachment.

(8) Guru Yoga

Just to practice the guru yoga recitation, you must receive the root empowerment, the "Royal Anointment Empowerment."[7]

To practice guru yoga, directly destroy dualistic thoughts by proclaiming "Emaho!" and then rest in the unaltered natural state of rigpa. Visualize rigpa's self-radiance to be the Copper-Colored Mountain and the Palace of Lotus Light, and visualize yourself as Vajrayogini. Your teacher appears on the crown of your head in the form of Guru Rinpoche with his retinue. Then you invite Guru Rinpoche and the other deities from the pure field of the Glorious Copper-Colored Mountain. They arrive, merge with the forms you have visualized, and remain indivisible from them.

In their presence, perform the seven-branch offering of accumulation and purification, The Seven Branches of Devotional Practice. Then, generating intense devotion as the foundation of your practice, recite the vajra guru mantra, receive the four empowerments, and merge your mind inseparably with the mind of the lama.

It is crucial to begin any recitation retreat with guru yoga. This is because guru yoga carries the blessings of the deity to us and causes them to enter us swiftly, just like the sandalwood trees covering the slopes of Mount Malaya that spread their sweet fragrance far and wide on the wind.

b) The Way to Practice the Guru Yoga Approach Retreat

(1) Before the Retreat

Generally, before beginning a retreat, we must "marshal the forces of merit" by spending as much time as possible on practices such as:

- Proclaiming the sutras in the four directions,[8]
- Offering water tormas, *sang*, and *sur* to the deities above and the guests below, and
- Reciting practices such as the Three Sections of Offerings from Samsara and Nirvana (*Khordé chöpa cha sum...*).

These practices are necessary in order to remove obstacles and to ensure that we accomplish the siddhis quickly.

A retreat begins when the boundaries are set on an auspicious astrological date during the waxing phase of the moon. The evening is the time of day associated with magnetizing activity, as this is when circumstances (*tendrel*) make it easy to bring gods and spirits under control. Therefore, carry out the preliminary practices that are not part of the actual retreat in the afternoon. It is up to you to decide whether you are going to include protectors' practices or stop for a tea break.

To set the limits of the retreat with the posts of the four great kings and their retinues (*gyalto*),[9] practice the self-visualization of Rigdzin Düpa and recite at least three malas of the approach mantra (the vajra guru mantra). Continue with offerings, confession of mistakes in practice, and dissolution, which includes rearising as the deity, up to the end of prayer for auspiciousness.

Then, in the state of vajra confidence, the result of arising as the deity, perform the preliminary tormas practice, recite the offering and request for fulfillment of wishes, which begins with the line: "All those who dwell in this place—gods and *nagas*,..." ("gang dag dir né..."). Add other relevant practices as you wish. Then bless the torma to the obstructing forces (*gektor*), offer it, and issue the command to leave.

Next, either you or your retreat attendant should go to the places where the altars of the four great kings are set, and arrange and bless the regular offerings[10] and the post torma (*totor*) in front of each post. The altars transform into the palaces of the four kings, and you invite the four kings and their retinues into their palaces. Make offerings to them, entrust them with activity, and request them to remain.

Then return to your seat, and recite and actualize the protective-spheres section. After this, offer prayers of auspiciousness, either briefly or elaborately. The teachings say that it is crucial to recite verses of auspiciousness during every session of the retreat in order to make circumstances auspicious and prevent obstacles to accomplishments from ever arising.

From this point on, do not venture outside the boundaries and do not let people in. If you see anyone, it will "puncture" your retreat; and if you are seen by others, that will "rip" or "tear" it. Therefore, do not meet with anyone whom you have not anticipated meeting.[11] And don't bring things in or send them out either,[12] with the single exception of siddhi substances.[13] If for some reason you have no choice but to allow something or someone inside the boundary, meditate strongly on the protection spheres. Whenever you let anything or anyone into your retreat, you need to purify any accompanying negativity that might be caused by inauspicious conditions or samaya breakage (*nyam drip*). This is done with cleansing vase water (which must have been blessed previously through a specific practice that blesses the vase for cleansing activity, such as Vajrasattva or the Bhurkumkuta practice of the "Cleansing Vase"[14]). Sprinkle the water on the newly arrived items, and either sprinkle water on the person coming in or give him or her some water to drink. Then drink some yourself. Some people also bless the water by generating the deity and reciting a few mantras, sprinkling it, and drinking some every morning.

(2) The Guru Yoga Practice

Then divide up your day into the sessions you will follow during the retreat and begin the morning session with the ngöndro. It is important to recite "Secret Path to the Mountain of Glory, A Prayer of Aspiration for the Glorious Copper-Colored Mountain"[15] at the end of every session.

During the next day's early-morning session, recite the ngöndro. It is best to accumulate 108 recitations of the hundred-syllable mantra without interruption, and you must definitely recite it at least twenty-one times. Apart from the vajra guru mantra, it is not necessary to accumulate anything else. At the end of the session, receive the four empowerments and complete the practice. Then recite the four-line prayer beginning, "In all of my lives..." ("kyé wa kuntu..."),[16] and conclude with "Secret Path to the Mountain of Glory."

You can start the rest of the day's sessions with either refuge or guru yoga itself, but guru yoga is always the main focus of the practice. At the end of the evening session, recite all the aspiration and dedication prayers.

During all sessions of guru yoga, in fact during any practice of approach (*nyenpa*) and accomplishment (*drubpa*), do not let negative attitudes caused by distraction and other such obstacles creep in. Reject them, because they produce constant suffering in both this life and lives to come. Contemplate the wonderful and extraordinarily precious opportunity you have to lead yourself and others to the lasting happiness of perfect liberation through the means of this supreme path, without having to waste your life on all kinds of negative activities like business or farming. Develop joy and enthusiasm by thinking along these lines. With a spacious, calm, and relaxed attitude, do all that you can to recall the meaning of every word of the text. This is an extremely important point.

2. Rigdzin Düpa Recitation Retreat

a) Introductory Comments on the Rigdzin Düpa Recitation Retreat

In the evening offer the preliminary tormas—the *kator*, *gektor*, and *gyalto* tormas—and then visualize the protection spheres and recite verses of auspiciousness, as previously explained.[17]

At the start of the session, focus on bringing out the key points of guru yoga by remembering the meaning of the practice as you recite the words. Then start to practice the Rigdzin Düpa sadhana text. At the end of the evening session, offer *tsok*. From this time on, throughout the retreat, tsok needs to be offered only on the tenth day of the waxing and the waning phases of the moon (i.e., on the tenth and twenty-fifth days of the lunar calendar).

(1) The Significance of the Rigdzin Düpa

(a) Lama Rigdzin

Here, we need to know that there are both male (*yabka*) and female (*yumka*) lama vidyadhara (Lama Rigdzin) sadhanas. In terms of the male vidyadhara practices, there are peaceful and wrathful practices. Regarding the peaceful practices, there is the outer practice, Lamé Naljor; the inner practice, Rigdzin Düpa; the secret practice, Duk-ngal Rangdrol; and the innermost lama practice, Tiklé Gyachen. For the wrathful aspect, there are both dark-blue and red forms, which are Palchen Düpa and Takhyung Barwa, respectively. The female practices are Yumka Dechen Gyalmo from the root sadhana, *Yumka Dechen Paltreng*, and the secret sadhana of Sengé Dongma.

Most of the practices of the Longchen Nyingtik terma cycle, including the practices I just mentioned, are sadhanas of the Lama Rigdzin.[18] Therefore, if we devote ourselves to practicing them, we will be able to reach the most supreme accomplishment in this very lifetime. Even those who do nothing more than simply respect the samaya, have faith and devotion, and develop the habitual tendencies of approach and accomplishment[19] for these practices will be able to reach the pure land of Lama Rigdzin, the Glorious Copper-Colored Mountain. This crucial point is shown in the *Seal of the Prophecies from Lama Gongdü*:[20]

> In the south will appear a *tulku* named Özer[21]
> Who will liberate beings through the profound teachings of the
> Nyingtik.
> He will lead whoever is connected to him to the pure land of the
> vidyadharas.

The root of this cycle of teachings is the practice of the Lama Rigdzin. This is illustrated in the Palchen Düpa practice of the Longchen Nyingtik, where there is an explanation of how to practice the deities of the Kagyé sadhanas. There, the passage beginning "Outwardly this is practiced..."[22] says the deities of the Kagyé sadhanas are, on the outer level, bodhisattvas; on the inner level, they are the vidyadharas; and on the secret level, they are the blazing, wrathful Kagyé deities. What this means is that on the inner level, this practice of the Drupa Kagyé is the practice of the vidyadharas—Rigdzin Düpa. This example shows us that the Rigdzin Düpa is the most important of the three-roots practices. It also shows us that there are many ways to practice the Rigdzin Düpa.

(b) Lama Kagyé

Also, in terms of Lama Kagyé, it is said that this practice is like the innermost essence of the Kagyé Rigdzin Yongdü[23] and the elaborate path of the Dröltik.[24] The signs foretelling the revelation of the Longchen Nyingtik cycle of teachings were brought to light when the habitual tendencies of Ngari Panchen awakened in Jigme Lingpa. He recognized that in a previous incarnation he had been Ngari Panchen, the revealer of the greatest earth-treasure transmission of the Kagyé, the Kagyé Rigdzin Yongdü. The interdependent connection of the revelation of the Longchen Nyingtik by Jigme Lingpa as a rediscovered mind treasure of the innermost essence of the profound terma Kagyé Rigdzin Yongdü makes the Longchen Nyingtik practices very special.

(2) The Way to Practice the Sadhanas of the Longchen Nyingtik

My revered master, Dodrupchen Jigme Tenpe Nyima, said that the sadhanas of the Nyingtik cycle are not actual kyerim practices, but are in fact guru yoga practices. At the same time, however, he indicates in the *Rain of Siddhis*, the lineage prayer that he composed for the Rigdzin Düpa, that we can follow this path by practicing these sadhanas as kyerim, with all the crucial points of the three aspects of purifying, perfecting, and maturing. By doing so, we mature our mindstream, and then actualize the wisdom of dzogrim through the practice of tsalung and the path of skillful means.

However, the way of meditating according to the Nyingtik tradition is a special and unique path. In other Highest Yoga tantras practitioners begin with kyerim practice to mature the mindstream before they practice dzogrim. But it is not like that in the Nyingtik tradition. Here, we are first introduced to the clear light of rigpa, and recognize that the mind of the lama and our own rigpa are indivisible. Then we rest in that recognition and train so that our rigpa arises as the mandala of the deity. This approach therefore includes the special key feature of uniting kyerim and dzogrim. It is a very powerful means for directly bringing about the wisdom of realization in which you unite your own mind indivisibly with the lama's wisdom-mind.

(3) Developing Confidence

To practice this profound yoga, we need to have confidence in three things: the teachings, the lineage of the masters, and ourselves.

(a) Confidence in the Teachings

> In the Gandhola temple of Samyé, the manifestation of Akanishtha,
> In the Blazing Turquoise Palace on the second floor,
> The profound meaning of the Nyingtik cycle was entrusted
> To the three heart disciples: the king, the subject, and the friend.[25]

As this and other quotations[26] show, it was Guru Rinpoche himself who gave the Dharma king and his son[27] the empowerments and instructions for these profound teachings. Though few in words, the Dzogchen Nyingtik contains the complete meaning of Dzogchen; the Nyingtik teachings are easy to practice yet wholly effective, bringing fortunate disciples to liberation within a single lifetime.

Then Guru Rinpoche sealed the Dzogchen Nyingtik instructions into the all-pervading space of the wisdom-mind of clear light, and concealed them as a terma. Among the many rebirths the Dharma king Trisong Detsen took as a tertön, one was as Omniscient Jigme Lingpa. In the earlier part of his life, Jigme Lingpa received the four empowerments from a footprint Guru Rinpoche had left on a road. This allowed Jigme Lingpa to see within the inner basic space of his own mind the liberation that is endowed with the six extraordinary features of Samantabhadra.

Later, Jigme Lingpa was blessed by Manjushrimitra, and from this time on, the secret treasure of his wisdom-mind was revealed. These and other events recorded in Jigme Lingpa's biographies show how he realized the absolute nature of Dzogchen. The biographies relate how his mind merged with the mind of Guru Dewachenpo ("The Guru of Great Bliss"). The result was that the Longchen Nyingtik cycle of teachings previously entrusted to him (during his previous incarnation as King Trisong Detsen) was awakened in his mindstream. He could then decipher them and set them down in writing. Therefore, we can develop confidence that these are profound teachings from the Nyingtik tradition of Dzogchen Pith-Instructions.

(b) Confidence in the Lineage

The sacred lineage of these teachings remains unbroken from Guru Rinpoche onward. Therefore, we can be certain that the power of its blessings remains undiminished. As the omniscient lord of siddhas, Dodrupchen Jigme Tenpe Nyima said, "The lineage is exceedingly short, as there is no one in this Nyingtik lineage between Guru Rinpoche and myself, save Zhabdrung Rinpoche (Jamyang Khyentse Wangpo)."[28]

(c) Confidence in Ourselves

We can be certain that if we first receive the empowerment, practice according to the text, and always keep the samayas, we will reach accomplishment.

Therefore, at the beginning of the retreat feel deep regret for any breakage or degeneration of the samayas, and confess and repair them with the four powers. Then receive the four empowerments, complete the practice, and be certain that your samayas are restored.

During the actual practice of approach and accomplishment, trust and be confident that the practice will be successful. Never doubt that your past faults and breakages of samaya have been purified, and that they will not come between you and accomplishment.

b) Arranging the Shrine

At the beginning of the Rigdzin Düpa text, when it tells us to arrange "the mandala, the material offerings, and lavish presents as you like"[29] in front of the shrine, it is referring to the accomplishment phase.

Here, for the approach, place the torma in the center of the mandala, with the amrita on its right and the rakta on its left. In front of them arrange the regular offerings, the fulfillment torma, the dharmapala tormas, and so on.[30] It is said that if you arrange the offerings in a pleasing and beautiful way, you create the auspicious circumstances for receiving the blessings. Once you have arranged everything, including the accomplishment torma, bless the offerings before the end of the day.

3. The Actual Practice of Approach and Accomplishment

1. The Stages of the Practice

a) Lineage Prayers

We pray to the lamas of the lineage with intense devotion to prevent any obstacles to the practice from arising and to receive the blessings quickly.

b) Blessing the Vajra and Bell

We visualize ourselves in the form of Vajradhara in union with Dhatvishvari in order to purify the attachment we have to our ordinary physical appearance.[31]

The Highest Yoga Tantra vehicle purifies confused perceptions and all attachment to them, and the fruition of the great dharmakaya is realized by taking as the path the great primordial wisdom, which is the union of wisdom and skillful means. We hold the vajra and bell to symbolize this union.

We consider that the essence of the vajra is skillful means and great bliss, and its nature is the five wisdoms, arising in the form of the five-spoked vajra. We recite OM MAHA VAJRA HUNG while holding the vajra at the level of our heart.

We then consider that the essence of the bell is wisdom and emptiness, which then manifests in the form of the bell. The bell naturally resonates with the sound of emptiness, waking beings from the sleep of ignorance. As we recite OM VAJRA GHENDE A we ring the bell and then rest it on our hip.

Through uniting the male and female aspects in this way, we rest in the unity of great bliss and the space of emptiness and recite OM SARWA TATHAGATA MAHA ANURAGANA VAJRA SOBHAVA EMA KO HANG as we perform the mudra of union.

c) The Seven Preliminary Sections

(1) Invoking the Field of Merit

You can visualize the field of merit as it is described in the prayer of invocation beginning "**At my heart is a letter HUNG . . .**"[32] However, according to the oral lineage of my peerless teacher, Lushul Khenpo Könchok Drönme, the deities of the field of merit have always been present in the sky before us. Therefore, reciting the samadza mantra[33] simply reawakens us to this view, just as bringing butter lamps into a richly painted temple at night immediately reveals all the deities. Lushul Khenpo also said that we can visualize the field of merit as it is described in the ngöndro, in spite of the practice text specifying that we visualize "**all the deities of the Mahaguru's mandala.**"

(2) Taking Refuge

So who is it who takes refuge? **I and all infinite beings.**[34]

What do we **take refuge in?** Those who wish to attain final liberation take refuge in the Buddha, Dharma, and Sangha. We take refuge in **the** lama, who in **essence is the Three Jewels**—his body is the Sangha, his speech is the sacred Dharma, and his mind is the Buddha. So we take refuge in the lama, surrounded by his retinue of vidyadharas, who appear **in the form** of **the mandala of the multitude of vidyadharas.** How do we take refuge in them? We recall that all sentient beings, ourselves and all others, live in dread of the three fears. Therefore, we take refuge **with** intense **devotion from the depth of our hearts** and with the complete conviction that the field of refuge has the capacity to protect us. As we do so, we think, "I take refuge until I attain enlightenment!"

The absolute refuge of the nature of phenomena is to rest in the natural state in which all phenomena, including the objects of refuge, have never existed from time without beginning.

(3) Bodhichitta

Lord Maitreya said,

> Arousing bodhichitta is: for the sake of others
> Longing to attain complete enlightenment.[35]

Why **have I entered** the practice of approach and accomplishment of **this** profound **mandala** of the Lama **Vidyadhara** Assembly? Because when **I recall** my own dear **father and mother,** I see that they are constantly tormented by the three types of suffering, which are the direct result of their negative actions and destructive emotions. This makes me realize that **all beings throughout the six realms** of existence, who have also been **my father or mother,** are suffering in the same way. Looking at the infinite number of beings from the perspective of the four immeasurables—the **immeasurable compassion** of wishing that all of them may be free from suffering and the causes of suffering, the immeasurable love of wishing them to be happy, and so on—**I generate the awakened mind** of bodhichitta.

I awaken bodhichitta in aspiration by wishing to attain enlightenment in order to liberate all beings from the fears of samsara and nirvana. I also awaken bodhichitta in **action** by pledging to train continuously in the altruistic activities of a bodhisattva. Arousing bodhichitta in aspiration and in action is the awakening of the supreme **relative** bodhichitta.

I awaken **absolute bodhichitta** by resting in the recognition that in the unaltered nature of mind nothing has any inherent existence, including the mind of enlightenment, the one arousing it, and the act of generating it.

As these practices of the generation of bodhichitta are the keystone of the Mahayana paths, we simply cannot leave them out. We must meditate on bodhichitta wholeheartedly and transform our minds.

(4) The Accumulation of Merit and Wisdom—The Seven Aspects of Devotional Practice

The oral advice of my peerless teacher for this section is to follow the usual method of emanating bodies as numerous as atoms in the universe and then prostrating and so on. But, as in *The Casket of Siddhis*,[36] he did not speak about the meaning of the root sadhana, because he knew that this would be too difficult for beginners to assimilate. I received the following explanation as personal advice from the great master Lushul Khenpo Könchok Drönme, which I then recorded in my notes.

(a) Prostration

Just **like bubbles arising from** clear **water**, the entire display of the mandala palace and **deities manifests** as the self-radiance or creative energy of **wisdom expanse**, the great dharmakaya of our own mind. This clear light nature of mind has always been the very essence of the three kayas of the buddhas. This, and nothing other than this, is what arises as the deity. Paying homage with this **direct recognition**, or by means **of rigpa**, **is** the ultimate **prostration** of the natural state, the supreme prostration of encountering the view. Recognizing rigpa in this way, and recognizing all its manifestations as dharmata nature, is the "direct realization of dharmata," the first of the four visions of tögal.

(b) Offering

By coming to know, through the path of tögal, wisdom and its manifestations, which have been introduced directly (as was just explained), there is "increasing experience" (*nyam gongpel*), the second of the four visions of tögal. This process continues until the kayas are perfected, so that they are actually present in our reality.

Increasing experience is referred to as "offering to the deities of the field of merit," because making offerings is pleasing to the deities. Here, through the power of exerting ourselves in the practice, the primordial wisdom of clarity, bliss, and nonconceptuality blazes within us more and more. The more it blazes, the more our experiences develop and increase, and this pleases the deities.

(c) Confession

Directly realizing emptiness, the all-pervading space of rigpa, and perfecting its manifestation so that the kayas and deities are actually present in our reality, is called "**awareness reaching full maturity**," the third of the four visions of tögal. To rest in this union of clarity and emptiness is the king of all **confessions**.

(d) Rejoicing

The "**exhaustion of phenomena into the nature of reality**," the fourth of the four visions of tögal, is brought about through the natural interruption of the inner and outer aspects of delusory perception—the outer appearances of objects created from the primary elements, and the habitual tendencies (or karmic seeds) of the confused conceptual mind and its mental states. In this state, we remain in dharmata without ever separating from a vast ocean of untainted bliss. As this is the culmination of the path of training, we really have something to **rejoice** in. Even those who are not yet on this path (of "no more learning") can meditate by rejoicing for those who do abide there.

(e) The Request to Turn the Wheel of Dharma

We then request the deities of the mandala to **turn the wheel of Dharma**, according to the capacities and karmic fortune of individual beings. The request is made to those who have reached the bhumis, or those who, having reached the end of the four visions of tögal, have attained the rainbow **body of great transference** and can turn the wheel of Dharma out of the expanse of their realizations.

(f) The Request to Remain

We also pray that those who have attained this **great rainbow body** may **remain** until samsara is totally emptied, and that they do not pass into nirvana, but stay to bring benefit continuously to beings.

(g) Dedication

Dedication without conceptual reference is to rest in a state that is beyond the notion of there being something to dedicate or an actual act of dedication. In this way, we **dedicate all the merit ever accumulated** through these seven branches to the attainment of **the youthful vase body**, the inner luminosity of manifest enlightenment, which is attained **with** the six extraordinary features of Samantabhadra.

(5) Dissolution

Then, like the moisture from breath evaporating off the surface of a mirror, the deities of the field of merit dissolve into Orgyen Dorje Chang and into you. You then also melt into light and then into the seed syllable; the seed syllable dissolves into the *nada*; the nada dissolves into the primordial space of the indestructible tiklé; and you rest in the basic space of emptiness.

(6) Torma to the Obstructing Forces

First, we give the command for any obstructing forces that may be present to leave, and expel them. We then prevent any negative forces from entering in the future by meditating on the protection spheres.

(a) Self-Visualization

Out of emptiness you **instantly** arise as **Hayagriva**. He is red in color, with one face and two arms. On the crown of his head a green horse's head neighs resoundingly. Hayagriva brandishes a cudgel in his right hand. The top of the cudgel is made from a human corpse. He makes the threatening mudra with his left hand. Masses of fire and tiny wrathful deities emanate from the tips of his left hand's little and index fingers. Visualize yourself in this **majestic** form, in the midst of a **blazing** expanse of **fire**, so wrathful and fearsome that it is difficult for others even to look at.

(b) The Offerings

The torma offered to the obstructing forces is placed on a lower level than that of the practitioners. As you recite the activity mantra, sprinkle the torma with water from the activity vase (*lebum*). An infinite number of vajras, as fine as minute particles, emanate from Hayagriva's heart. They strike and shatter the torma and its container, which are scattered like dust dispersed on the wind. Then, bringing to mind the state of emptiness, recite the sobhawa mantra[37] and rest in its meaning.

Out of the absolute, an enormous, capacious vessel made of precious metals and gems appears in front of you. It contains the torma, which is exactly what every negative influence (*dön*) and obstructing force (*gek*) desires. The torma transforms into an inexhaustible source of nectar.

Recite the seed syllables OM AH HUNG three times:

- The first time, visualize the three syllables arranged on the gektor.
- The second time, the three syllables emanate rays of light that please all the buddhas and invoke the nectar of wisdom from the buddha fields. The light then dissolves into the three seed syllables.
- The third time, the syllables melt into light and dissolve into the torma. The torma is transformed so that its essence becomes the nectar of wisdom, while it appears in the form of whatever objects of enjoyment the obstacle-making guests desire. This offering has the capacity to satisfy them completely.

As you say HO, make the *garuda* mudra,[38] all the guests receive these offerings peaceably and are satisfied.

Then recite the mantra that summons the obstructing forces.[39] Hayagriva sends out a swarm of the four goddesses Hook, Lasso, Chain, and Bell from his heart and summons the negative spirits and obstructing forces, who create obstacles to the practice of approach and accomplishment, into your presence.

As you recite the sky treasury mantra[40] three times and perform its mudra, the gektor is transformed into whatever it is that the guests desire. All karmic debts are repaid; all grudges are dissolved. The harmful spirits and guests are satisfied and they depart filled with joy.

(c) Issuing the Command

For those with extremely negative and unruly minds who seek any opportunity to cause harm and simply refuse to leave, issue the command through wrathful subjugating activity.

Starting with **HRIH**, the seed syllable of Hayagriva, say:

> "Now, we are practicing the profound **mandala** of primordial
> wisdom where the environment of the **universe** manifests as the
> palace **and beings manifest** as the deities of Lama Rigdzin Düpa.
> Therefore, **all you malicious** negative influences and **obstruct-
> ing demonic forces** who became various kinds of demons
> and elemental forces (*jungpo*), the creators of obstacles to the
> accomplishment of the profound mandala, **take the torma** we
> give you. Do not stay here, but quickly **go elsewhere!** Go away!
> I am Hayagriva, and the mind of this display is indivisible from
> primordial wisdom. From its expanse I will manifest weapons,
> mountains of wrathful fire, and an immeasurable gathering of
> **vajras** that will **crush you into dust**, you can be sure of that!"

Then, as you recite the mantra of the four HUNGs,[41] wrathful emanations, weapons, and sheets of flame stream out from your heart. They expel
all the obstacle makers so completely that not even their names remain.

This is the relative expulsion of obstructing forces.

(d) The Absolute Approach

The absolute expulsion is to recognize that harmful influences and obstacle
makers are merely temporary delusory appearances and do not exist in the
basic space of the great primordial purity of inseparable rigpa and emptiness. By resting in this state of recognition, we purify the delusory appearances of harmful influences and obstacle makers into the dharmadhatu.

(7) The Protection Spheres

(a) The Relative Protection Spheres

i) Formation

Your heart sends out wrathful deities, weapons, and sheets of flame and
the wrathful weapons and flames you sent out earlier to expel the obstructing forces now head back toward you. At the point where these two sets of
emanations meet, the vajra sphere is formed, as if liquid metal were being
poured into a cast.

ii) The Ground

The ground transforms into a great crossed vajra. Small and even very small vajras fill all the space around and inside the main vajras, so that there is not even one tiny gap remaining.

iii) The Inner Layer

Arising around the edge of the circular ground is a solid and unyielding wall of standing vajras. Again, all the gaps in this perimeter fence are filled with very small vajras.

iv) The Outer Layer

Outside this fence is a spherical net made of interlaced vajras. Its surface is smooth and even.

v) The Vajra Canopy

Above this net lies the vajra canopy, which is formed by a large double vajra. Again, all conceivable gaps are filled with tiny vajras. At the four tips of the double vajra are small half vajras that point slightly upward.

vi) The Intermediate Layer

In the space between the first and second layers of the protection spheres there is another net of vajras, hanging down like a curtain from the top of the vajra canopy. It looks like a cup with a sealed top.

vii) The Vajra Tent

The vajra tent has the shape of a dome and covers all the other layers of the sphere. It is formed from a crossed vajra. The four spokes of the vajras slope downward, all the way to the ground. As before, any space is totally filled with tiny vajras. The tent covers the spokes of all the vajras, including those of the standing vajras, and looks like an iron helmet. A blue vajra with outspread spokes stands at the summit. The fires of the end of time[42] blaze all around the perimeter of the sphere.

An infinite number of wrathful deities and weapons spread outward from the protection spheres, scattering and annihilating all negative influences.

viii) The Qualities of the Protection Spheres

The various layers of protection spheres do not obstruct each other, so each layer is as clearly visible as a butter lamp inside a glass vase. Every layer is solid, strong, and impregnable to obstacle makers. The essence of this structure is the mind of the buddhas, the primordial wisdom of omniscience. This is the kind of pride and confidence we need to cultivate.

ix) The Gyalto Practice

Outside, in the midst of the raging fires that surround the protection spheres, are the altars of the four kings.[43] They are placed in the four cardinal directions and then transform into palaces. We invite the four great kings and their retinues into their palaces, present them with the torma, and request them to remain. The kings and the retinues face outward to protect the practitioners against all obstacles.

This is the relative protection spheres.

(b) The Absolute Protection Sphere

Even though **appearance and existence** manifest in an impure form, their nature is nothing other than our own rigpa, the all-pervading space of great simplicity that is free from conceptual elaboration. These extraordinary self-manifesting appearances that arise unceasingly out of this space-like expanse, have always been spontaneously perfect; they are the deities of the mandala of **infinite purity. Not even the name of the negative forces** (*dré*) and those of the various **obstacle** makers, who arise as the embodiment of deluded thoughts due to the circumstances created by the three types of ignorance, actually **exist**. So remain in meditative equipoise, and leave in the dharmadhatu, the great unborn nature of phenomena, all negative and obstructing forces that arise due to mistaken thoughts—the **adventitious** grasping at characteristics. By doing so, **deluded** appearances are confined to the **basic space** of dharmadhatu, and **the boundary is set**. This is the absolute protection sphere.

(c) Conclusion

The Rigdzin Düpa text clearly presents the command from the relative point of view, and presents the protection spheres from the absolute point of view. The relative command itself demonstrates the need for practicing the relative protection spheres. The description of the absolute protection spheres indicates that the absolute command is also necessary. They should both be practiced daily, and this is especially important toward evening, since it is the time when gods and demons are on the prowl.

(8) Descent of Blessings

By expelling obstructing forces and visualizing the protection spheres, we have eliminated unfavorable circumstances that could hinder the accomplishment of the practice. Now we create favorable circumstances with the descent of blessings and the blessing of the offerings. The first of these two practices is a general blessing of the practice site and articles, and the second is a specific blessing of the offering substances.

(a) The Visualization of the Descent of Blessings

The visualization for the descent of blessings is as follows: You are Hayagriva. Countless rays of red light emanate from your heart in the form of iron hooks that invoke the wisdom-mind of all the buddhas and bodhisattvas throughout the ten directions. The blessings of their enlightened body then descend in the form of deities, all of whom possess the major and minor marks of a buddha. The blessings of their enlightened speech descend in the form of seed syllables, while the blessings of their enlightened mind descend in the form of hand implements such as vajras and wheels. The blessings arrive and utterly fill the vast expanse of space and the surface of the earth. They dissolve into you, your place of practice, and the materials and implements you are using. They bless everything into its inherently pure nature.

(b) The Descent of Blessings in the Rigdzin Düpa Text

i) Invoking the Blessing of the Mind-Transmission Lineage

Since dharmata, the wisdom of the dharmakaya free from conceptual elaboration, is the basis from which *rupakaya* manifestations arise, it is referred to here as a **palace**.[44] Therefore, all the deities of the mandala, starting with the **primordial buddha, Samantabhadra**, who is also known as Vajradhara, the lord of the sixth family,[45] arise from the dharmakaya palace. The **buddhas of the five families in union**, the male and female bodhisattvas, and so on, their wisdom-minds inseparable from Samantabhadra, arise with him. Up to this point in the lineage, the realization has been transmitted within a single wisdom continuum, so these lineage holders are referred to as "**lamas of the mind direct-transmission lineage**." We ask these deities to **shower down** the **blessings** of their enlightened body, speech, and mind onto us, our place of practice, and our practice materials.

ii) Invoking the Blessing of the Sign-Transmission Lineage

The vidyadhara **lamas of the sign-transmission lineage**, the *nirmanakaya* vidyadhara **Garab Dorje**, the master Manjushrimitra, the vidyadhara **Shri Singha**, and the masters **Jnanasutra** and Vimalamitra, arise from the **Vajra Palace**. In other words, they are the illusory manifestation of Vajrasattva and arise as his display (*namrol*).

The oral tradition says it is not necessary to chant the following lines every day, because they were added:

> Garab Dorje, Manjushrimitra,
> Shri Singha, Jnanasutra, and so on . . .

However, my precious teacher Lushul Khenpo Könme said it is well known that Gyalse Shenpen Tayé, also known as Kushok Gemang, put in these lines. Also, their inclusion was confirmed by Jamyang Khyentse Wangpo, who, during a recollection from a past life,[46] remembered that these lines were included in the original text and omitted at a later date.

iii) Invoking the Blessing of the Oral-Transmission Lineage

From the palace of the nirmanakayas who train beings, who train students according to their capacity and appear in the form of great vidyadharas, manifest the **eight vidyadharas,** such as the master Hungkara, **Pema Jungne, the king** Trisong Detsen **and the subjects, the twenty-five disciples,** such as Vairochana, Yeshe Tsogyal, and so on, and the eighty mahasiddhas of Yerpa, who are the lamas of the oral-transmission lineage of superior individuals. As before, we request them to **shower down their blessings** on us, the place of practice, and our practice materials.

iv) The Blessings Descend

Make the following requests:

> "**Make** my practice **mandala glow in** magnificent and **vivid splendor! Make the practice articles**—amrita, torma, and so on—**glisten, sparkle,** and **bubble! Ignite** and increase the experience and realization of the wisdom of **great bliss in our body, speech, and mind,** and **grant us siddhis, supreme and ordinary,** right here and right now!"

v) The Mantra

To invite the masters of the lineage and bring them into your presence, recite the mantra:

> OM AH HUNG, the seed syllables of body, speech, and mind;
> VIDYADHARA, "holder of rigpa";
> E A RA LI, "give your blessings"; and
> PEM PEM, "here," as a way of saying, "We implore you, please bring them here."

(9) Blessing the Offerings

(a) The General Method for Blessing Offering Substances

Visualize yourself as Hayagriva with the syllable HRIH in your heart. RAM, YAM, and KHAM shoot out from the seed syllable and strike the offering substances. The three syllables purify the offerings into emptiness by burning, scattering, and cleansing them. Out of emptiness arises DROOM, which transforms into vessels made of precious materials that contain the offering substances. In essence these offerings have the nature of untainted primordial wisdom, and in appearance they arise as offering goddesses, such as the Goddess of Flowers.[47] Each goddess emanates countless other goddesses. They all hold immeasurable offerings of flowers, incense, and so on, and present them to the buddhas. Through their very nature the offerings have the capacity to please and delight the buddhas.

As for the inner offerings, imagine that three *kapalas* arise from the syllable AH. One of the kapalas contains the amrita, and the three syllables OM, AH, and HUNG are arranged on top of it. The syllables emanate and reabsorb rays of light, which transform the amrita into clouds of nectar that have the potency to satisfy the buddhas.

On the torma is the syllable OM, from where the torma sends out and reabsorbs rays of light. Goddesses, such as Vajrarupa, the vajra goddess of form, who by their nature delight all the deities of the mandala, manifest and fill the whole of space.

The syllable RA appears on the rakta and shoots out rays of light. The light rays gather all the desire and attachment of the three realms in the form of an ocean of blood, its waves thick with the corpses of men, horses, and so on, and are reabsorbed into the rakta. All this is blessed, so that the nature of the rakta becomes great bliss. From this radiance of bliss an infinite number of offering goddesses, all of whom have the ability to delight the buddhas, spread out into space.

(b) The Blessing of the Offerings in the Rigdzin Düpa Text

By saying OM AH HUNG, we directly destroy any thoughts of clinging to the offering substances as being impure. We rest in the naked state of inseparable rigpa and emptiness, and all impure ordinary perceptions of the offering substances dissolve into the dharmadhatu. The offerings then arise exclusively as the illusory manifestations of Samantabhadra, our own rigpa.

All phenomena, **all that appears and exists,** are blessed into what they have always intrinsically been, the display of **offering clouds,** whose nature is the **amrita of** primordial **wisdom.** Their appearance is the five kinds of **outer offerings:** flowers, the fragrance of sweet incense, light, scented water, and food. The **inner** offerings are the five sensual stimulants, such as form,[48] and the **secret offerings** are amrita, torma, and rakta. Essentially, all phenomena are transformed into the vast offering of primordial wisdom, which manifests as clouds of **offerings,** like those of **Samantabhadra.**

Now recite the offering mantras. Sometimes the part starting with **SARWA PENTSA**... is said three times, after the offering mantra has been recited. But my teacher[49] said that since the text of the Rigdzin Düpa places this mantra inside the "casket" of the three syllables OM AH HUNG, it should be recited three times *together* with the offering mantra, starting with OM VAJRA... and ending with... AH HUNG.

You might wonder why it is not enough for impure reality and perceptions to be purified through the cleansing, scattering, and burning actions of the syllables RAM, YAM, and KHAM. Why should we also have to arrange the seed syllables OM AH, HUNG and bless the offerings through the emanation and reabsorption of light rays? The answer is that for those who are able to practice this genuinely, purifying with RAM YAM, KHAM is actually enough. We bless the offering substances to purify ourselves of our ordinary fixated perceptions of the offerings, and this transforms them into a pure offering of primordial wisdom. If we can actualize this transformation and rest in meditation so that all phenomena arise naturally as the great dharmakaya, then there is no need for anything else. However, acknowledging that this is difficult to accomplish for all but those of extremely sharp faculties,[50] the oral teachings stress that we should apply ourselves to the blessing through the general method for blessing the offering substances.

d) The Main Section: Generating the Deity

(1) Kyerim Practice

(a) The Uncommon Path of the Secret Highest Yoga Tantra

The approach of the uncommon path of secret Highest Yoga Tantra, or Dzogchen, does not involve only the generation of deities that is a development of the coarse proliferations of thought we usually experience and taking them as the essence of the path. Rather, this approach consists of taking the very nature of the mind as the essence of the path. The nature of mind is present continuously, for the whole time that we are ordinary beings and until we become enlightened, without ever ceasing even for a single instant. It has never experienced any adventitious obscurations that need to be eliminated. The nature of mind is similar to the wisdom of the great dharmakaya, and it is this that, at the time of fruition, becomes the essence of the dharmakaya. It is called "the innate wisdom of the nature of mind" and it is not revealed in other sutras and tantras, but is hidden. It is this nature that is taken as the path in both its profound and its vast aspects.

Therefore, this approach is similar to all paths of the Highest Yoga Tantra in teaching that we must purify even the subtlest impurities of the mind and its perceptions and arrive at the supreme fruition. However, it is very different from these other approaches in the way the innate wisdom of the nature of mind is brought forth and put into practice.

(b) The Path of the Other Highest Yoga Tantras

i) The Way It Is Brought Forth

In the other tantras, where the innate nature of the wisdom of clear light is hidden, such as the other Highest Yoga tantras, it is taught that when elaborations of conceptual mind and mental states are present, the ground of the natural innate wisdom is not manifest, but latent, like a seed. Therefore, it needs to be revealed in order for it to become the path. To do this, these tantras explain that we have to halt gross thoughts, which is accomplished by bringing the *prana*-mind into the central channel. The skillful means used for this is to strike the vital points of the channels, wind-energies, and essences of the vajra body. For this to be fully effective, it needs to be preceded by the generation phase (*kyerim*).

The clear light manifests when the mind is matured through kyerim and then the prana-mind enters the central channel by means of the yoga of prana and *bindu*. When this happens, the clear light simply arises through the force of halting the prana-mind.

ii) The Way This Path Is Practiced

Therefore, the profound aspect of the path is practiced by connecting with the primordial rigpa and emptiness, while the vast aspect is practiced through the arising of the illusory body of the deity from the perpetuating or causal prana riding the clear light. And based on the path of these two accumulations, the fruition of the two kayas is obtained.

(c) The Dzogchen Approach

i) The Way the Innate Wisdom of the Nature of Mind Is Brought Forth

However, here, on the Dzogchen path, even when coarse thoughts proliferate in the mind of sentient beings, each thought is permeated by the cognizant aspect of the primordial wisdom of clear light, just as oil is everywhere within a sesame seed. Therefore, without going through the complex procedures of practicing *prana* and *nadi* (*tsalung*), and so on, if you now put the authentic introduction that you have received from your teacher into practice, all the important points of the path of the two accumulations that lead to the fruition, the two kayas, are gathered in the best possible way.

ii) The Way the Dzogchen Path Is Practiced

The profound aspect of the path is practiced when we are introduced to and take to heart the essence of rigpa, the aspect of primordial space beyond all thought and all conceptual limitations, such as the notions of being existent, nonexistent, and so on. Since all the qualities of the fruition, such as the kayas and wisdoms, have always been perfect and complete in their cognizant nature, all the key points of the vast aspect are brought together when we actualize the basic condition of all appearances as the nature of the deity and take this as the path.

(d) The Approach to Kyerim in the Rigdzin Düpa

Having clearly distinguished the different ways of establishing and bringing the great dharmakaya wisdom onto the path, we now turn to the Rigdzin Düpa. This practice is said to fall into the category of Anuyoga within Highest Yoga Tantra, because we practice by generating the deity with the four fully awakening meditations mentioned in the Mother Tantras. Concerning them, the Heruka Galpo Tantra says:

> First is emptiness and bodhichitta,
> Second is placing the seed syllable,

Third is perfecting the form of the deity,
And fourth is placing the syllables.

Since in the Rigdzin Düpa the deity mandala is generated by relying on the seed syllable, the development of the deity, and so on—basically by following the four fully awakening meditations—it is considered to be Anuyoga. However, the actual way of generating is like that of Atiyoga, and is similar in that respect to Yumka Dechen Gyalmo, the dakini practice of the Longchen Nyingtik.

Therefore, as we utter **HUNG**, all our thoughts and concepts are destroyed directly, and we rest in the sky-like state of rigpa, free from any reference or objective. With this all our thoughts, including our deluded perceptions, dissolve into the indivisibility of rigpa and emptiness, the all-pervading space of great primordial purity. In other words, we recognize nakedly the utter simplicity free of all conceptual elaboration, the state of **rigpa**, **unaltered** by thoughts, **empty yet luminously clear**. At this time all the essential points of the samadhi of suchness, in which the concept of holding things as real is purified into emptiness, are perfectly complete.

Out of this **state** of rigpa, from the **interdependence** of the rigpa **of vipashyana** and the unimpeded clear radiance of the appearance aspect, rigpa's self-radiance naturally arises, like rays shining from the sun. **All that appears** and exists has always been **spontaneously** present (*lhundrup*) without being created anew by causes and conditions, and is the infinitely pure **great mandala** of the victorious ones. It abides, **spontaneously** present and with all the qualities of the fruition already **complete**.

And all the key points of kyerim, the path of the three kayas that purifies birth, death, and the bardo, are also complete when we remain without moving from the unaltered state of rigpa, as its self-radiance arises as the deity. This is explained by the omniscient lord Dodrupchen Jigme Tenpe Nyima in his *Notes on Yumka Dechen Gyalmo*:[51]

> The essence, the utterly nonconceptual primordial space, is, at the time of the ground, the cause of the clear light of death, and at the time of the fruition, the cause of the arising of the ultimate dharmakaya.
>
> The nature, the aspect of unimpeded radiant clarity of primordial wisdom, is, at the time of the ground, the cause of the luminosity of the bardo of dharmata. At the time of the fruition,

it is the cause of the arising of the sambhogakaya with its seven inherent aspects.

The compassionate energy of rigpa, which appears dualistically as subject and object, is, at the time of the ground, the basis for the creation of the continuous and inexhaustible manifestations appearing from the bardo of becoming onward. At the time of the fruition, it is the pure cause of the nirmanakaya with its activity.

As these three aspects are complete within a single instance of rigpa, if they can be changed into the utterly pure deities, mantras, and wisdom,[52] all the crucial points of purifying, perfecting, and maturing are also complete.

We have to know this. However, for beginners who do not have the capacity to meditate like this, I have given in my Notes on the Palchen Düpa a short yet complete presentation of how to meditate according to individual capacity. Based on the oral instruction lineage, the notes describe how to practice the dissolution and then rest in the equality free of any reference point, remaining in the pride of the dharmakaya and so on, all in accordance with your capacity. So please refer to them.

In his *Notes on the Palchen Düpa*, Khenpo Chemchok says:

For Those of Lesser Capacity

Here you first visualize yourself as the deity and send out rays of light from your heart. They melt the whole universe and its inhabitants into light, which dissolve into you. You yourself melt into the core seed syllable by dissolving from above and below. The seed syllable in turn gradually dissolves into the nada, and you rest evenly in the state free of reference points, giving rise to the vajra confidence of the dharmakaya.

In general, the nada can be translated into sound as A. But A alone doesn't convey any meaning, in spite of its being a component of all words. In the same way, the appearances of samsara and nirvana do not exist, and the nature of all things is simply emptiness without focus. You need to rest in this state of emptiness free of reference points, because there is no way of meditating on pure deities without dissolving ordinary appearances, since phenomena—ordinary pillars and so on—are not the pure deities.

It is said that here it is important, at the very least, to practice the dissolution, and it is not enough to remain in the mere absence of thoughts. It is also not right to praise the absence of thoughts or comment on it excessively.

FOR THOSE OF INTERMEDIATE CAPACITY

Those of intermediate capacity bring in the view of Madhyamika and so on and rest evenly in the emptiness of true existence of all things, considering it as the natural primordial wisdom (*nyukmé yeshe*). They do not need to go through the stages of dissolution.

FOR THOSE OF SUPERIOR CAPACITY

Those of superior capacity follow the approaches of the *Guhyagarbha Tantra* or of Dzogchen. According to the *Guhyagarbha*, they rest in the basic space of rigpa, which doesn't exist as anything whatsoever. According to Dzogchen, having distinguished between the mind and rigpa, you directly enter the unaltered state of rigpa and rest. This is the specific way of practicing the samadhi of suchness in the Longchen Nyingtik. However, those who are not ready to do this should use one of the methods I have mentioned above.

---

(2) Visualizing the Great Mandala of the Lama Rigdzin Düpa

On the ground in the middle of the protection spheres is an immense thousand-petaled lotus. Its anthers support a crossed vajra with a square hub. The vajra has either twenty spokes to symbolize the elimination of the twenty views of transitory collection, or twelve spokes to represent the purification of the twelve links of interdependent origination.

(a) The Palace and Its Characteristics

i) The Palace

Visualize the inconceivable **palace** on top of the crossed vajra. It fits completely, from top to bottom, within the petals of the lotus when it is a closed bud. Made of precious substances, this palace is **inconceivable** to our ordinary mind and **delightful** to behold. It is **square**, hence it has four corners, and the walls are made of five layers of colored light; the innermost layer is blue, and then there are separate layers of green, red, and yellow lights. The outer layer is white, which is the same color as the main deity of the mandala, as is sometimes the case.[53]

In each of the **four** directions is a **door** and a gateway comprised of three parts: portico, side walls, and trefoil aperture. Surrounding the bottom of the palace is a red terrace called the pleasure terrace where innumerable offering goddesses stand, each sending out infinite clouds of offerings from their hands.

ii) The Four Friezes

Jutting forth from the top of the outer wall are four friezes. The lowest is the yellow brick frieze which is one *chatren*[54] high and inset with jewels. Above the golden brick frieze is the colonnade frieze. It is comprised of sixteen pillars that are one *chachen* wide and two chachen tall. There are four pillars set in each of the four directions. On the outer face of the pillars are gargoyles (*cipatra*), and four parallel golden chains that run around the perimeter of the colonnade. Hanging chains are suspended from the gargoyles' mouths, and looping chains are hung in loops from one mouth to another.

The flat golden beam frieze is above the colonnade frieze. The four vajra beams lie on top of the flat golden beam frieze. These four beams dissect and extend beyond the four corners of the palace. They also extend inward and support a central, circular, vajra root beam, which is also supported by eight pillars, two on each side. The four vajra beams support twenty-eight half-beams, seven in each quarter. These half-beams are covered by a flat roof that is aligned with the four cardinal directions. In the middle [on top of the vase structure, four] crossbeams leave an empty square where the roof lantern is. The half-beams support rafters made of precious substances that are in turn covered by smaller beams that form a net.[55] Above the extremity of the smaller beams, all around the walls, are the sloping sides of the roof of a pagoda.[56] Sharbu ornaments hang under the pagoda roof. They look similar to the traditional round water vases used by monks when they are turned upside down. The edge of the pagoda roof is ornamented with traditional square or lotus motifs. The third frieze is the sharbu ornament level, while the fourth is the pagoda roof.

iii) The Roof Lantern

A pillar stands where each of the four beams supporting the roof lantern cross. These pillars carry four flat beams that form a square. Above the flat square is a pagoda roof with a four-petaled lotus that surrounds an eight-sided jewel at its center. The very top of the palace is decorated with an ornament formed by a vase that is shaped like an incense censer, on top of which is a five-spoked golden vajra.

iv) The Gates

Four gates stand in the four directions. There are four toranas above each door: the golden cornice, the jeweled cornice, the cornice of sharbu ornaments, and the pagoda roof. On top of each of the cornices is a four-petaled lotus that supports a wheel of Dharma that is flanked to the right by a crouching deer and to the left by a crouching doe. There is a parasol over each Dharma wheel.

v) The Surroundings

There are trees made of precious substances, and celestial bathing pools around the outside of the palace. Beyond the thousand-petaled lotus are the eight great charnel grounds.

In this way the mandala is **complete** and has all of its characteristics.

(b) Symbols, Meaning, and Correspondence in the Palace

i) Symbols

The word "symbol" denotes the many different aspects of the palace that have just been mentioned, such as its four corners.

ii) Meaning

The meanings of the symbols correspond to the wisdom-mind of the buddhas, which arises as the various aspects of the palace:

- The palace is made from precious substances, signifying that this wisdom fulfills the hopes of those to be trained.

- The four corners of the palace illustrate that all phenomena have the same dharmata nature.
- The different colors of the floor and the gates placed in the four directions are an expression of the four wisdoms.
- The four gates are an expression of the four immeasurables.
- The eight causal torana (this means the doorway, which has eight steps) are an expression of the eight vehicles of the gradual path.
- The four resultant torana (the four cornices above the door) are an expression of the four ways of attracting students.
- The Dharma wheels, the deer, and so on are an expression of the constant and unceasing turning of the wheel of Dharma.

How the Palace Symbolizes the Thirty-Seven Aspects of Enlightenment

The thirty-seven aspects of enlightenment[57] are symbolized in the structure of the palace in the following way:

- The four sections of the pleasure terrace are an expression of the four applications of mindfulness.
- The four pillars that support each torana cornice are an expression of the four genuine restraints.
- The four gates are an expression of the four legs of miraculous powers.
- The five layers of the wall are an expression of the five powers.
- The four friezes and the central pavilion are an expression of the five strengths.
- The looped and hanging chains of precious substances, garlands of flowers, hanging silk ornaments, mirrors, crescent moons, and tail fans are an expression of the seven elements of enlightenment.
- The eight pillars are an expression of the noble eightfold path.

Other Enlightened Qualities

- The eight capitals distributing the weight of the beams on top of the pillars are an expression of the eight perfect freedoms.
- The four vajra beams are an expression of the four fearlessnesses.
- The twenty-eight half-beams are an expression of the ten strengths and the eighteen unshared qualities of a buddha.
- The pagoda roofs are an expression of the inconceivable positive qualities of a buddha.

· The four columns of the skylight pavilion are an expression of the four perfect knowledges.
· The top-ornament is an expression that all the qualities of fruition are included within the vast expanse of our own rigpa.
· The silken canopy is an expression of the perfectly pure dharmata.
· The parasol is an expression of the protection of all beings.
· The pennants are an expression of great compassion.
· The victory banner is an expression of the conquering of the maras.
· The bells are an expression of the lion's roar that proclaims the Dharma of emptiness.

The thirty-seven factors of enlightenment are the qualities of the primordial wisdom of the buddhas. They are perfectly complete in the very nature of the celestial palace and correspond to the meanings of the different aspects of the palace.

iii) Correspondence

Correspondence refers to associating symbols with their meaning. In a palace such as this, all **symbols, meanings, and correspondence** are **perfectly complete**. Since the palace arises in the wisdom of great bliss of the lama's mind, it is **vast** and appears as **unimpeded clarity**, with all features clearly visible and without any one feature obscuring the other. This is how to visualize this immeasurable palace.

(c) The Seats and the Seed Syllable

The eight-petaled **lotus** on which the deities reside is **in the center** of the palace. Covering its anthers at the center of the lotus is a second, delightful, and **multicolored** lotus. To demonstrate the purification of birth from warmth and moisture, sun and moon disk seats sit on top of the lotus. The sun seat signifies heat, the moon seat signifies moisture, and the syllable HUNG signifies the bardo. Visualize that the **HUNG**, the wisdom of the inseparable union of the lama's and your own mind, rests on top of the **sun and moon** disk seats, signifying also skillful means and wisdom.

This is how we meditate on the seed syllable at the beginning of the generation of the deity. As the *Guhyagarbha Tantra* says, all phenomena are solely the manifestation of names, words, and letters; so all the phenomena of samsara and nirvana are merely labels created by means of sounds and

concepts. In reality, none of these things exist; they are space-like emptiness. This is the realization we take as the basis for the paths of kyerim and
dzogrim. This is taught to make us realize that even the mandala of the
deities is nothing more than a manifestation of the root seed syllable, and
has no independent existence in its own right. Through this realization, it
is possible to understand that the fundamental nature of all phenomena is
enlightened in the form of the self-appearing deities of unbiased experience
(*rang nang rimé kyi lha*).[58]

(d) The Deities

i) Guru Rinpoche

Here it is not necessary to send out and reabsorb rays of light from the seed
syllable. Instead, **as soon as you think of it**, the seed syllable **instantly** and
completely transforms into the fully and perfectly visualized forms of the
deities.

The clear light of natural innate wisdom, which is indivisible from the
lama's mind, is the very subtle basis for the imputation of an "**I**," which we
visualize as **Pema Jungne**, the physical or outer form **of all the buddhas**, in
the aspect of **Prevailing Over All That Appears and Exists** (Nangsi Zilnön). He is the embodiment of all the buddhas, for as Guru Rinpoche said:

> See me and you see all the buddhas,
> For I am the gathering of all the sugatas.

Guru Rinpoche's single **face** is a sign of his realization of the one taste of
all phenomena and the dharmata as suchness. His **two hands** symbolize the
inseparability of skillful means and wisdom. His complexion, **white tinged
with red**, is a sign of the union of bliss and emptiness.

Regarding the three yanas, **as a sign of his complete mastery of the**
Shravakayana, Guru Rinpoche wears the traditional, patched **Dharma robe**
(*chögö*). His **silken cape** signifies his perfection of the Bodhisattvayana. Of
the two types of capes, a riding cape and a throne cape, Guru Rinpoche
is wearing a throne cape. As a sign of his complete mastery over the Mantrayana, he wears a great **gown** called the gown of ritual dances. He wears
the Dharma robe as the outermost layer, the gown as the innermost layer,
and the silken cape as the middle layer.

He **wields a five-spoked** golden **vajra** in his right hand. This is a sign that he has attained the level of a spontaneously accomplished vidyadhara, the essence of the five kayas, which is buddhahood in the Mantrayana, and is the perfection of all the qualities of elimination and realization. He holds the vajra **in the threatening mudra** because he accomplishes the activity of eliminating all harmful influences by terrifying and putting to flight all the demonic forces of dualistic thoughts.

In his left hand he holds a skull-cup filled with amrita, which contains a **long-life vase** (*tsebum*) filled with the wisdom nectar of deathlessness, its open top ornamented by the branch of a wish-fulfilling tree. This is a sign that Guru Rinpoche matures and liberates beings by means of the unsurpassable yana, and that he cares for students through the great siddhi of a vidyadhara with power over life.

Cradled in his left arm is the beautiful goddess Mandarava, the embodiment of the three kayas endowed with the seven attributes. She is white, wears silk and jeweled ornaments, and holds a long-life arrow in her right hand and a long-life vase in her left. Completely alluring, she embraces Guru Rinpoche outside his robes.

On his head, Guru Rinpoche wears a lotus hat, which demonstrates that he has perfectly accomplished the signs of realization of the empowerment of the five buddha families. It is said that the hat indicates the lord of the buddha family to which a deity belongs. As Guru Rinpoche is part of the Lotus family, all of his many hats include the word "lotus" in their name— the Lotus That Liberates Upon Seeing, the Lotus Bud, and so on. The hat he wears here is the Lotus That Liberates Upon Seeing, which was offered to him by the king of Zahor.

He sits with his two legs **in the graceful posture of royal poise**, a sign that Guru Rinpoche has entered the service of others, having accomplished his own benefit. Usually the posture of royal poise refers to sitting with the left leg slightly extended, but most ancient drawings show Guru Rinpoche sitting with his right leg extended. What I heard the All-Knowing Lord Dodrupchen Jigme Tenpe Nyima say is that here it is his left leg that is extended.

ii) The Lineage Masters

As a sign that Guru Rinpoche is guiding those to be tamed on the path of Dzogchen, the summit of all yanas, both Samantabhadra, the teacher of the summit of all yanas in Akanishtha, and Garab Dorje, who taught Dzogchen in the human world, sit **above his head.**

Garab Dorje sits in shimmering spheres of rainbow light, on lotus and moon disk seats, complete with all the **sambhogakaya adornments**, the eight jeweled ornaments and the five silken garments. His body is **brilliant white**, and **he holds a vajra and bell crossed** at the level of **his heart**.

Above Garab Dorje's **head**, on lotus, sun, and moon disk seats, is **the primordial protector Samantabhadra. He is** dark-blue in color, sitting with his two legs in the vajra posture and with his hands in the mudra of equanimity. **His consort** Samantabhadri is sitting in his lap. She is a lighter shade of blue, although both are still referred to as **sky-colored**.

Meditating on these three enlightened beings (Guru Rinpoche, Garab Dorje, and the Samantabhadra in union with Samantabhadri) one above the other is totally acceptable, because this method illustrates the close lineage (*nyegyu*) of Dzogchen. As it is said, "Padmasambhava went to see Garab Dorje, . . ."[59] and received many teachings from him, including those on the seventeen Dzogchen tantras.

iii) The Eight Vidyadharas, Twenty-five Disciples, and So Forth

The eight vidyadharas surround Guru Rinpoche's seat. **On each of the eight petals of the lotus is a sphere** made **of** layers of rainbow **light that enshrines one of the vidyadharas, who stand on lotus, sun, and moon disks. Each layer of light is made from one of the five colors** and encircles the previous layer. It is the eight bodhisattvas, the pure aspects of the eight consciousnesses present at the time of the ground, who arise as **the eight vidyadharas,** all of whom accomplished one of the deities of the Kagyé sadhanas **of the Glorious Heruka.** In essence they are the eight Kagyé deities, but they appear as the eight vidyadharas. In the eastern direction is Yangdak (Vishudda) in the form of the master Hungchenkara, also known as Hungkara, and so on. The rest are easy to figure out.[60] All of them appear semiwrathful, with two eyes, lines that look like tiger stripes on their foreheads, and with their mouths slightly open. The vidyadharas wear the **heruka costume** of a tiger skin skirt and bone **ornaments,** and their long hair is tied up in a topknot. They **play damaru and bell** with their **two hands** as they leap and dance. The vidyadharas are in union with their **mudra**—in other words their consorts—and manifest the play of vajra **dance.** The consorts wear leopard-skin skirts, the five bone mudras or ornaments, and hold curved knives and skull-cups. The **colors of** the deities in union who are in **the four cardinal directions** are white in the east, and so on.[61] The deity vidyadharas and their consorts **in the four intermediate**

directions—southeast, southwest, northwest, and northeast—**are dark blue**. As explained above, visualize the eight vidyadharas while recognizing that **in essence they are the eight** glorious **Kagyé deities** of the **Sadhana** Section of the Mahayoga.

All around Guru Rinpoche are a vast number of vidyadharas, such as **the vidyadharas of India**, the eighty mahasiddhas, such as Saraha, Luipa (also called Nyatopa), and so on; the **Tibet**an vidyadharas, such as the mahasiddhas of Yerpa, as well as **the twenty-five great incarnate** beings—**King** Trisong Detsen **and the subjects**, such as Vairochana. Their physical **appearance and styles of dress vary**, and they move assuming **all kinds of gestures of vajra dance**.

Above is the gathering of deities: the **yidams, dakas, and dakinis** of the **tantra section** of the Secret Mantra, along with the assembly of practitioners who attained accomplishment by relying on them. There are either **four** or six sections of the Secret Mantra: the four are Kriya, Upa, Yoga, and Anuttarayoga Tantra, or Highest Yoga Tantra; while they are **six** if Highest Yoga Tantra is divided into the three categories of father, mother, and nondual tantras. Visualize them appearing **like a pod of sesame seeds**, meaning packed with seeds, but still with space in between every seed.

iv) The Protectors

Concerning the "**outer pathway**," in one of his drawings, the powerful siddha, the omniscient Jigme Tenpe Nyima, drew a pathway or a terrace outside the palace for the protectors who obey the sacred commands. Actually, if this pathway were inside the palace walls, it would be called an intermediary pathway.

Also, as is well known, in the section of the *General Overview of Empowerment*[62] that shows how to draw the dimensions of a mandala, the Rigdzin Düpa mandala is used as the example. The text states that the outer circle surrounding the palace appears to touch the four corners of the square palace, thus forming four equal quarters. This is how we know there is no intermediate pathway, and why the pathway is outside the mandala, he said.

On this terrace are the **seventy**-five **glorious protectors, the twenty**-eight *ishvaris*, the mantra protectress Ekadzati, the five sisters of long life, and so on. These protectors received the profound empowerments of the vajra mandala from Palchen Heruka, Guru Rinpoche, and others. The vajra, the sign of empowerment, was placed in their hands and they came to reside within the borders of the mandala, **obey the commands** of the vajra speech, and be **bound** by samaya. The protectors **whirl about like the wind**, dispel the obstacles that hinder practitioners, and carry out limitless activities to ensure that practitioners are protected and accomplish the siddhis. To protect the practitioner from obstacles entering the mandala, they face outward.

At the **four gates** of the mandala are the **four** classes of **great ging**, who stand on corpse-seats in a protective stance. They all wield a corpse-club in their right hand and hold a skull-cup filled with blood in their left hand. Their appearance is semiwrathful, and their long hair is tied in a topknot. They wear a triangular pennant pinned in the middle of their hair, the ear ornaments that are characteristic of the ging,[63] and red silk skirts. They too face outward to protect practitioners from obstacles.

(e) The View of the Visualization

The nature of all the supported deities, as well as the mandala that supports them, is simply the wisdom of the great bliss-emptiness, the wisdom-mind of the lama, Guru Rinpoche. Consequently, the deities and the mandala appear and yet their nature is insubstantial: they arise as the display of emptiness. Recognizing this, meditate so that even the details of the white and dark parts of their eyes are precise and clear, and understand them to be spontaneously present and perfect from the beginning.

(f) The Extent of the Mandala

The extent of the mandala of deities is extremely vast. It encompasses the whole of samsara and nirvana, arising solely as the mandala of Lama Rigdzin. Since **all** samsara and nirvana is complete within the vast expanse of rigpa, nothing exists outside of rigpa. As all impure samsaric phenomena are just the numerous inventions of the conceptual mind, there is no reality to any of them. They are just **empty** forms **appearing**. When someone's bile disorder is cured, the yellow color that they perceived while looking at a white conch shell disappears. In the same way, when we rest in the primordial state of the inseparability of the nature of our own mind and the thought-free wisdom of Lama Guru Rinpoche's mind, conceptual thoughts and deluded perceptions are purified into primordial space. The pure phenomena of nirvana—all the qualities of the kayas, buddha fields, and so on of the buddhas of the ten directions and the three times—are all complete within the wisdom of our own rigpa, the vast expanse of Guru Rinpoche's mind. Indeed, the symbolic mudra in the form of the deities of the mandala of Guru Rinpoche is the manifestation of the absolute deity, dharmata.

As for the extent of the qualities of this mandala, everything that appears—the deities and their supports—are not merely a reflection. They are the wisdom of our own rigpa, which is the same as the mind of the Lama Guru Rinpoche, the wisdom of great bliss and that which arises from it. In the same way, not only the nature of the main deity and entourage, but also that of the seats, the palace, the trees around the border, everything down to the most minute particle is truly awakened. This is because their nature is dharmakaya wisdom—the result of complete elimination and realization, endowed with the three qualities of wisdom, love, and power.

(g) The Jnanasattva in Guru Rinpoche's Heart

Meditate on the jnanasattva, the vidyadhara Vajradharma (Dorje Chö) in Guru Rinpoche's heart. Of the different forms of Vajradharma, such as the body-Vajradharma and so on, here his speech aspect appears. He is red in color, with **one face**, a semiwrathful expression, **naked,** and wearing **bone ornaments.**

i) The Bone Ornaments

a. The Bone Wheel

Vajradharma wears a bone wheel on his head. It is formed from a small bone circle that sits around the crown of the head, surrounded by a second, larger circle. The two circles are attached to one another by eight bone spokes. On each of the five spokes at the front, above the forehead, stands a dried skull that supports the jewel, which is the crest ornament. From the lower part of their jaws, looped chains and hanging decorative chains extend downward to the space between Vajradharma's eyebrows and to the tips of his ears. On the back of each skull is a multicolored vajra with a crescent moon placed to the left. The deity's long hair passes up through the hole in the middle of the inner bone circle and is tied in a topknot.

b. The Earrings

There are five parts to the earrings. There is a main circle of bone, which is like a bangle. From the bottom of the circle hang two smaller rings, each one attached to the larger ring above them by a semi-circle of bone.

c. The Necklace

The necklace is made of two strings of bones bound together with hair taken from both a corpse and a living person. At the front is a square central hub. The hub forms the base for a T-shaped triple vajra. There are two more triple vajras placed at the two points where the strings of the necklace reach the shoulders.

d. The Bracelets

The deity wears a bracelet on each ankle, wrist, and upper arm, making six in total. Each bracelet is made from two strings of bones that have been bound together. There are three vajras on each pair of bracelets, one at the knot in the upper string, one at the knot in the lower string, and one opposite the knot in the upper string.

e. The Brahmin's Bone Thread

Next is the Brahmin's bone thread, or investiture thread (*yajnopavita*). On the front of the body, above the navel, is a bone wheel with either eight or four spokes. There are holes in four of the spokes and two parallel strings of bone pass through each of them. Two of these strings go over the shoulders, and two pass under the armpit. On each of these strings are two vajras on the shoulder and another two under the armpit, making eight in total. Sometimes there is a second bone wheel on the back, to which all the strings are tied; if not, all the ends of the strings are knotted together.

Together, or with the thread of hair from a slain thief,[64] these bone ornaments are called the ornaments of the five mudras.

f. The Bone Belt

The bone belt, or apron, hangs from the waist. It is made, as before, of two parallel strings of bone. The strings have five vajras attached to them—one at the front in the center, one on each hip, and one on each side of the center, halfway to the hips. Hanging chains and looped chains decorated with small silver bells and small bone spearheads hang from the tips of the vajras. The chains end at the point where the calf muscle begins to taper.

According to oral tradition, the necklace we just mentioned is ornamented with five vajras at the heart. Although I have consulted many descriptions of the bone ornaments, I have never seen this stated anywhere else. There are many traditions concerning the bone ornaments, but here I have presented that of the oral tradition taught by my master.

ii) Vajradharma

In his two crossed hands, Vajradharma **holds a vajra and bell**. He is embraced by **the blue yogini**. She holds a **hooked knife** in her right hand and **skull-cup** in her left and she wears the five mudras; in other words, the bone ornaments.

In the **heart** of the male deity, **upon lotus, sun, and moon** seats, is the *samadhisattva*; a dark-**blue** syllable HUNG the size of a mustard seed. It is surrounded by the revolving **mantra-garland**, which is also dark blue, and **as fine as if written by a single hair**.

The syllables of the mantra-garland are arranged counterclockwise, their heads turning slightly inward toward the core seed syllable, HUNG. The head of the syllable is the point at which we start to read them (i.e., from the left) as is explained clearly in *Notes on Takhyung Barwa*.[65]

As Guru Rinpoche belongs to the Lotus family of speech, his core seed syllable is usually HRIH. Nevertheless, as part of Invoking Inspiration and Blessing, we recite HUNG nine times: HUNG is the core seed syllable because the lama is the Kagyé.

Here I have presented the meditation of the three nested *sattvas*, according to the oral lineage.

(h) Invoking the Deities of the Mandala

In Guru Rinpoche's **three centers** are the **three syllables**, OM AH HUNG: on a moon disk seat in his crown chakra is the white syllable OM, the essence of the **vajra** body of all the buddhas; on a lotus seat at his throat is a red AH, the essence of the vajra speech of all the buddhas; and in the hub of a vajra in his heart is a dark-blue HUNG, the essence of the vajra mind of all the buddhas.

Visualize them clearly, and see them as being the **vajra** body, speech, and mind.

Rays of light, great bliss in nature, blaze and emanate with great **intensity** from the three syllables and the core seed syllable, invoking the wisdommind of all the buddhas and bodhisattvas throughout the ten directions. In this way we **invite** all the deities of the mandala of Rigdzin Düpa, together with their "supports" (the palace, their seats, and the environment), into this practice mandala. We invite them from the **supreme** sacred place of Akanishtha, the natural, **self-existing dharmadhatu.** We also invite them from Oddiyana, the nirmanakaya pure field to the **west** of the vajra seat. When the Buddha was in this world, he himself went to the **land of Orgyen.** He gave many teachings to King Indrabodhi and his retinue on the Highest Yoga Tantra, such as the *Guhyasamaja*, which resulted in the king and his entourage departing to the levels of the vidyadharas. The land then ceased to be the dwelling place of humans and became the residence of dakinis, the principal among them being those such as Guhyajnana (Sangwa Yeshe); the fields of power places and secondary power places such as the twenty-four sacred places, the thirty-two **sacred lands** like Jalandhara, **the eight great charnel grounds,** such as The Cool Grove (Shitavana), and so on; **and especially from the** field of the Palace of Lotus Light with its three levels representing the three kayas, located at the summit of **the Glorious Copper-Colored Mountain** in the center of **Ngayab Lanké Ling.** We say to them, "**Deities of the mandala of the Rigdzin Düpa,** together with your supports, I invite you from all these places to the practice mandala." We say, "Please come **to this place! SAMADZA!**" because samadza is an extremely respectful way of saying, "Assemble!" or "Please come here."

(3) The Invitation

The invitation purifies us of the mistake of thinking, "The deity I visualize is just a fabrication of my mind, so it must be inferior to the actual mandala of the Lama Rigdzin."

The invitation is chanted as a melodious song of yearning that is as plaintive as a young child crying out to its parents. As Guru Rinpoche said:

> Pray to me at all times during the six periods of day and night,[66]
> As harmoniously as the pleasant sounds of stringed lutes and flutes.

With a sweet-sounding voice, sing the invitation with intense longing and devotion.

"In the past, during the first kalpa" is a reference to times of supreme joy and happiness at the time of the first kalpa, like a golden age, when an immeasurable number of beings to be trained were matured and liberated through the unsurpassable vehicle. The expression "at the very beginning of this age" can also refer to the primordial buddha or primordial enlightenment. Primordial buddha is the ground before the onset of any delusory thoughts or concepts, the original kalpa of the manifest nature of things. This is the awakened state of a buddha that is the essence of the Lotus family of speech. When bringing benefit on a limitless scale to those beings to be trained through enlightened body, speech, and mind, the awakened state manifests for some time as vidyadharas. This, I think, is another way to explain this line.

The expression "at the very beginning of this age" also refers to the original time of the realization of the actual nature of the ground. This is the time before the onset of any delusory thoughts and concepts, which is what is meant by the expression "primordially enlightened." All the adventitious stains are purified and the natural state of the primordial ground is completely manifest. The awakened state of a buddha is the essence of the Lotus family of speech; in other words, we bring benefit on a limitless scale to those beings to be trained through our enlightened body, speech, and mind. So, "the time at which we manifest as a vidyadhara" is, I think, another way to explain a line. We say:

> "On **the northwest** border **of the** western **land of Oddiyana,** on an island in Lake Dhanakosha, you, Guru Rinpoche, were miraculously born on the anthers **in the heart of a blossoming lotus flower.** You did not rely on causes and conditions, such as a father and mother, but were born in the manner of rigpa arising instantaneously.
>
> Relying on the accomplishment of the level of vidyadhara with power over life, **you have attained the** five kayas and so on, which is **most marvelous:** you attained the **supreme siddhi,** the wonderful fruit. **You are renowned** throughout the sacred lands of dakas and yoginis **as the "Lotus-Born,"** the name you were given because of the way you took birth, and because you belong to the Lotus family of speech. You are **surrounded by your retinue of**

many dakas and **dakinis, and ocean-like hosts of the vidya-dharas and siddhas** of India and Tibet.

We invite all of you here, to our place of practice."

Why do we need to invite Guru Rinpoche and his retinue? Because, as Guru Rinpoche reached the supreme level of fruition by relying on the unsurpassable and profound vehicle, by **following** in his footsteps and practicing as he did, we too will accomplish the supreme and ordinary siddhis. We ask him to **come** and inspire **us** with his **blessings** so that we may quickly give rise to the extraordinary wisdom of realization and perfect the siddhis. Then we make this request:

> "**Shower down** the inconceivable **blessings** of **your** body, speech, and mind **on this supreme place** where the Lama Rigdzin Düpa is being practiced! Ripen our mindstreams by conferring on us, the supreme practitioners, the four empowerments! **Remove** the obstacles—unfavorable circumstances, and **any negativity that obstructs and disturbs our practice**—by destroying them! Quickly **grant us** all the siddhis: the **supreme** siddhi, the attainment of the five kayas of enlightenment in this very life, **and the ordinary siddhis**, such as the eight great ordinary siddhis, and so on."

After the music, we recite the mantra many times. When we call Guru Rinpoche "Tötrengtsal," we call him by his secret name, so he cannot help but respond quickly. Just as it says in the visualization section, rays of light stream out from the three seed syllables OM AH HUNG and the core seed syllable in Guru Rinpoche's heart to invite the assemblies of deities. They all arrive in the sky in front of us, flowing together like converging rivers of lava.

(4) Requesting the Deities to be Seated and Remain

The **mandala** of the support and the supported is **generated through the skillful means** of the samadhi of the ultimate vehicle, which uses the result as the path. We **invite** the jnanasattvas into this mandala, from Akanishtha and other pure realms. In the all-pervading **space of wisdom**, also called the "all-pervading space of dharmakaya," absolutely all phenomena are seen in their pure nature and in all their multiplicity. Without moving from the space of wisdom, the jnanasattvas arise in a limitless display of rupakaya manifestations. All the **deities of the** complete **mandala of Lama Rigdzin** descend. Like water poured into water, they merge and remain in one taste with us, the *samayasattvas*. We then pray to them: "**Stay contentedly in the absence of duality.**"

The invited deities spiral down in a clockwise direction. They dissolve into the visualization, beginning with Guru Rinpoche, the principal deity, who dissolves into the visualized Guru Rinpoche. One after the other, the deities of the retinue then dissolve into their visualized forms, and the palace dissolves into the palace. The jnanasattvas remain firmly and inseparably united with the samayasattvas.

The mandala arises as the self-radiance of our own great dharmakaya, inseparable from the lama's mind; it is the mandala of the actual Copper-Colored Mountain. If we hold this certainty clearly in our mind, we do not need to do anything else to invite the deities. Neither do we need to request them to be seated and remain.

(5) Symbolic Prostration

(a) The Importance of Paying Homage and Making Offerings

If we want the help of a king or another powerful person, then in order to present him with our request, we first need to invite him to our home. Then we need to show our respect by bowing down and by paying homage through whatever means is appropriate. We please him with food and drink, we offer him praise, and only then do we make our request. Here, we follow the same principle: before making our request to the deities of the mandala, we prostrate, paying homage, and make offerings.

Then, we emanate an identical deity, the activity deity from our heart (the heart of the principal deity). The activity deity moves to the eastern door of the mandala. He turns toward the center of the mandala and with his body, speech, and mind he offers the symbolic prostration of "seeing."

(b) Prostration

All the deities of the mandala, even the activity deity, are none other than our own mind, the great dharmakaya wisdom arising in these forms. Equally, we and the activity deity who prostrates arise as the absolute deity, the indestructible wisdom of dharmata. We prostrate to the fundamental, abiding nature of all the deities of the **mandala,** who **manifest** from the wisdom of the **self**-existing dharmakaya, by resting evenly in the state of knowing that there is **no good to adopt, nor bad to reject** in the one who prostrates, the object prostrated to, and so on. This is the absolute prostration of realization. The **symbolic prostration** of seeing is to understand that on the absolute level neither good nor bad exists, while maintaining respect by "seeing" the **interdependence** of practitioner and deity.

A TI PU HO means "I pay homage!" With PRA TI TSA HO, we consider that the deities slightly bow their heads in acknowledgment.

(6) Offerings

(a) Outer and Inner Offerings

Innumerable offering goddesses stream out from the heart of the activity deity and all the offerings on the pleasure terrace. They hold up the countless offerings that arise like Samantabhadra's magical display of offerings, delighting the deities of the mandala.

As we say OM AH HUNG, we keep in mind that the nature of the offering substances is the body, speech, and mind of all the buddhas. The display of these **clouds of offerings** appears as the totality of the universe, **outer vessel and inner contents**—both the **environment and the beings** within it.

The goddesses offer the five kinds of **desirable objects:** the Goddess of Flowers offers flowers to adorn the head, the Goddess of Incense offers fragrant incense to delight the sense of smell, and so on; **the five** kinds of inner **sensual stimulants:** for example, Vajrarupa, the goddess of form, offers mirrors to the eyes; the eight **auspicious objects,** such as the mirror, gorocana[67] medicine, and so on; the eight **auspicious symbols,** such as the parasol and the vase; **and** the **seven emblems of royalty,** such as the wheel, and so on. Offerings beyond calculation appear and are presented to the deities, delighting them. These offerings relate to the outer vase empowerment.

(b) Secret Offerings

Next we present the secret offerings: **amrita, torma, and rakta.** To offer the amrita we imagine, just as we did before, that innumerable offering goddesses holding amrita emanate from the offerings. With their thumbs and ring fingers, they scatter tiny drops of amrita that fill the sky, like clouds, causing an enormous rain of amrita to pour down from the clouds and delight the deities with great bliss-emptiness. From the torma, as before, innumerable goddesses such as Vajrarupa emanate. They offer tormas that delight the deities. From the waves of rakta stream out the corpses of human and nonhuman beings. At the same time innumerable goddesses of sensual offerings emerge from the foam on the waves, making offerings that delight the buddhas. These offerings relate to the secret empowerment. We offer the amrita, torma, and rakta **purely and joyfully.**

Even the briefest of glances at one of the goddesses is enough to ravish the mind. Their bodies are **seductive** and beautiful; they **laugh** and **sing,** moving their hands and feet in dance. Joining in union with them leads to the wisdom of great bliss, which is why they are called **the "wisdom consorts of** great **bliss union." Hundreds of thousands** of celestial **consorts** stream out. By making their offerings, they join in **union** with the deities, delighting their minds with **great bliss.** This offering relates to the wisdom empowerment.

The **offerings** of flowers and so on, **those who offer,** such as the activity deity, as well as the deities of the mandala, who are the **recipients of the offerings, are all utterly pure,** since they are **the** luminous great dharmakaya **space of wisdom,** in which nothing whatsoever exists. To rest in this utterly pure state is the **great mudra of offering.** This offering relates to the word empowerment.

With deep conviction we say, "All this **I offer** with devotion **to you, the deities of** the mandala of **Rigdzin Düpa. Accept** it with immense delight, **then grant us** the four **empowerments** that ripen and the instructions that liberate. Having established this basis, quickly confer the supreme siddhi and all the ordinary **siddhis!**" Following this, we recite the offering mantras.

The end of the mantra MAHA SUKHA DHARMADHATU A means "great bliss dharmakaya." All the offerings dissolve back into the space of wisdom and all that appears and is experienced brings satisfaction and becomes the fuel that causes the radiance of the wisdom of great equality to blaze. This is the vital point concerning the path of offering.

Finally, the activity deity is reabsorbed back into the principal deity's heart.

(7) Offering Praise

Praise and homage can be offered in three ways:

- The retinue can praise the principal deity of the mandala.
- The offering goddesses can emanate and praise the deities of the mandala.
- Or it can be offered by means of the self-resounding praise of dharmata.

The third method is the one we practice here. As we bring words of praise to mind, we imagine that the unborn, self-resounding empty sound of dharmata pervades in every direction.

(a) Praise to Guru Rinpoche

First, we say HRIH, which is the core seed syllable[68] of the buddha family of speech. Then we say:

> "**Lama** Guru Rinpoche, you are endowed with the **dharmakaya**, which you actualize by resting in meditation, never separating from the dharmadhatu, which is the **great simplicity** free from all conceptual elaborations, unfabricated by causes and conditions, and **unaltered** by thoughts. The rupakaya that **experiences great bliss (the sambhogakaya)**, which is like an ocean of immaculate treasures, is the **lama**—you are the **lord** of all the rupakayas, the sambhogakaya who resides in the self-manifesting Akanishtha. **Born from a lotus** flower on Lake Dhanakosha, **nirmanakaya lama, you** appear to all those to be trained, pure or impure. Guru Rinpoche, you are the unity of the **three kayas**, the precious teacher who attained buddhahood in the state of the great **vajradhara**. With devotion, **I offer** you **praise** and **prostrate** to you.

(b) Praise to the Eight Vidyadharas

> Great mahasiddhas, a long time ago **at Enchanting Mound** Stupa (Dechetsekpa), the dakini Lekyi Wangmo gave the

empowerments and instructions of the eight Kagyé deities to you. **You** then **ripened** the **siddhis** through following this **profound and vast path** that leads to buddhahood in one lifetime. **In the eight** great **charnel grounds,** such as Cool Grove, **you seized the stronghold of realization, master**ing **the** Highest Yoga tantras, especially the 6,400,000 sections of the tantras of Dzogchen—**an infinite, ocean**-like collection **of mandalas. To the eight supreme** great **vidyadharas,** Acharya Hungkara and the rest, **I offer praise** and prostrate to you!

(c) Praise to the King and Subjects

Your realization **soared into the vast expanse of** spaciousness when you actualized the mind of the buddhas—the nature of Dzogchen, which is the sky-like, vast expanse of rigpa, the utter simplicity free from all conceptual elaboration. Skilled in means, manifesting **all manner of** bodily forms and costumes, with diverse activities and conduct, you lead and **guide** all those to be trained on the path of ripening and liberation. **You** took as your practice the absolute view **of the extraordinary** short path of the luminous **vajra essence,** the Dzogchen, and you taught it to others. In this way, you up**held** the teachings and prevented their **life-force** from diminishing. To Guru Rinpoche's **heart sons, the king and subjects—the twenty-five disciples—I offer praise and prostrate to you!**

(d) Praise to the Protectors of the Dharma

To the protectors of the Dharma, we say: "You were brought under control by Guru Rinpoche's compassion and placed within the **mandala.** You uphold the samaya pledges that you took in this **spontaneously** appearing **mandala,** which manifests from the wisdom-mind of the Lama Rigdzin Düpa."

Essentially, in devotion we **offer praise** to all the **deities of the three roots**—the lama, root of blessings; the yidam, root of siddhis; and the dakini, root of activity—to all the **Dharma-protect**ing guardians, with their retinue of **messengers** manifested from the **wisdom space** of the lama's mind, and **to all the deities** of this completely perfect **mandala.**

(8) The Mantra Recitation

(a) Approach

Although the recitation manual (*The Casket of Siddhis*)[69] does not mention that we need to visualize the jnanasattva during the approach stage, according to the oral instructions of the lineage, we should visualize the jnanasattva. Therefore, we recite from *The Concealed Instructions* (*Gabjang*) the lines starting with, "**In the heart of Padmasambhava, subduer of all that appears and exists...**" and visualize the three nested sattvas, as previously explained.

i) The Mantra

a. The Mala

Once your mala has been blessed,[70] don't place it on the ground, don't show it to others, and don't let it part from the warmth of your body. When you go to urinate for example, consider that your mala manifests as a wrathful deity and leave it to guard your meditation seat. Recite the mantra at all times, and don't let your meditation seat get cold.

b. The Nature of the Mantra

It is said that "the nature of the mantra is the deity and the nature of the deity is luminosity." What is meant here is that we must be aware that the mantra is the deity. It is the great dharmakaya wisdom of our own mind that appears as the deities and the environment of the mandala, and the sounds of the mantra-garland are the deities of the mandala of the lama arising in the form of speech and mantra.

ii) The Visualization

The mandala of supported deities and the supporting environment, in particular the jnanasattva and the mantra-garland, is nothing other than the wisdom of great bliss manifesting in all these different forms. Therefore, simply by directing our focus toward them, we will have irresistible experiences of bliss. Actualize this as you consider that your visualization, which is clear down to the white and black parts of the deities' eyes, blazes intensely with rays of light, brighter than the light from hundreds of thousands of suns.

If you are not able to do this, recite the mantra while focusing your mind on the main deity, the mantra-garland, and the jnanasattva, and do the intermediate breath practice.

Once the visualization is clear, the experience of bliss blazes intensely in the core seed syllable and the **mantra-garland,** the garland of letters of the mantra. From this, **rays of** five-colored **light** (primarily red due to the interdependence of mastering the deity)[71] **stream out** to all the buddha fields throughout the ten directions. As soon as the light touches them, the buddhas and bodhisattvas are delighted with great bliss-emptiness, the enlightened mind. This invokes the blessings of their body, speech, and mind, which return to us in the form of light. As the light dissolves into the core seed syllable in our heart, the four types of obscurations are purified, we receive the four empowerments, and we actualize the four kayas. The experience of great bliss blazes even stronger, naked rigpa overflows, and we rest without fabricating anything.

Just as we take food into the body through the mouth to sustain all the elements of the body and to allow it to develop, the blazing of the experience of bliss in the principal deity, Guru Rinpoche, increases the blazing of the experience of bliss in the deities of his retinue. In this way, both the support and the supported are the single display of great bliss. So actualize this and rest in unaltered rigpa.

Now rays of light flow downward and touch all sentient **beings** throughout the three realms, **purifying** their negative karma, destructive emotions, and habitual patterns. They completely purify **the environment and all beings.** Now **everything has become pure:** the environment is the palace, and the beings within it are the mandala of the deities of the Rigdzin Düpa.

According to the oral tradition, we should visualize that all the deities are reciting the mantra. Even though we cannot multiply the number of recitations by the number of deities and add them to our accumulation total for the purposes of the recitation retreat, visualizing this way does greatly increase the power of the practice. This is a very profound point and we should definitely apply it.

iii) How to Recite Mantras

Regarding the correct way to recite mantras, the *Tantra of Magnificent Lightning* (*Ngam Lok*) says:

> Not too loudly, not inaudibly;
> Not hurriedly, not slowly;
> Not forcefully, not feebly;
> Not adding or subtracting syllables;
> Not distractedly, not while chattering;
> Not while obstructed by yawning and so on.

Accordingly, we should eliminate these ten defects. Abandoning all faults, like coughing, sneezing, yawning, and speaking, we should practice the approach continuously, like the uninterrupted flow of a river.

iv) The Vajra Guru Mantra

OM AH HUNG are the seed syllables of the three kayas.

VAJRA is dorje in Tibetan.

GURU means lama, or teacher. The word guru comes from the Sanskrit roots *guna*, meaning positive qualities, and *ru*, heavy with. So a lama is someone who is heavy with positive qualities.

PADMA: One of Guru Rinpoche's names is Padmakara, which means "lotus-born," and refers to the fact that he was born inside a lotus flower on an island in Lake Dhanakosha, and that he belongs to the Lotus family. The special significance of this is that Guru Rinpoche carries out diverse activities to benefit those to be trained, but he is not tainted by the faults of samsara, just as the lotus grows in mud but is not stained by it.

SIDDHI means accomplishment.

HUNG is the syllable of the three kayas, having three parts: the root syllable HA, the vowel U, and NG, the nasalization.

In brief, what we are saying when we recite this mantra is, "Guru Rinpoche, you who are the embodiment of the three vajras of all the buddhas: vajra body, vajra speech, and vajra mind," or "you who are heavy and replete with all the immeasurable great qualities of the three sacred vajras, Powerful

Sovereign Padma, I implore you: grant me the supreme siddhi, the level on which the three great kayas are actualized!"

v) The Song of HUNG (HUNG Lu)

Occasionally, send out and reabsorb rays of light because, as already explained, this increases the blazing of the experience of great bliss in all the deities. As you do so, consider that the soft murmuring sound of the song of HUNG arises. Then practice the song of the appearance of HUNG, and simply allow the mind to rest without reference, unaltered in rigpa.

vi) Lama Guru Rinpoche

It is very important to see your teacher at all times as inseparable from Guru Rinpoche. The general explanation for this is that we need to rely on the lama for the supreme siddhi and the ordinary siddhis to arise. More specifically, when you receive the empowerment your lama himself appears as the mandala of Rigdzin Düpa. Then when the wisdom deities are invoked from the Copper-Colored Mountain and the other places in which they reside, your lama becomes indivisible from them; it is from this state that he blesses your mindstream as the mandala of Rigdzin Düpa. Meditating in this way renews the potency of the empowerment.

Essentially, it is vital to never part from the yoga in which whatever appears arises as the mandala of the Lama Rigdzin Düpa, where we hear all sounds as the sound of mantra, and where all concepts or thoughts arise as the display of the wisdom of great bliss.

vii) The Vajra Chain

When the Rigdzin Düpa "notations"[72] says, "In the interval, persist in the vajra chain practice," it is referring to tögal meditation. Even if you haven't done all the required retreat recitation,[73] my teacher said[74] that no problem will arise from meditating like this.

viii) The Benefits of this Practice

The meaning in the "small writing" from "The yogi who practices this…" onward is easy to understand and refers to the benefits that arise from prac-

ticing in the way described. When practicing the approach, it is not necessary to practice the *do-li*, or "palanquin recitation."[75]

ix) The Duration of the Practice

As for the duration of the approach practice, it is one hundred thousand recitations for each syllable, which makes a total of thirteen hundred thousand
recitations. Reciting the mantras in order to pacify bad dreams and other
problems, reciting while your mind wanders, or adding the mantras you
recite during breaks between sessions to your total—none of these kinds of
practice should count toward the fulfillment of the recitation requirement.
Many benefits flow from the recitation of the mantra: the power of the mantra arises, obstacles are eliminated and obscurations purified, deficiencies
and excesses regarding your mantra commitments are repaired,[76] and the
invocation of the wisdom-mind of the deities is actualized. This practice
is called "approach," because, through your becoming intimately familiar
with the deity, it brings the deity's wisdom-mind into your mind.

x) Concluding a Session of Approach Practice

To conclude a session of approach practice, recite the vowel and consonant mantras, the hundred-syllable mantra, and the mantra of the essence
of interdependent origination three times each. This will amend faults of
lacking or excess and will ensure that the result of your practice remains
firmly with you. We should offer the merit created by reciting the mantra
to the deities. This protects the merit from being lost after its positivity
has ripened, or if we are overcome by anger, become boastful about our
recitation, or feel regret about it. Continue by blessing the offerings,[77] and
then recite the offerings and offering praise sections before jumping to the
confession of mistakes in practice, and recite from the dissolution to the end
of prayer of auspiciousness. After this, recite the "Secret Path to the Mountain of Glory: A Prayer of Aspiration for the Glorious Copper-Colored
Mountain."[78]

xi) Dividing Your Day into Sessions

Practice like this in three or more sessions every day, according to your
wishes. Don't make your early morning session or any other session longer

than the rest. Make them equal in length, and never recite less than a thousand mantras in any session. However many sessions you do on the first day, do the same number on subsequent days. Also, during breaks between sessions, recite a quarter of the number of mantras that you are reciting within a session. Unless you have stable diligence, do not at first promise to practice for too long in retreat. This is because there is a danger that you might bring harm on yourself by letting your initial commitment go. Instead, gradually increase your commitment and prolong your practice sessions. Your retreat should follow the shape of a grain: round in the middle and tapering at each end. What this means is that your retreat should be slightly loose or relaxed at the start and the end, but firm in the middle.

xii) What Not to Do in Retreat

When in retreat, don't do such things as give empowerments or blessings, perform exorcisms, or explain the Dharma to others. What is more, don't:

- Talk to those whose samaya has degenerated.
- Shake out your seat.
- Change the place where you sit.
- Talk about or show such things as the deity, the mantra, signs of accomplishment, and practice substances to others.
- Cut your hair or shave.
- Blow onto fire.
- Put sharp utensils into your mouth.
- Wash your bowls or clean your food.
- Eat food given to you by lepers, samaya breakers, and impure or negatively inclined people.
- Let such people go on the roof of your retreat cabin.
- Give your leftover food to dogs.
- Repair damaged cups and plates.
- Or let someone sit on your bed and cushion, and so on.

You should also know and apply all the usual instructions mentioned in recitation manuals.

(b) Accomplishment

Go through the practice text as was just explained and recite three malas (or as many as you feel is appropriate) of the vajra guru mantra as you actualize the approach visualization, including the emanation and absorption of light rays. After this, replace the visualization of the vajra guru mantra—the approach mantra—with the mantra called "essence of the accomplishment of the life-force of the vidyadharas," which embodies all the vidyadharas.[79] This mantra starts with OM and ends in HUNG. Elegantly nestled in between are twelve syllables. Finely written, as if by a single hair, and beautifully arranged, this is the mantra of accomplishment. It is the innermost essence of the life force of the Lama Rigdzin Düpa. Recite this mantra while resting in the understanding that deity and mantra are inseparable. As for the meaning of the mantra, MAHA means great, SARVA means all, and the meaning of the other syllables is as before. So very briefly what we are saying is: "You who are the embodiment of the three vajras, and who are heavy with their qualities, deities of the Lama Rigdzin Düpa, grant me all the siddhis, supreme and ordinary!" In terms of the number of recitations, since twelve hundred thousand mantras need to be recited in order to accomplish the siddhis, we should recite thirteen hundred thousand in total to make up for any deficiencies.

To practice the *do-li* or palanquin samadhi, we need to have attained clarity and stability in our visualization of the deities of the mandala by meditating without separating from the three awarenesses.[80] As the saying goes, "If there is no water in the dam, the irrigation channels cannot bring water to the land." This means that if the deities don't appear clearly, we cannot accomplish the emanation and the reabsorption of light rays. And, in particular, we cannot practice the palanquin visualization. The palanquin visualization is something we really do need to practice, because it is an extraordinarily skillful means for accomplishing the siddhis, as it gives rise to the wisdom of great bliss.

Visualize a red syllable BAM on a lotus and sun disk seat, as fine as if written with a single hair, at the heart of the yogini. As the core seed syllable and the mantra-garland in the male deity blaze with the experience of great bliss, their radiance and dazzling brightness increase infinitely. Like one butter lamp lighting another, an identical **mantra-garland streams out from the mantra-garland turning clockwise at the heart** of the male deity, forming an uninterrupted vajra **chain**. It is drawn along by the syllable OM, flows up through the body **of the jnanasattva, and** emerges **from** his **mouth. Entering the** yogini's **mouth, it descends and revolves counterclockwise around the** syllable **BAM at her heart, and** then **descends through** her body and exits through the opening of her **secret** place. Continuing on through **the path of the jewel** of the male deity, the mantra-garland moves upward and dissolves into the core seed syllable at his heart. Innumerable **mantra-garlands constantly revolve** in the same way, **like a** whirling **firebrand.** The firebrand has the nature of great bliss, and appears as a blazing luminous mass. As light spreads out in all directions, the almost unbearable experience of bliss grows ever stronger, causing **the experience of great bliss in the male and female** jnanasattva **consorts to blaze up unbearably.** This **causes light rays of compassion to stream out** from their bodies, which are in union, and extend everywhere throughout the ten **directions.** As these rays of light touch **the chief deity of the mandala** and **his retinue,** they **increase their experience of the wisdom of great bliss and emptiness.** Their bodies move in dance, **the hand drums** in their hands **rattle,** and their **bells ring.** Their speech **resonates** with the sound of the **song of HUNG.** Their minds overflow with the naked great simplicity of rigpa that is free from all elaboration. They remain, unwavering from the enlightened mind of clear light, indivisible **space and rigpa.** They also direct their rigpa so that the appearances of its dynamic energy, or its own spontaneous radiance, appear as **the complete perfection of this one** great deity **mandala** of infinite purity. They **rest without** ever **moving from this** state.

Ideally, by meditating in this way we destroy or interrupt the impure **perceptions of reality** caused by inner mistaken thoughts, namely the appearances of the **environment and beings,** or of **appearance and existence.** At this point we need to imagine that **the rays of light** emanating from the deities of **the mandala** stream out, pervade the whole environment and all beings, and purify these impure perceptions of reality. This is an important key point. The reason why this phase of the practice is called "accomplishment" is that, by practicing in this way, the potentials of both the supreme and ordinary siddhis actually become manifest, or are accomplished.

(c) How to Practice According to the Extraordinary Path of the Nyingtik

First, we distinguish between mind and rigpa. Then, rigpa, which is present as the nature of the three great kayas, is authentically introduced and held as the ground. Thoughts of subject and object are cut through instantly, and we rest without fabrication in the state of the great all-penetrating, natural rigpa. Unmoving from this, rigpa's own spontaneous radiance appears as the mandala of Lama Rigdzin Düpa, where jnanasattva and samayasattva are one. We rest in our visualization, with clear appearance and stable pride, recognizing that the mantra and the deity are indivisible. By practicing the three yogas of perceiving the body clearly as the deity, the speech as mantra, and the mind as clear light, we will progressively accomplish the three vajras of enlightened body, speech, and mind. In this way, never parting from these three mandalas—the mandalas of body, speech, and mind—by always applying mindfulness and awareness, and meditating by alternating between holding thoughts in mind with relaxing, rigpa will go on increasing in stability. As this stability increases, thoughts will become progressively subtler.

When we visualize the deity, there is an aspect of meditation being created by the mind. Therefore, we may find that visualization becomes more difficult as rigpa becomes more stable and the conceptual mind dissolves, meaning that thoughts appear less and less frequently and are less and less gross. At such a time, do not try to visualize more vividly, and do not let the appearance of the deity completely dissolve. Instead, train having a clear and stable[81] visualization of the deity by uniting the appearance of the deity with bliss. Invoke the wisdom of great bliss by practicing the palanquin recitation. By training in this way, you will directly see the face of the "natural great perfection" (*neluk dzogpachenpo*).

The key points of meditation that I have just explained show that the practice is not just about perpetuating the clear light, but also about the appearance aspect, the empty form of the mandala of the Lama Rigdzin, arising with it. When the clear light dawns in this way, meditation is nothing other than maintaining the experience of the great indivisibility of rigpa and emptiness. When you meditate like this, at some point dissolve the appearance of the palace and environment into the deities, and the appearance of the deities into the dharmata. This is known as merging inseparably into one taste, meaning that when all thoughts and delusory perceptions have been purified into all-pervading space, everything that appears becomes one thing only: the mandala of deities. This mandala of deities in turn becomes solely the magical display of self-aware rigpa, the great simplicity free from elaboration (*kadak trödal*).

As it says in the Palchen Düpa:

Deity, appearances, and dharmata—
When the nail of unity brings them together,
I have no doubt I will attain buddhahood
In the self-appearing absolute Akanishtha![82]

Fearing that a presentation on the paths and bhumis, as well as the ways to accomplish the fruition and so on would be a vast undertaking, I haven't elaborated on them much, as this can be understood by studying texts by the two omniscient ones, Longchenpa and Jigme Lingpa.[83]

To awaken the wisdom of the path and develop it, it is essential to meditate according to the instructions given in *The Scroll of the Oral Lineage*,[84] and on tögal.

Whenever you practice the approach and accomplishment according to the explanations given here, it is extremely important to hold the ground of the practice. This is achieved by training the mind in intense devotion, by knowing that your teacher and Guru Rinpoche are inseparable, and by training the mind in bodhichitta, after arousing love, compassion, and so on.

e) Conclusion: The Stages of the Tsok Practice

(1) Tsok

There are many detailed explanations of tsok that present the meaning of the word tsok, its etymology, and the different types of tsok, or "gathering": the gatherings of fortunate practitioners, abundant offering substances, and joyful deities, as well as the great gathering. So, rather than elaborating on these points here, I will briefly explain the tsok practice in the Rigdzin Düpa sadhana.

(a) Confession[85]

At the beginning of a tsok offering, it is important to purify impairments and breakages of samaya, because the deities will not accept offerings from anyone whose samaya has degenerated.

If you practice the *Inexpressible Ultimate Confession* (*Yeshe Kuchok*), you first say, "All the mandalas of primordial wisdom arise and pervade the whole of space,"[86] or, if you practice the *Emptying the Lower Realms from*

Their Very Depths (*Narah Kong Shak*), you begin with "Lama rigdzin . . . benza sama dza." As you recite one of these lines, the deities of the field of merit appear in the sky in front of you. Then you confess with the offering of the two sets of four causes of confession. The first set of four is related to confession and the second is related to fulfillment.

The four causes of confession are: (1) With the body, we pay homage by making full prostrations. (2) With the speech, we recite the verses of confession as a lament. (3) With the mind, we use the four powers to confess with remorse. (4) With the confession of the view that applies to the three other causes of confession, we rest in the great simplicity of dharmata, free from conceptual elaboration—there is no one confessing, no one to confess to, and so on.

The four sections of fulfillment are the offerings of medicine, rakta, torma, and the lamp.

If you practice the Inexpressible Ultimate Confession, which comes from the *Rampant Elephant Tantra*,[87] recite the hundred-syllable mantra, preferably one hundred times and certainly no fewer than twenty-one times. As you recite, confess all general faults and downfalls as well as the particular degenerations and breakages of the samayas of the Secret Mantrayana by making use of all four causes of confession. Consider that all the negative actions and obscurations accumulated throughout every part of your body gather into a black pile on your tongue. Then the deities of the field of merit send out light rays that strike the pile of accumulated negativity and purify all obscurations. Not a single trace of negativity is left; just as if all the dust were being blown off the surface of a mirror. At this point, rest in unaltered rigpa.

For the second set of four causes of confession, recite the brief fulfillment offering of the four sacred substances that begins with "HUNG! Within this wondrous mandala of secret instructions . . ." ("ka sang mé du . . ."), and make the offerings. This heals all degenerations and breakages of samaya, and restores and fulfills the samaya. Then you recite, "Sentient beings are as limitless as the whole of space . . ." ("namkhé tartuk . . ."), and the field of merit dissolves back into you.

(b) The Tsok Offering Itself

For the tsok offering itself, arrange as many outer, inner, and secret offering substances as you can afford. They should be made from every possible kind of offering of sensual stimulants that the world has to provide. In particular, meat and alcohol are specific samaya substances of Highest Yoga Tantra and are absolutely essential components of the tsok offering.

i) Blessing the Offering

In order to bless the offerings, sprinkle the three inner liquids[88] onto the offerings. As you do so, it is necessary to visualize rays of light emanating from HUNG, the core seed syllable. This is an important point. Visualize yourself clearly as Guru Rinpoche, with **the letter HUNG** at your **heart**. From this seed syllable, **RAM, YAM KHAM emanate**: From RAM, fire bursts out and burns away all imperfections and defects in the tsok. From KHAM, water pours out and washes away all imperfections and defects. And from YAM arises a wind that scatters and disperses **all imperfections and defects**.

Then everything dissolves into emptiness.

Out of this state, the letter KHAM arises as the self-manifesting appearance of the great inseparability of rigpa and emptiness. From KHAM emanates a tripod that supports a kapala. The tripod is made of three human heads, each one as large as Mount Meru. The kapala, whose forehead points toward you, is white outside, red inside, and as vast as the billionfold universe. **OM AH HUNG transform** the tsok substances inside the kapala into an abundance of the five meats and five **nectars**.

Beneath the kapala is fire in the form of the seed syllable RAM. Below RAM is YAM, the seed syllable of air, appearing inside the crescent-shaped mandala of the wind. Wind rises from YAM and strikes the syllable RAM, causing fire to blaze up. The nectar in the kapala boils and vapor rises from it. The lid of the skull-cup is a moon, on top of which stands a half-vajra with five spokes. The cavity inside the hub of the vajra is ornamented with the syllables OM AH, and HUNG, which are arranged vertically. When the vapor touches the syllables, rays of light radiate out from them. The light pervades the buddha fields of the ten directions, to which all respond by sending out wisdom nectar that is reabsorbed into the nectar inside the kapala.

The nectar is now in essence wisdom and has the appearance of nectar. It transforms into tsok offerings of every sensual stimulant that could possibly be desired and **fills the whole of space**. The offerings are purified with RAM YAM KHAM, and then blessed by OM AH HUNG.

ii) Inviting the Field of Merit

The invitation begins with the core seed syllable, **HUNG**. Where do the deities we invite come from? They come from Akanishtha, the **realm of great bliss**, with the Buddha Field of Dense Array (Tukpo Köpa) in the center, the Buddha Field of Manifest Joy (Abhirati) in the east, and so on. They also come from **Orgyen**, the **land** of the nirmanakaya emanation Guru Rinpoche **in the west, and, especially,** from the land of **Ngayab** in the southwest, with the realm of the **glorious** Copper-Colored **Mountain** in the center. Many come from the twenty-four **sacred places**, the thirty-two sacred **lands,** the **eight** great **charnel grounds, and so on.**

Who is invited? **All** the **deities of** the mandala of **Rigdzin Düpa.** How do we invite them? With intense and yearning devotion, we say to them, "We invite all of **you to this** place where the **tsok offering** is being made. As you already know this because of your unobstructed wisdom, **come** quickly, **we pray!**"

Where are they invited? To **the** joyful **tsok shrine** of the great, spontaneously manifesting mandala of the buddhas, which is located within the **charnel ground.** The charnel ground is the state free of the eight consciousnesses, which are all mistaken, deluded thoughts, once they have been liberated into all-pervading space. This is just the right place to hold the tsok; it's **so full of joy!**

It is **heartwarming and inviting and,** thanks to **the** vast **gathering of dakinis** from the sacred places and sacred lands, the experience of great bliss increases. The tsok place is extremely **pure,** because **the yogins and yoginis** who are gathered there protect their Mantrayana **samaya** perfectly. It is **bright and pleasing** because **the** sensual stimulants **of the offering** have been transformed into untainted wisdom nectar. This is why you should come to this place!

Having come here, what do we ask the deities to do? To **shower down** their great **blessings** of body, speech, and mind upon the gathering of practitioners, and **grant** them the **supreme and ordinary siddhis.** At this point, Guru Rinpoche invites countless deities by sending light streaming out from the core seed syllable in his heart. The deities form the field of merit in the sky in front of you. If there is a front-visualization however, dissolve it into this field of merit. A front-visualization is practiced only in the case of gathering practices[89] and the receiving of the siddhis. In all other cases there is no need for it, because we practice with the front-visualization indivisible from the self-visualization.

iii) Offering the First Portion of the Tsok

When a wise man needs the help of a king or someone else in a position of power to help him bring a plan successfully to fruition he will first establish a connection with him by taking an oath of allegiance and pledge to help him with his body, speech, and mind. If the king becomes displeased with him or holds a grudge against him, the wise man will also change his behavior and reestablish a good connection. By first creating a solid relationship, the wise man will then be able to accomplish his wishes. Similarly, in order to accomplish our wishes and aims, we offer the first portion of tsok to the wisdom deities to establish a close connection with them.

Visualize a vast array of offering goddesses emanating from your heart. A vast multitude of tsok offerings—forms, sounds, and so on—arise from their hands and fill the whole of space. We offer all this to the deities of the three roots. We particularly offer it to the **ocean**-like assembly **of** deities of the mandala of the lama **vidyadhara** assembly, to the hosts of **dakinis** from the sacred lands and sacred places, **and** to the ocean-like assembly of **protectors who keep the samaya** vows and guard the sacred teachings. We **offer** this **sumptuous and abundant tsok offering of sensual stimulants** to all of them, in the way explained above. Then we request them: "In return, please **grant us** the **siddhis, ordinary and supreme.**"

Regarding the literal meaning of the mantra:

> GANA means "gathering" or "assembly,"
> CHAKRA means "wheel,"
> PUJA (or PUTSA) means "to offer," and
> KHAHI means "enjoy!"

The offering pleases the deities by bringing them the experience of great bliss. Then the offerings and the deities who made them are reabsorbed back into your heart.

iv) Confession

The practice of confession is for purifying any displeasure we have caused the deities through breaking our samayas and allowing them to degenerate. For this purpose, we emanate offering goddesses as before. They present an unimaginably vast offering of the five meats, five nectars, and so on. As they do so, we think:

"I sincerely regret all the negative actions and downfalls I have ever committed, **in all my lives without beginning**. Especially, I regret whatever **root** downfalls and **violation of the branch samayas** I have committed since **I** first **passed the door of the Secret Mantra** Mahayana (maha means "great," or "as vast as space") by receiving empowerment. With the support of this **offering of sensual stimulants, I now confess**. Please grant me the supreme siddhi, the fruition which is free from obscuration."

In this way, we express our sincere regret to the deities, and then make our offering. Our offering completely satisfies the deities and all breakages of samaya are purified. Then, as we say VAJRA SAMAYA AH, we actualize the great vajra samaya of resting in unborn space.

v) Annihilation

a. Liberation Through Annihilation

The practice of annihilation is a special activity of the Highest Yoga Tantra.

The principal activity of the Mahayana path is to bring benefit to all beings. All vehicles from the bodhisattva vehicle up to and including Highest Yoga Tantra teach that the way to benefit those beings to be trained who are not already practicing Dharma is to bring them to the Dharma through the four ways of attracting students: generosity, pleasant speech, giving beneficial guidance, and acting in accordance with one's speech. However, none of these paths teach the skillful means for bringing malevolent beings to the path of Dharma—beings who are so corrupt that they cannot be trained through the four ways of attracting students. In this practice, even malevolent individuals who have committed all ten misdeeds, and who are considered enemies, can be subjugated through the special activity of annihilation.

What is the method of liberation through annihilation? As it is said:

The great samaya of liberating through compassion
Is neither killing (out of anger) nor suppressing (out of ignorance).
My whole body is transformed into vajra,
And my consciousness is transformed into its true nature.[90]

This shows that annihilation is realization, and that it is not the same as killing someone with a weapon when motivated by destructive emotions such as attachment or anger. Instead, by relying on the key points of focusing on life, cleansing, and place,[91] and by relying on the special four immeasurables as taught in the *Lha Gyü*,[92] what annihilation actually liberates is our karma, negative emotions, and thoughts. The activity of annihilation makes our naturally present wisdom manifest and brings us to the level of Lama Rigdzin.

We will not have the capacity to liberate others through compassion unless we first liberate our ego through realization. And even if we can annihilate others, our act of annihilation would only be annihilation in the ordinary sense of the word and would bring no benefit to the one being annihilated. It would only cause our own faults to increase, and create obscurations on the path.

But, when grasping at a self and its confused perceptions have been liberated into the dharmadhatu by the wisdom that realizes the nature of things, we gain the extraordinary wisdom of the realization of dharmata. At that point, even if we do not liberate others through compassion, enemies, demons, and the like will not be able to harm us. As it says in the *Way of the Bodhisattva*:

> Since all violence and harm,
> Fears and sufferings in the world
> Arise from grasping at self...[93]

As these three lines show, if there is no grasping at a self, there will be no violence, and so on.

In terms of liberation, the main approach of Rigdzin Düpa is the liberation of self through realization. The principal obstacles to our attainment of enlightenment are factors such as the three types of ignorance and mistaken dualistic perceptions. To annihilate these obstacles and actualize our inherent dharmakaya is the root of the Highest Yoga Tantra path. Consequently, the steps for the activity of annihilation are the main steps necessary for performing the tsok.

b. The Actual Practice

For the annihilation, take either an effigy or a portion of the tsok, and put it to one side when blessing the tsok. If you have already blessed the annihilation portion of the tsok, then it is important to reabsorb the offering goddesses from the annihilation offering back into your heart. Next, place the effigy or tsok portion in the triangular box in front of you. Sprinkle rakta onto it and recite a *gukpa*, to summon harmful forces through the power of truth, three times. This summons those who are to be liberated, and they then merge indivisibly with the substance.

Who or what is to be summoned? **Ignorance** and the elements, aggregates, and so on, which circle in samsara through the force of **karma, destructive emotions, and dualistic grasping.** We also summon all the **rudras** of **ego-clinging,** the imputed ignorance that **breeds** all the enemies and negative forces of deluded appearances.

Where are they summoned? **Into the effigy** or tsok substance. **NRI** is the seed syllable of the consciousness of the enemies, and **TRI** is the seed syllable of the consciousness of the obstructing forces. As we say these two syllables, followed by **DZA**, we visualize the negative forces becoming indivisibly united with the **bod**ily support (i. e., the effigy or the tsok substance). Then, as we say: "The dualistic **consciousness** is **sent** into rigpa, the all-pervading **expanse of** primordially pure **dharmadhatu—PHAT!**" the consciousness is ejected upward and dissolves into rigpa. We then rest, free from grasping, in the great natural simplicity that is beyond any elaboration.

Next, we sprinkle amrita and *tsok chang* onto the effigy, which is the manifestation of ordinary confused perceptions. The blessing transforms the effigy into wisdom nectar, which we offer to the deities of the mandala as the **tsok offering. They enjoy it and** are satisfied.

RUDRA SARWA HALA refers to the flesh and blood of the rudras of dualistic grasping that are liberated. With **PENTSA**, these impure appearances are transformed into wisdom nectar. **PUTSA KHAHI** means "enjoy these undefiled offerings!" These words fill the deities of the mandala with great bliss. They are delighted and satisfied by the offering.

The method for quelling the three faults of reversibility, attractiveness, and sympathy through the three visualizations, as well as the method for compassionately liberating others through life, cleansing, and place are explained in texts such as *Notes on Drupchen*, by my revered teacher Dodrupchen Jigme Tenpe Nyima.[94] For this reason, I will not elaborate on them here.[95]

At this point, recite the *The Vajra Lute—A Brief Fulfillment for the Lama Rigdzin Düpa*,[96] or any other appropriate fulfillment practices.

vi) Enjoying the Offering Substances

It is crucial to view all the offering substances—those offered at this point as well as those offered at earlier or later stages—as the lama's wisdom-mind arising as clouds of offerings. This wisdom-mind is the wisdom of bliss and emptiness inseparably united with our own rigpa.

As you enjoy the tsok, you can consider that you are receiving the siddhis, although there is no fault or anything lacking if you do not. Enjoying the tsok while recognizing that it is wisdom nectar causes the great bliss experienced by the deities of the self-visualization to blaze. These deities send out rays of light to the deities of the field of merit who, in the state of great bliss, melt into light and dissolve back into the deities of the self-visualization. The entire mandala of the support and supported becomes the display of incomparable great bliss. Enjoy the tsok as you actualize this.

vii) Remainder Offering

First we bless the remainder offering and transform it into wisdom nectar. This is done either by spitting on it or, to do it on an aspirational level, by sprinkling the offering with water from the vase, whichever is appropriate.[97] At the same time, we recite the akaro mantra.[98] Then we make the offering.

During recitation retreats, the remainder offerings are always gathered together and confined to the northeast of the mandala until the siddhis have been received. This is because the remainder guests are attached to the remainder offering, so by keeping it we ensure that they remain part of the retinue and continue to protect us.

a. The Preparation of the Remainder Offering

After receiving the siddhis, offer the remainder.

How is the pure remainder—the fourth offering—combined with the impure remainder that is gathered from the feast offering enjoyed by the assembly? Mixing the pure remainder into the impure is like placing the subjects higher than the king. In this arrangement, auspiciousness and power are weak. On the other hand, mixing the impure remainder into the pure is like placing the king above the subjects. Although the power is increased, it is still an inauspicious arrangement.

To remedy these two faults, first mix a little of the pure remainder into the impure, and then mix all of the impure remainder into the pure. Next, take a portion of the tsok offering substances from the mandala, which is called the "magnificent remainder offering." Place it on the remainder offering and bless the remainder offering in the way that has just been explained.[99]

b. The Recipients of the Offering

To whom do we give the remainder? To the ocean-like gathering of samaya-bound protectors who keep the sacred commands and **dwell** at the **edge of the great mandala** of Rigdzin Düpa: the twenty-eight **ishvaris**, the eighteen great **ging**kas, the seventy-five glorious protectors, the hundreds of thousands of **langkas**, and the rest. We offer the **remainder torma** of wisdom nectar and ask the samaya-bound protectors to **accept** it. Why do we do this, and what should they accomplish in return? We entrust them with activity when we entreat, "May I attain enlightenment through the practice of this samadhi" or "Always **protect us yogins from** all the **obstacles** that prevent us from **accomplish**ing enlightenment!"

c. The Mantra

> UTSITA means "remainder,"
> BHALINGTA means "torma," and
> KHAHI means "accept, enjoy!"

As we recite the mantra, we make the offering. This satisfies the recipients and they accomplish whatever activities we entrust to them without hindrance. We then dedicate with the prayer beginning, "Through the merit of this tsok offering…" ("tsok chö pulwé…").[100]

(2) Summoning

First, we summon those to be annihilated by reciting a *gukpa*, to summon harmful forces through the power of truth, three times. Next, in the summoning prayer in the sadhana text, we say, "**Rise up!**" Who do we ask to rise up? **The deities** of the mandala **of Rigdzin Düpa**. From where do they rise? **Out of the dharmadhatu**, the great freedom from elaboration. Without stirring from the dharmakaya, they **arise** as the lama vidyadhara in the blazing **form** of wrathful Hayagriva. Once they have arisen, what do we ask them to do? We make this request of them:

> With your wrathful activity, please **crush any obstacle to** our practice of the path that leads to great **enlightenment**. Please pacify and dispel sickness, famine, warfare, and so on. **Halt the**

degeneration of the continuum of the **elements in the environment and in beings. Heal any** weakness or **deterioration** in the **channels** (*nadi*) and the **wind-energy** (*prana*) of the vajra body—the special support for following the path of the Highest Yoga Tantra—and in our **wang tang**, "authentic presence."[101] Having healed them, restore their strength and make our **practice** of this great mandala bring the **results** of the supreme and ordinary siddhis. Protectors, do this right now!

Through this request, we entrust these activities to them. Briefly, the visualization is as follows: while visualizing yourself as Guru Rinpoche, consider that many Hayagrivas emanate from your heart. They annihilate all those to be annihilated, leaving not even the slightest trace behind, not even their names. Their flesh and blood is then blessed and transformed into nectar that has the essence of wisdom. This is offered to the guardians of the teachings, and it delights them. Completely satisfied, they accomplish without any hindrance whatever activity we entrust to them.

(3) Covenant (Cheto)

Sprinkle the *cheto* torma with amrita and rakta, and bless it so that it transforms into wisdom nectar. Who are the recipients of this offering? The protectors of the teachings who reside at the boundary of the mandala. Here, in the spirit of the lines:

> Since I belong to the lineage of vidyadharas,
> And you belong to the families of gods and demons…

…we remind the protectors of how they were bound under oath by Guru Rinpoche and others. We repeat their solemn oaths and samayas so that they remember and uphold them. This is why we offer them the torma, and why this section is called cheto, or "covenant."[102]

When the text says, "**Long ago, in the Akanishtha heaven of great bliss**," it means "the Buddha Field of Dense Array, or Tukpo Köpa, and **the three god realms**—Tushita, the Heaven of the Thirty-Three, and Akanishtha—from among the five pure abodes, and so on." **In** these pure, **pleasant places**, when teachers such as Vajradhara **revealed the great secret tantras** of **Vajrayana**, especially the Dzogchen tantras, Ekadzati and others were specifically empowered and established as their **protectors**. They were granted empowerments and took the **solemn samaya commitments** of the Secret Mantrayana. They were then **given a seat** on the boundary of the mandala behind the deities to remain as the guardians of the teachings.

Later on **in Tibet, the land of snows, the master Padma Tötrengtsal turned the wheel of Dharma of the Secret Mantra** teachings, the Clear Light Heart Essence (Ösel Nyingtik) teachings, and so on. At that time, all the worldly **gods and spirits** of Tibet, such as Nyenchen Tanglha, offered him **the essence of their life-force. He seized it**, empowered them, and established them as guards of the Vajrayana. Therefore, they are considered to be **guardians of the teachings.**

Finally, "in the pure field of clear light" corresponds to the experience that Jigme Lingpa recounts in his autobiography, *Dancer Like the Moon in Water*, when he writes:

> In the pure state of clear light, I met the king of Dharma from Orgyen, Manjushrimitra and others, in the sky before me . . .[103]

Here in the practice text, the essence of **clear light**, which is the basic space free of any adventitious stain and without any inherent existence, is called "**pure field.**" **Great bliss**, the cognizant nature, corresponds to **the palace.** I think the reason for this is that the extraordinary natural self-radiance of these two—the empty and clarity aspects—gradually becomes the pure land and the palace. **Within** the state of luminosity, **Lotus-Born** Guru and the omniscient **Drime Özer** (Longchenpa) revealed their face to the **vidyadhara** and mahasiddha **Pema Wangchen**, which is another name for Jigme Lingpa. They entrusted him with the teachings of the ultimate **profound** and vast pith-instructions of the Dzogchen **Longchen Nyingtik**, and they encouraged and inspired him. When the appearance of walking along the eastern walkway of the great stupa at Boudhanath arose in his mind, Jigme Lingpa immediately met the dharmakaya **wisdom dakini** face to face. She **handed him** the scriptures of the **radiant expanse of Longchen Nyingtik** in **symbolic** script, and Za Rahula, "**Life-Force Razor of Wild Rahus**," along with **other** guardians of the teachings, offered their help.

Entrusting these guardians with activities, we say:

> "All of you, who on these three occasions—in front of Palchen Heruka, Guru Rinpoche, and Jigme Lingpa—promised to dispel obstacles and create favorable circumstances for us practitioners

of this profound mandala, **accept this offering torma with all its ornaments** that is blessed into wisdom nectar and be satisfied. Swiftly **accomplish** all of the actions, which comprise **the four kinds of activity**: pacifying, enriching, magnetizing, and subjugating."

Consider that the protectors and guardians then carry out this command and accomplish their activities as we have requested, without any obstacle.

(4) Offering to the Tenma

Although Shabdrung Pema Trinlé[104] said not to put a torma on the shrine for the Tenma[105] and offered only the "rinsing water," in the practice tradition of Longchen Nyingtik we offer a torma. Pour the rinsing water from the cheto torma over the torma for the Tenma, sprinkle it with amrita and rakta, and bless it into nectar. To whom is this offering being made? To those who **obey the sacred commands of the** great **glorious** lama himself[106] and who were established as great female guardians to **protect Tibet**. They are the twelve *mamos* of supreme bliss, who come as **the twelve Tenma mothers and sisters**[107]—the four female demons, the four menmos and the four yakshinis. We say to them: "All of you, together with your retinue, please **come** here! **The rinsing water of the torma** and this torma have been blessed into nectar. We offer it to delight you completely. Enjoy it, **and** quickly **carry out** whatever **activities we demand of you!**" We recite MAHA HRING HRING, the life-force mantra of the Tenmas, then BALINGTA KHAHI and make the offerings. We consider that this delights them all and that they carry out whatever activity we demand, without any obstacle.

(5) Horse Dance—Suppression

Place the plate from the cheto torma upside down, and summon those to be suppressed with a *gukpa* to summon harmful forces through the power of truth. Who is being suppressed? Those practitioners "already associated with me from previous samaya." These practitioners were our vajra brothers and sisters and received empowerments and other transmissions with us, but later became demons. Since the protection spheres could not block them, we now need to suppress them. We say and consider:

"Now, on this occasion of practicing the profound **mandala** of the victorious **lama vidyadharas**, the demons of the **samaya breakers** who **lead astray** and have a negative influence **are suppressed** beneath the vessel of the torma, which is clearly visualized as Mount Meru. They are **buried beneath the seal of the nine yanas and never rise again!**"

(6) Receiving the Siddhis

(a) The Day Before

When you finish your practice after seeing signs in the approach and accomplishment practices, or after you complete the set numbers of mantras, you need to do the following: On the day before you receive the siddhis, at the close of the afternoon session, arrange the substances for receiving the siddhis, replenish the old offerings, and make some new ones. During the evening session follow the text of the practice up to the end of the offering praise section. Say the mahaguru mantra, with DROOM BISHO BISHUDDHE at the end to "divide the mantra-garland," which means that you visualize a front-visualization that is identical to the self-visualization that separates out from the front-visualization. This is done by visualizing that a jnanasattva mandala emerges from the self-visualization and sits in the sky in front of you amid a mass of flames. Considering that there is a jnanasattva in both the self-visualization and the front-visualization, recite and actualize the mantra visualization section. Recite as many vajra guru mantras as you wish, and just enough mahaguru mantras. Next, recite the lines beginning with "**From the mantra-garland turning clockwise at his heart...**," and recite as many mahaguru mantras as is appropriate. Then recite the mantra for receiving the siddhis,[108] which is the main mantra we recite here. Multicolored rays of light stream out from the mantra-garland in the self-visualization, touch the deities of the front-visualization, and invoke their wisdom-mind. From their three centers stream out all the siddhis of body, speech, and mind in the form of white, red, and blue rays of light respectively. These rays of light enter the three centers of the deities of the self-visualization and the siddhi substances. You obtain all the siddhis, supreme and ordinary, while the siddhi substances transform and become wisdom by nature, and gain the capacity to bring liberation when they are swallowed.

After reciting the mantra for receiving the siddhis, continue with the offerings section and offering praise section. Then do confession by reciting the hundred-syllable mantra 108 times—strengthening each recitation by preceding it with VAJRA SAMAYA DZA.

Next, chant receiving the siddhis and with deep respect make the request to receive the siddhis by reciting the mantra twenty-one times. Continue through the rest of the practice as usual, except that during consecration (*rabné*), you request the front-visualization to remain in the images.

(b) The Actual Day of Receiving the Siddhis

Early morning is a good time to practice because that is when the clarity of rigpa is untainted. It is also a meaningful time because early morning is when our Compassionate Teacher, Buddha Shakyamuni, became enlightened. For these reasons, it is important to receive the siddhis in the early morning.

Therefore, a little before dawn, go straight through the root sadhana and practice the division of the mantra-garland and so on, as in the previous session. Then recite the offerings section, and offering of praise section, and do an extensive practice of tsok and fulfillment.

Recite the confession and fulfillment practice known as *The Spontaneous Vajra Song of Fulfillment and Confession*. After the last line, "**Into the vast expanse of natural Dzogchen AH**" ("neluk dzogpa chenpöi long du AH"), say VAJRA SAMAYA DZA.

Then recite the *Inexpressible Ultimate Confession* through to the end, and accumulate twenty-one or 108 hundred-syllable mantras, each strengthened by being preceded by VAJRA SAMAYA DZA.

Next, expel the obstructing forces from the siddhi substances[109] and meditate on the protection spheres. After that, send the invitation by reciting the seven-line prayer three times, followed by "HUNG! Rise up Padmakara..."[110]

Recite the descent of blessings section, and receiving the siddhis, followed by the mantra for invoking the siddhis twenty-one times. Touching your three centers with the practice support torma or accomplishment torma[111] and the siddhi substances, receive the siddhis while visualizing in the manner that has just been explained. Maintain the visualization and receive the siddhi substances in a respectful way by slightly raising yourself off your seat and enjoying them.

Then, briefly perform the offerings, and offering praise sections, and enjoy the tsok. From this point on, follow the order of the root text.

As for the meaning of the words in the sadhana, as you say **HO**, rejoice that you have had this opportunity to receive the supreme and ordinary siddhis. Continue by saying:

> "By relying on **all the deities of the mandala of** the lama **vidyadhara** assembly, I have **fulfilled** the **samaya** commitment of reciting the set number **of approach and accomplishment** mantras. Now, **the dawn of** the body, speech, and mind of the Glorious Lama **Vajrasattva is breaking** and **the time has come to grant** us **the** supreme and ordinary **siddhis.** Through the **secret** of the mind of the victorious buddhas (**from** Lama Vajrasattva's secret **mandalas of body, speech, and mind**), the **wisdom** of our own rigpa that does **not dwell** in the extremes of samsara and nirvana, which is the supreme **vajra body, speech, and mind**—inspire us with your blessings, **and grant** us all **the siddhis, supreme and ordinary,** without exception, at **this very instant!**"

Here we chant the mantra beginning with **OM AH HUNG**. Only share the accomplishment substances, such as siddhi substances, with those whose samaya connection to you is pure, such as retreat attendants.

(7) Confession of Mistakes in Practice

Send out the activity deity to the eastern door of the mandala. To whom do we make the confession? To the deities of **the mandala of Rigdzin Düpa.** What do we confess? Such things as **incomplete offerings, distraction** during approach and accomplishment **practices,** lack of clarity in our **meditation** due to **drowsiness, dullness, and lifelessness.** We confess **all confusion, mistakes and** whatever negativity has arisen during the practice of this profound path. How do we confess? With intense regret, saying: "Through this confession may all the deities **forgive** us!" Thinking this, we purify all degeneration and breakages of samaya by reciting the hundred-syllable mantra. Once we are purified, we are completely free of any obscurations and the supreme siddhi is bestowed on us. The activity deity then dissolves back into the heart of the self-visualization.

(8) Dissolution

(a) Dissolution Itself

If we consider the main part of the practice primarily in terms of the yogas of enlightened body, speech, and mind of the three kayas, then: the generation of the deity is the yoga of the mudra of the form of the deity; the recitation is the yoga of speech as mantra; and suchness is the wisdom-mind yoga of the great clear light. We practice these increasingly subtle yogas to purify the extreme of permanence, or existence. The mandala of the deities—the support and the supported—manifests from the primordial wisdom of the great dharmakaya, which is my own rigpa. In other words, **the mandala and the deities are self-arisen**, or naturally present. **Like bubbles on the surface of the water dissolving** back into the water, as we say VAJRA MU! the mandala and the deities **dissolve into the** unaltered **space of primordial wisdom** free from elaboration, the vajra space of inseparable rigpa empti-ness. Rest as long as you can in the unimpeded clarity without reference point, in all-pervading space, which is nothing whatsoever, free from elab-oration. Rest in clear light.

When you come out of this state, **the form of the deity,** Guru Rinpoche, **arises** instantaneously **in postmeditation** like the sudden appearance of a magical illusion. See the environment and beings as the display of Guru Rinpoche's **body,** speech, and mind. Always maintain the awareness of yourself as Guru Rinpoche, with the three seed syllables present in your three centers, and remember that their nature is the body, speech, and mind of the buddhas. They are the armor equal to the deity. This is important.

(b) General Postmeditation Advice

Between sessions, seal all that appears to the mind—all the activities of postmeditation, dreams, and so on—with the yoga practiced during the sessions. Once you are used to doing this, everything you do is the contin-uous flow of the approach and accomplishment practices. If you act like this, accomplishment is close at hand and the power of the blessings will increase greatly.

Otherwise, even if you practice to the very marrow of your bones during the formal sessions, but cast the continuity of the practice to the wind during the breaks by getting caught up in irrelevant conversations and distractions, then the next practice session will be just like starting from the very beginning again. Since you will lack any skill or stability, your approach and accomplishment practices will not have much power, and it will take much longer to reach accomplishment. No matter how many days, months, or years you spend in retreat, there will not be even a hair's breadth of improvement within you and you will leave the retreat as just another ordinary being; and that really would be a tragedy. Rigdzin Jigme Lingpa's *Mountain Dharma* says:

> How difficult it is to obtain a human body!
> How difficult it is to meet the Dharma!
> How rare is a qualified teacher!
> How numerous are the gateways to evil!
> There is no one who will not die one day!
>
> It is necessary to reflect deeply on the torture endured by people living an ordinary life, and to feel the same revulsion for samsara that someone with bad indigestion feels for greasy leftovers.[112]

Reflecting on this, give rise to strong renunciation, the longing and determination to be free from samsara. As Shantideva's *Compendium of Trainings* (*Shiksasamuchaya*) says:

> Crazed by destructive emotions, blinded by delusion,
> On a treacherous pathway alongside steep ravines,
> Stumbling with every step we take...

Generate immense compassion by contemplating on how all sentient beings, our former mothers, are confused about which actions to adopt and which to abandon and are afflicted by constant and unrelenting suffering. Then generate bodhichitta, the wish to accomplish the fruition of great enlightenment for the sake of all beings. With your mind infused with these thoughts, reflect in the following way:

> "Now I possess this unique opportunity because I have excellent support and am blessed with all the freedoms and advantages. This is entirely the result of relying on the great compassion and kindness of my precious lama. I must follow his profound

instructions precisely, because they will guide me on the mirage-like journey to buddhahood! I have the same precious chance that the omniscient Longchenpa, Jigme Lingpa, and the other victorious teachers had in the past! This is an incredible opportunity. It is not just a dream!"

Thinking this, feel joy beyond measure.

Practice the path with extreme diligence, regardless of whether you perceive deities or demons, have good or bad dreams and meditation experiences, endure illness, and so on. Whether you hear pleasant or unpleasant words, think good or bad thoughts, or if anything such as attachment to your retreat place or signs of accomplishment arises, do not let hope or fear inhibit one thing and encourage another. Instead, by maintaining the awareness that the nature of all phenomena is the three mandalas, allow your rigpa to expand and increase. As was already explained, never separate from the three yogas that bring form, sound, and thought onto the path.

(c) Concluding the Retreat

Once the practices of approach and accomplishment are finished, we should perform a fire offering (*jinsek*) for reparation of mistakes, and completion for what was omitted. If you do not make a fire offering, recite the hundred-syllable mantra for a week or more after you have received the siddhis. This is important, because it will magnify the power of the deities of the Rigdzin Düpa. It will also remove any negativity that would have been dissolved by the fire offering.

Then, after dark, make offerings to the protectors without anyone else seeing you. In postmeditation, from within the state of the deity, offer the gyalto torma (*totor*) and the prayer to depart,[113] and take down the boundary posts.

In the initial stages of the post-retreat period, protect your place for the first three days or so by not seeing people too quickly. Meet those who have the purest samaya connection with you first.[114]

(9) Prayers of Dedication and Aspiration

Dedication and aspiration prayers are very important because they multiply the merit we have accumulated by the number of sentient beings we dedicate it to, and because they are the cause for enlightenment. As it is said:

Dedication is the way to make things inexhaustible:
It multiplies and transforms.

The difference between dedication and aspiration is that during dedication we think of the sources of our merit and give them away, while during aspiration prayers we simply wish, for example, "May all beings have happiness." There are three possibilities: we can recite dedication prayers on their own, aspiration prayers on their own, or combine them.

(a) Dedication

For the dedication we say,

> "All the positive acts performed in the past, all those that are bound to be performed in the future, together with all the positive actions carried out in the present moment—in short, **all** the **virtues of** positive actions performed with or without concepts throughout **the three times**—I gather together and **dedicate** them **to be the cause of realizing** the **omniscience** of Samantabhadra, the **primordial** lord, the sacred helmsman and guide for countless beings."

(b) Aspiration

The aspiration is, "**May I and all those gathered** in this profound mandala, the male and female practitioners assembled **here, attain enlightenment together in one mandala!**" Recite the prayer three times and seal it with the dedication free from concepts.

(10) Prayer for Auspiciousness

Imagine that the lamas, buddhas, and bodhisattvas in the sky before you sing beautiful songs of auspiciousness resonating everywhere throughout the three worlds. They scatter flowers that float down in a soothing shower and accomplish the intention expressed in the songs that say:

"**Through the blessing of the** compassion of the lamas of the **lineage,** the unbroken chain **of vidyadharas** from Samantabhadra until the present, through the immense power of **the truth of Buddha, Dharma, and Sangha,** and the power of **the** auspicious interdependent **circumstances** of practicing the approach and accomplishment of **the profound Secret Mantrayana** teaching of Lama Rigdzin:

May all be auspicious to quell swiftly **the eight fears** of drowning, thieves, lions, snakes, fire, flesh-eating demons, captivity, and elephants![115]

May all be auspicious to increase our **longevity and merit** ever further!

May all be auspicious to bring all things—the **appearance** of the environment and beings—effortlessly **under our control!**

May all be auspicious to bring about a glorious abundance of joy and happiness in all beings by **annihilating negative forces**—enemies and so on who lead us astray—through wrathful activities such as killing, expelling, and paralyzing!

May **all appearances and grasping** at impure confused **perception,** the many manifestations of the aspect of appearance, be **perfected** into the play of **the mudra of the form** of the **deities** of the Lama Rigdzin.

May **all sounds,** whether natural or produced by sentient beings, be **purified** into mantra through arising as the play of the **mantra,** the spontaneous radiance of the wisdom of **great bliss.**

May all dualistic **thoughts** be purified **into the** space of unaltered natural rigpa, **matured** into the wisdom of the vast **clear light of dharmakaya.**

Finally, may **we attain the rainbow body** of great transference in this very life, and continuously accomplish the welfare of sentient beings—**may all be auspicious** in **unimpeded** clarity!

2. Afterword

Born like a wondrous stream of nectar from the two accumulations,
Spontaneous white light of permanent and all-pervasive actions,
You who dispel the darkness of samsara and nirvana and bestow the
  majesty of great bliss,
Incomparable and supreme lama, always care for me!
The vital points of the pith-instructions
Of the most profound Heart Essence of Dzogpachenpo gathered here
Are easy to practice, yet extraordinarily effective.
Like the wish-fulfilling king of jewels, the rain of blessings from this
  sadhana of the vidyadharas
Satisfies all hopes and desires for liberation!
An ocean of amrita, these pith-instructions
Carry the blessings of the lineage of transmission—an unbroken chain of
  vidyadharas.

Like the sweet spittle of the great masters who have fully experienced them,
They are the nectar of the very essence of the practice!
Even so, our childish minds, caught in the net of destructive emotions and
    karma,
Have difficulty understanding the meaning of this profound text.

Therefore, whatever negative actions and faults I have committed, which
    have obscured me throughout time without beginning,
In the presence of the supreme sources of refuge who are endowed with
    wisdom, I confess!
Just as the powerful bodhisattvas have dedicated,
I dedicate all the merit from this virtuous action,
Along with those accumulated by myself and others throughout past,
    present, and future, to the perfection of good action,
So that all beings may cross the ocean of existence!

May those who are a refuge for beings and who carry the responsibility of
    upholding the teachings,
The supreme lineage holders who increase the study and practice of these
    extraordinary teachings,
Have long and stable lives!
And may the goodness and virtuous qualities that arise through the
    enlightened activity of these teachings increase!

From this day forward,
Throughout all my lives,
May I follow my incomparable lama.
Practicing according to his instructions, may I actualize realization
And hold the treasury of the sacred Dharma, the sole fortune of beings.
May I spread and develop the Dharma, and accomplish the benefit of
    beings on an extremely vast scale!

Just as Manjushri dedicated,
Through perfect actions and intentions,
May I establish all beings on this most secret path,
So that the sun of the teachings may blaze in every direction!

*Wanting to benefit the Nyingtik teachings, I thought to compose these
notes on the Rigdzin Düpa Inner Sadhana that I called "The Words of the*

Vidyadhara That Bestow the Majesty of Great Bliss." On top of that, some vajra brothers and sisters and Dharma friends strongly requested it. So, thanks to the kindness of many great masters I, the indolent beggar Lobsang Jampa, or Chemchok Thonduptsal, put this together. May the teachings of the buddhas, and specifically the teachings of the Vajra Essence of Clear Light, spread and extend throughout every direction and remain forever. Virtue! Virtue! Virtue! Sarva mangalam!

The Light of the Sun and the Moon— Generation and Perfection Stages

Notes Explaining the Words of the Rigdzin Düpa,
the Inner Sadhana for the Longchen Nyingtik Cycle

By Khangsar Tenpe Wangchuk

Lotus-Born, Dharma king who rules over the three realms,
Longchenpa, holder of the treasury of the three sections of
    Pith-Instructions,
Jigme Lingpa, owner of an ocean of profound termas—
O self-arisen rigpa, the sole union of these three masters, I pay homage to
    you.

A. Introduction

Here, I will present briefly the way to direct the practice of kyerim and dzogrim for the Rigdzin Düpa sadhana, based on the following texts:

> *The Ladder to Akanishtha, the Instructions on the Generation Phase
> of Deity Practice*, by the great vidyadhara Jigme Lingpa;[1]
> *Melody of Brahma Reveling in the Three Realms: Key Points for
> Directing the Practice for the Four Nails That Bind the Life-Force
> of the Practice*, by Orgyen Jigme Chökyi Dawa Palzangpo, also
> known as Patrul Rinpoche;[2]
> *The Casket of Siddhis, A Recitation Manual for the Rigdzin Düpa*, by
> Jigme Lingpa;[3]
> *The Words of the Vidyadhara That Bestow the Majesty of Great
> Bliss: Notations on the Rigdzin Düpa*, by Khenpo Chemchok
> Thonduptsal.[4]

Patrul Rinpoche said:

> Anyone who follows this path will reach complete liberation
> Without effort, just like iron transmuted into gold by an alchemist,
> The sole extraordinarily skillful approach for covering the path in an instant—
> This is the supreme king-like vehicle.

Anyone who has the good fortune to **follow this path** of the union of kyerim and dzogrim **will reach complete liberation,** which will occur **without** the practitioner having to exhaust him or herself by making great **efforts.** Patrul Rinpoche gives the example of **the alchemist transmuting iron into gold.** Liberation occurs without taking any time—**in just an instant. This** extraordinary skillful means for **covering the path** to buddhahood in a single lifetime is a special and unique feature of the Mantrayana, the **king** or **supreme** of all **vehicles.**

All the approaches of this vehicle are gathered in the vajra path of union. "Union" refers to the union of skillful means and wisdom, of kyerim and dzogrim.

The other schools only present the path of kyerim alone, which is an approach involving mental fabrication. They do not emphasize the view of the great equality and purity of environment and beings, an extraordinary and crucial point of the long transmission teachings of the Nyingma school.[5] As an antidote to ordinary attachment and perceptions that we currently experience, and as a means to stop the ignorant mind from grasping at things as truly existent, which must be interrupted, we emphasize the sole view of the great equality and purity of environment and beings by means of these three aspects of practice: clear appearance, recollection of purity, and stable pride in oneself as the deity. It is extremely important that we give rise to this view within ourselves, with a certainty that nothing can undermine—Patrul Rinpoche repeated this again and again.

The Four Reasonings

In its fifth chapter, the root *Guhyagarbha Tantra* says,

> Same basis, the way seed syllables are formed,
> Blessing, and direct experience—

These are the four excellent realizations
That lead to the great king of universal perfection.[6]

As the tantra states, we need to rely on the four reasonings, or four "realizations," to eliminate our ordinary, impure perceptions and realize the higher two truths in their indivisibility. All the key points of kyerim are included within this skillful means. What is the ultimate objective or goal to be attained through applying these four reasonings? "The great king of universal perfection," in other words to attain, based on the path of the union of kyerim and dzogrim, the level of the Truly Perfected King, the embodiment of the four kayas and five wisdoms, also known as the great universal Buddha Vajradhara.

So how, according to the long transmission of the Earlier Translation school (Nyingma), should we establish the great equality and purity of the universe and beings with these four reasonings?

1. The Reasoning of Same Basis

The object of refutation of these reasonings is the grasping at the self. The way to refute it based on the reasoning of similarity with the cause is as follows:

We identify the object of refutation as the string of stubborn thoughts that grasp at the self, the habitual tendencies our negative mind has been cultivating from time without beginning in samsara. They are refuted by the reasoning that comes from the Madhyamika tradition that follows the sutra path, and that goes: "A pillar is devoid of true existence because it is similar in kind to its basis, which is emptiness." Applying the reasoning of same basis works like understanding that all reeds are hollow inside when realizing that one reed is hollow. Similarly, we should come to the conclusion that all phenomena are unborn, and give rise to an authentic certainty about this.

On the sutra path, this reasoning of same basis only brings one to the conclusion that things are not real but are emptiness. However, all conventional appearances are still seen the way they appear to us now, that is to say impure. They are not considered to be infinite purity. In these teachings that present the Vajrayana approach, however, the same basic reasoning leads one not only to the realization of the lack of inherent existence, or emptiness of all phenomena, but also to the fact that all conventional appearances— the universe and beings within it—are infinite purity, the spontaneously present great equality and purity of a universe and beings. This is also knowing that all-pervading space and wisdom are indivisible, and realizing the indivisibility of the higher two truths, which is the way to follow the path of kyerim and dzogrim.

2. The Reasoning Based on the Way Seed Syllables Are Formed

The reasoning of the formation of seed syllables shows that although things are empty, they appear unceasingly. When a few causes and conditions come together, things arise unimpededly, interdependently, while empty. So the sutra path uses, for example, the way A, O, and M can come together to form a syllable OM[7] to demonstrate the way empty, interdependent phenomena arise unimpededly. Here on the path of the union of kyerim and dzogrim, the reasoning of the formation of a seed syllable must also lead to the realization of how primordial wisdom and its display arise unimpededly as deity and realization. Therefore, we need to use this reasoning to come to the realization that all phenomena—the universe and beings within it—that arise from the dynamic power of great emptiness wisdom, are pure appearance and existence, and the equality of all universe and beings. In other words, this reasoning needs to make you realize the unity of the higher two truths. It is said that without knowing this, to say without any reason that appearances are the deity is like pretending that charcoal is gold, or that a donkey is a horse.

3. The Reasoning of Blessing

The reasoning of blessing shows that between the great emptiness wisdom of our own rigpa and all phenomena that arise as its power and display, every single one is "sealed" by the other.[8] This is the oral instruction from Gyalse Changchup Dorje, or Khenchen Lungtok Tenpe Nyima, whose wisdom power was developed to the full, and who was such a great master that he was like the full moon among the garland of stars that were students of Patrul Rinpoche of Dzogchen Monastery.

Here again, for example, on the sutra path, this reasoning allows the practitioner to establish that the way things are empty and the way they are interdependently originated are one and the same. But here it also shows that the great wisdom of our own rigpa and all phenomena—the appearances arising from its energy—are indivisible. Phenomena are the display of wisdom; there is not a single atom that exists apart from wisdom. Wisdom and phenomena are like the ocean and the waves: the waves are never different from the ocean. To offer another example, when water is in its ice form, it is not anything other than water. In the same way, the impure appearances that we perceive only exist as the display of the essence of great wisdom.

Therefore, since we can be certain that these impure appearances, when they appear, are in essence the display of great wisdom, appearances are not made empty, nor is there a need to turn something that is empty into appearances. Right from the very beginning, the deities have always been the display of wisdom, and deities and realization are indivisible. It is extremely important to have an unshakeable confidence in this, which happens to be the way things are.

4. The Reasoning of Direct Experience

The indivisibility of the deity and realization, or indivisibility of the higher two truths, is perceived directly from the first bhumi onward. It is the direct experience of the wisdom of the aryas in meditative equipoise. Just as it can be perceived directly by the aryas, the presence of the wisdom of our own rigpa as it is right now can also be established through reasoning. Although we do not currently experience it directly in this way since we are beginners, we must at least give rise to a correct understanding of this realization.

So, in the realization of the dharmakaya, which is the indivisibility of the higher two truths, there is a direct experience of the essence of the wisdom of our own rigpa and, incidentally, of the pure relative aspect in which deity and realization are inseparable. We must understand this by reflecting on the conventional level, and develop complete conviction in the conclusion.

The great abbot Lungtok Tenpe Nyima repeated again and again that if we follow the Madhyamika approach of not holding appearances to be truly existent, while at the same time considering impure appearances to be just as they appear, then we are actually apprehending the higher relative truth incorrectly. Therefore, it is extremely important for those on the Vajrayana path to apply these methods to make sure to gain stable confidence in the indivisibility of the deity and emptiness.

Why Kyerim Is Taught

You might wonder why, here in the Vajrayana, the practice of kyerim is taught. It is in order to purify impure perceptions, the habitual patterns of the four modes of birth.

Rigdzin Jigme Lingpa said,

> The four modes of birth are the basis of purification,
> While the means of purification is the kyerim practice of
>   habituation
> In those who have the kind of body to support mantra
>   practice.

Also, the *Guhyagarbha Tantra* states,

> Because we need to purify the four modes of birth,
> Generation is also of four kinds—
> Very elaborate, elaborate, simple,
> And very simple.

The Four Kinds of Kyerim Practice

1. The very elaborate practices of kyerim are to purify the habitual patterns of egg birth and are for those of lesser capacity whose minds are more conceptual.
2. The elaborate practices of kyerim are to purify the habitual patterns of womb birth and are for those of ordinary, middling capacity.
3. The simple path of kyerim is to purify the habitual patterns of birth by heat and moisture and is for those of superior capacity who develop gradually.
4. The extremely simple path of kyerim is to purify miraculous birth and is for those of superior capacity who are instantaneous realizers.

1. The Very Elaborate Practices of Kyerim

The very elaborate practices of kyerim to purify the habitual pattern of egg birth, for the more conceptual mind of those of lesser capacity, are quite extensive kyerim practices.

Indeed, in these practices, the causal "heruka," which is the seed syllable, arises as the vajra holder. Then one meditates on the various aspects of "one's own child" and "another's child," as practiced in the Kagyé Deshek Düpa and the Gyutrül Shyitro sadhanas.

This meditation involves making "another one's own child": Because samsara and nirvana are born of the great qualities of rigpa or buddha nature, by meditating in this way we gather the quintessence of samsara and nirvana and make it our own child.

To make oneself the child of another means that since the lineage of the buddha family is uninterrupted, we visualize the heruka deities in union. They are the pure manifest result of the causal heruka, the seed syllable. Then the female deity prays to the male to give birth to the heir. As a result, the practitioner's aggregates, elements, and sense-sources dissolve into light that becomes a tiklé that the male deity inhales through his nostrils. It mixes in one taste with the great bliss tiklé of bodhichitta, which enters the secret space of the female deity. Then the other deities come out of the secret space of the female deity and appear clearly with all the ornaments, garments, and hand implements perfectly complete, and finally take their place in the mandala. The wisdom deities are invited, the seal applied, and so on. This is explained in more detail in *The Ladder to Akanishtha*.[9]

2. The Elaborate Practices of Kyerim

The elaborate practices of kyerim to purify the habitual tendencies of womb birth for those of ordinary, middling capacity emphasize the stage of generation, the skillful means aspect. Say you want to tame an elephant crazed with wine, you can tame it with a hook or a crowd. Similarly, to eliminate habitual tendencies of womb birth there are two methods: For our deluded perception of the outer environment, which is the support that is created through all sorts of habitual patterns, the means of purification is to visualize the palace as the support. And to eliminate attachment to the reality of the body, the supported, there is the skillful means of "generating" our body as the deity. As for the mind, we bind it to the stake of profound samadhi to prevent it from going after objects, by meditating on the samadhi of suchness, the samadhi of universal manifestation, and the causal samadhi, which matures bodies into deities.

The way to first "put up the tent structure" of the three samadhis, and then to generate the support (the palace) and the supported (the deities) in accordance with their nature, is presented in detail in the Nyingmapa kyerim and dzogrim teachings, such as the *Guhyagarbha Tantra*. In the father tantras, this is done by means of the three vajra rituals; in the Mother Tantras it is by means of the five fully awakening meditations; in Yoga Tantra, with the five outer fully awakening meditations; and in Mahayoga Tantra, the five inner fully awakening meditations, and so on—so the generation stage is taught in many ways.

In brief, these teachings present various approaches to dealing with our different habitual tendencies; there are practices that deal with our present situation and purify our aggregates and eight collections of consciousness, some that deal with the bardo and purify the aspects of prana-mind, sperm and ovum, and others that deal with the habitual tendencies of faculties awakening to the objects, focusing on them, and experiencing them.

3. The Simple Path of Kyerim

The simple path of kyerim to purify the habitual tendencies of birth from heat and moisture, for those of superior capacity who develop gradually, which is also called the illusory form of the deity that is the indivisible union of the expanse of Samantabhadri—great, empty, basic space of wisdom— and the appearance of the naturally arising mudra of the deity.

The *Tantra of Self-Arising Rigpa* explains,

> What does it mean to "practice gradually"?
> To take the steps of basic space and primordial wisdom.

As this indicates, in Anuyoga, it is the creative expression of indivisible space and wisdom that arises as the deity. Deities are visualized clearly and completely by simply saying the individual names and remembering the nature of the palace (the support) and the deities (the supported). It is called the kyerim of the union of bliss and emptiness.

4. The Extremely Simple Path of Kyerim

The extremely simple path of kyerim to purify miraculous birth, for those of most superior capacity who are instantaneous realizers, is the path that emphasizes the union of kyerim and dzogrim in which we do not rely on words but on the nature of mind, which has always been the perfect essence of the form of the deity. This is the path that we are teaching here.

It is said,[10]

> The deity is oneself, oneself is the deity,
> It is born together with oneself—
> Samayasattva and jnanasattva are indivisible,
> So inviting deities and requesting them to be seated are unnecessary
>   here.

Oneself is emanating from oneself, oneself empowered by oneself.
Our own rigpa abides as the three roots.

The Omniscient Longchenpa said,[11]

Just as through miraculous birth there is instantaneous appearance,
Just so, we don't need to meditate on the stages of generation and
completion from words.[12]

The *Tantra of Self-Arising Rigpa* says,

What does it mean to "practice directly"?
To perfect the deities by remembering their essence, not by
generating them.

Practice for those of the very highest acumen emphasizes the indivisibility of all-pervading space and wisdom. In the view of the Atiyoga of natural simplicity, rigpa is the kaya of the dharmakaya while rigpa's dynamic energy is the dharmakaya's display. The practitioner meditates on the path knowing this, remaining in the natural state of the ground where dharmakaya and dharmakaya's display abide primordially as great purity and equality of all that appears and exists—this is the way to rest in meditation.

In general, it is taught that what purification eliminates is the habitual samsaric patterns of the four modes of birth; the means of purification are the two paths of kyerim and dzogrim; and the basis for purification is nothing other than the single wisdom of clear light. So, in order to purify the habitual patterns of the four modes of birth, the means used are the four paths of extremely elaborate, elaborate, simple, and extremely simple approaches, with the first three mainly emphasizing the practice of kyerim. They appear to us to be extremely difficult to grasp because we don't have much understanding, experience, or realization of kyerim practice.

Therefore, you may think that since you don't understand the kyerim and dzogrim practices for those of lesser, middling, and superior capacity, it goes without saying that you haven't developed any familiarity with the realization of the most superior approach since you are not an instantaneous realizer of most superior capacity. Generally, this may be so. However, outer and inner causes and conditions[13] lead us to gain some understanding and experience, to see and hear a great deal of the extremely unelaborate Atiyoga path; that is why I am going to explain the sadhana mainly on the basis of the extremely unelaborate Atiyoga approach.

Generally speaking, the Rigdzin Düpa Inner Sadhana falls into the tantric category of Anuyoga. The text says, "in the unaltered state of rigpa—empty yet luminously clear,"[14] which corresponds to Anuyoga meditation in which the focus of your meditation appears as the expression of indivisible space and primordial wisdom. Yet practitioners who are somewhat accustomed to realization can emphasize the Atiyoga approach, since the life-force of kyerim is dzogrim, and the Rigdzin Düpa is a lama practice, and the lama is the root of blessings, among the three roots. The text of the dakini practice of Yumka in this cycle explicitly shows the Atiyoga approach of generating the deity the moment the practitioner thinks of it.[15] These are the explanations of Patrul Rinpoche.

B. The Practice Text of Rigdzin Düpa

Now, I will explain the Rigdzin Düpa practice, from refuge and bodhichitta down to the concluding prayer of auspiciousness, by presenting both elaborate and unelaborate approaches.

1. Preliminaries

a) Refuge

(1) The Absolute Approach to Refuge

First we say,

> *At my heart is a letter HUNG that sends out rays of light. As a result, from the natural abode arise the lama and the ocean-vast assembly of vidyadharas indivisible from him. All the deities of the Mahaguru's mandala, surrounded by all sources of refuge from all ten directions and four times without any missing, appear in the space in front of me—*
> *VAJRA SAMADZA!*[16]

Then we take refuge. The unelaborate, ultimate way of taking refuge according to the clear light Dzogchen, or Atiyoga, tradition is as follows:

Clearly establish that all phenomena are by nature empty and lack any individual identity; they are the wisdom of our own rigpa devoid of any basis or origin. Then, pledge never to part from that direct realization: everything is only ever the wisdom of your own rigpa's display of kayas and wisdoms.

As it is said,

> The mind purified, endowed, and free is the Buddha,
> Its unchanging and undefiled character is the Dharma,
> Its spontaneously perfect qualities form the Sangha—
> Our own mind is supreme indeed![17]

Jigme Lingpa wrote down,

> This rigpa, self-arisen and uncontrived,
> Is the very source of refuge.
> May all those who, in their ignorance, are drowning in the ocean of suffering,
> Be protected by realizing the three kayas![18]

So, one must know that the three-kaya wisdom of our own rigpa is the four kayas and five wisdoms, and resting in that natural state of recognition is the unelaborate, ultimate way of taking refuge.

(2) Refuge in the Rigdzin Düpa Text

We can also follow the words of the text.

> *Homage!*
> *I and all infinite beings*
> *Take refuge in the lama, the essence of the Three Jewels,*
> *And in the mandala of the multitude of vidyadharas,*
> *With devotion and from the depths of our hearts!*

Imagine that to your right is your father and to your left is your mother, in front and behind you are your enemies and obstacle makers, and **all** other **sentient beings** of the six classes, your parents, in numbers **infinite** like space, gathered around you in an enormous crowd.

In the space in front of you is the Palace of Lotus Light on the Copper-Colored Mountain. In its center presides Guru Nangsi Zilnön ("Guru Prevailing Over All That Appears and Exists"), indivisible from the **lama** who is **the essence of** the **Three Jewels** (Buddha, Dharma, and Sangha). To his right is Mandarava and to his left is Yeshe Tsogyal, and he is surrounded by the whole **mandala of the multitude of vidyadharas,** as well as the deities of the Eight Categories of Sadhanas (Drupa Kagyé) who have also assembled, the vidyadharas of India and Tibet, the twenty-five emanations who are the chief disciples of Guru Rinpoche, the yidam deities of the four or six classes of tantras, the seventy-five glorious protectors, the twenty-eight ishvaris, and so on. Visualize them all with vivid clarity, like a rainbow rising from the sky.

In front of them, all sentient beings, including yourself, give rise to an intense wish to be liberated—just like someone who is desperate to be released from the dungeon of his mortal enemy—and arouse strong devotion. Then, pay homage physically by prostrating with your body; recite the words of refuge to express respect with your speech; and filled with respect in your mind think, "I trust you! You know what needs to be done!", surrendering completely. This is what is referred to as taking refuge with trust and devotion from the depths of our hearts and the very marrow of our bones.

(3) The Crucial Point of Refuge

If you recognize that in fact you have never been separated—not even for an instant—from the mandala of the Lama Rigdzin Düpa, which is the actual essence of things, like oil in a sesame seed, you will be under the protection of the supreme refuge who will guard you from all adventitious thoughts and concepts that bind you. This is crucial.

b) Bodhichitta

(1) The Absolute Approach to Bodhichitta

The absolute approach is as follows. By means of the wisdom of discernment, determine the nature of all appearing phenomena, the universe and beings within it. This means that you come to the realization that these dualistic perceptions conceiving of things as having individual identity and holding them as real are in fact groundless emptiness wisdom. Then the state of the unqualified resolution of all samsara and nirvana (*khordé ubchub*),[19] in which there is nothing to be done and that is beyond all elaboration, becomes manifest. This is called generating bodhichitta by entering the womb of the natural state.

Determination by means of the wisdom of discernment, which is the actual nature of all samsara and nirvana, is bodhichitta in aspiration, while its result, the wisdom in which all is but a display in the unqualified resolution of samsara and nirvana, is bodhichitta in action.

(2) Bodhichitta in the Rigdzin Düpa Text

HO! I have entered this mandala of vidyadharas and
I recall all sentient beings in the six realms, my very own parents;
Moved by immeasurable compassion that aches for their liberation,
Aspiration, action, and absolute bodhichitta: fill my heart!

Bodhichitta in Aspiration

"Now I have entered the door of this great mandala, the assembly of the sugata vidyadharas, and I recall every single sentient being in the six realms—keeping in mind that every one of them has been my father or my mother—I am moved by immeasurable love, immeasurable compassion, immeasurable joy, and immeasurable equanimity. Inspired by these four immeasurables, I ache for their liberation from the ocean of suffering of existence in the three worlds of samsara. To achieve this, I will use skillful means of the profound and swift path of unsurpassable Secret Mantra Vajrayana like these ones to ferry them to the jewel island of liberation and omniscience." Think in this way to generate bodhichitta in aspiration.

Bodhichitta in Action

Bodhichitta in action is to train in the six paramitas, and to apply the profound skillful means of practicing deity meditation, mantra recitation, and so on.

Absolute Bodhichitta

Absolute bodhichitta is as I have just explained above.

c) The Seven Branches of Devotional Practice

(1) The Absolute Approach

The unelaborate, ultimate approach to the seven branches is as follows:

The supreme **prostration** of encountering the view is to come face to face with the absolute lama, our very own rigpa.

Offering delight in the great bliss of basic space is to recognize that all arising objects and appearances perceived by the six consciousnesses are but the ornaments of rigpa.

The absolute **confession** without words: when everything that arises is self-liberated upon arising, you are confessing within unbiased basic space.

For absolute **rejoicing,** let everything liberate naturally, carefree and beyond the conceptual mind, free of any focus on any positive action, whether tainted or not, and rest naturally without fabrication.

The unelaborate, ultimate **request to turn the wheel of Dharma** is to maintain deep, indwelling confidence while abiding by the great all-pervasive dharmadhatu free from the stains of dualistic thinking and beyond the nondual mind.

The absolute **request to remain** is formed by resting in the great continuous clear light, in which there is no transition or change throughout past, present, or future.

Absolute **dedication** is to dedicate any roots of virtue, whether with or without reference point, in the fundamental nature of the great youthful vase body, uncompounded, and free of elaboration.

(2) The Seven Branches in Rigdzin Düpa

Alternatively, if we turn to our text:

> *HO! Like bubbles bubbling out of water,*
> *The wisdom expanse emanates deities;*
> *Direct experience of rigpa is my prostration.*
> *Increase of experience is my offering.*
> *In the full maturity of rigpa, I confess!*
> *In the exhaustion of phenomena, I rejoice!*
> *Out of the expanse of great transference, please turn the Dharma*
> *wheels!*

In the great rainbow body remain, we pray!
I dedicate all merit gathered toward the youthful vase body!

(a) Prostration

Bubbles arise instantly from water; just so, the deities manifest out of dharmadhatu wisdom, the unborn expanse of great emptiness. It is the radiance of spontaneous presence, the appearance aspect, arising as deities. These arrangements in this limitless mandala are the union of basic space and primordial wisdom, the great purity and equality of samsara and nirvana, so when we have a direct experience of this fundamental nature of things—the vision of the direct realization of dharmata—we are offering the supreme prostration of encountering the view.

(b) Offering

By meditating based on the union of the two paths of trekchö of primordial purity and tögal of spontaneous presence, at some point our **experience** will **increase**. We will have a direct perception of the essence of the deities and kayas and appearances will arise as ornaments of rigpa. We call this "making the offering which has always been on display and needs no deliberate arrangement."

(c) Confession

When all appearances arise as kayas and pure realms as you experience the state of **rigpa reaching full maturity**, all impure aspects of experience that involve grasping at characteristics dissolve naturally into the expanse of purity and equality. This is called the unelaborate absolute confession.

(d) Rejoicing

To be immersed in the infinite state of the great transcendence of the ordinary mind, in which all deluded perceptions of conditioned phenomena are exhausted within the expanse of the great primordial purity of their nature, is the way to rejoice.

(e) Imploring the Buddhas to Turn the Wheel of Dharma

As the untainted expanse of great transference becomes manifest, we make the **request to turn the Dharma wheels** in the complete purification of the three spheres of subject, object, and action.

(f) Requesting the Buddhas and Teachers to Remain

When all the dregs of impurity have dissolved into the pure all-pervading space of the dharmakaya, the practitioner manifests in the untainted **rainbow body**, which remains in the great timelessness of the three times. This is the request to remain.

(g) Dedication of Merit

We then dedicate all the virtues—whether tainted or not—that have **ever** been **accumulated**. We dedicate these on behalf of all sentient beings, who pervade the whole of space, so that they may be liberated from the confines of their ignorant dualistic perceptions, and, having **realized** the wisdom of the three kayas present within their own rigpa, attain the ultimate stage of liberation of **the youthful vase body**, awakening as dharmakaya.

d) Expelling Negative Forces

(1) The Absolute Expelling of Negative Forces

Negative influences and obstructing forces are the dualistic grasping at subjects and objects that obscure the way suchness is, in other words the dharmata nature. As such, the benevolent worldly gods and spirits are all the positive conceptual thoughts that develop from dualistic apprehension; malicious harmful demons are all negative thoughts, with the subtle forms of conceptual attachment composing the different categories of obstructing spirits and the male and female owners of karmic debts. These are the only demons or obstacle makers, whether large, medium, or small; there is not even so much as an atom's worth of demons besides these. Therefore, the absolute expulsion of negative forces is to send away all appearances of deluded perceptions in the undeluded state of primordial purity, the great transcendence of the ordinary mind: unimpeded and clear emptiness.

(2) Expelling Negative Forces in the Rigdzin Düpa Text

If we now turn to the Rigdzin Düpa text, it says:

> HRIH! *In this emanation mandala of the universe and beings,*
> *All you malicious and obstructing demonic forces*
> *Take this torma offering and go elsewhere!*
> *Dare to disobey, and my vajras will destroy you!*

This mandala, the assembly of vidyadhara **emanations of** sugatas, is the manifestation of the union of primordial wisdom and basic space, the infinite purity of the **universe and beings.** In this mandala, you appear clearly in the form of the extremely powerful Hayagriva, dark red in color, with swirls of fire, unbearably wild and wrathful. At your heart is a letter HRIH that emanates infinite rays of light, dark red in color and shaped as hooks. **All the malicious and obstructing demonic forces,** the foremost of which is the king of obstacles Vinayaka, and all the eighty thousand kinds of obstructing forces, the fifteen great döns (negative influences) who strike children, Hariti with her five hundred children, and so on, and particularly all the groups of misleading negative and obstructing forces that create obstacles to this profound practice, are all summoned, powerless to resist. Inside a vessel made of extremely precious substances is **the torma**. It has the five sense-stimulating qualities—the most excellent shape, sound, smell, taste, and texture. From the samadhi of the magical display of the dharmata, we manifest offerings like "the enjoyments of triumphant Tushita," "Samantabhadra's display," and the "pleasurable objects of the sky treasury." They manifest in a way that fulfills the wishes of each. We give these offerings to them and tell them, "**Take** these **offerings, and go elsewhere! If you** refuse to go and instead **dare to disobey** this command, disrespecting the samaya, I, this manifesting Hayagriva indivisible from primordial wisdom, will send out from my heart great clusters of **vajras**, small wrathful emanations shooting out like sparks of fire, vast bombardments of weapons and masses of flames, all in infinite number, and expel you to the dark lands at the farthest limit of the outer ocean, destroying you completely and reducing you to dust!" This is the way to practice in relation to the elaborate kyerim approach.

e) The Protection Spheres

(1) The Absolute Approach

On the absolute level, recognizing that the whole of samsara and nirvana is the play of absolute bodhichitta, decide that all harmdoers and victims don't have any real existence and let them self-liberate naturally. Rest in the state in which everything arises only as the display of great emptiness and primordial wisdom without object.

(2) Protection Spheres in the Rigdzin Düpa Text

Furthermore, if we turn to our text,

> HRIH! *In the infinite purity of appearance and existence,*
> *Even the names "negative forces" and "obstacles" do not exist.*
> *Yet for delusional adventitious thoughts—the döns—*
> *The state of dharmadhatu sets the boundary.*

The whole of appearance and existence is infinite purity. It is the essence of the indivisible higher two truths and the mandala of the deities of the three seats. For the yogin who knows that this is the case, and always has been so, **even the names** of impurities such as **negative forces** and **obstacles do not exist**. Yet to **adventitious** dualistic perceptions, delusional mind appears as obstructing forces and negative influences (**döns**). To leave them in **the state of** the undeluded space of **dharmadhatu** is called "**setting the boundary.**"

The Relative Protection Spheres

In the elaborate practice of kyerim, or kyerim with characteristics, we imagine that the wrathful deities, weapons, and masses of fire that were sent out come back and form the vajra tent. The invincible protective tents made of precious substances, wheels, lotuses, crossed vajras, mountains of fire, and so on all form a protection tent that looks like an iron helmet that is sealed shut. I and all those in need of protection are inside, so that no harm can come to us.

f) The Descent of Blessings

(1) The Absolute Descent of Blessings

For the absolute descent of blessings, we ascertain all impure, delusive appearances and thoughts, and bring forth the state of the nature of things, the way they actually are. This is the descent of great blessings, through which the sun of the wisdom of rigpa shines its light on the vast realms that have been shrouded in the darkness of ignorance.

(2) The Elaborate Approach

The descent of blessings according to the elaborate kyerim approach is as follows: You are the samayasattva and the strength of your intense devotion sends out rays of light from your heart in all directions. The rays of light invoke the wisdom of the buddhas and bodhisattvas of the ten directions reminding them of their aspirations and pledges. Rupakayas arise from the dharmadhatu. The way they shower down their blessings is described in the Rigdzin Düpa text:

Invocation of the Lamas of the Mind-Transmission Lineage

> *HUNG! From the dharmakaya palace, free from conceptual elaboration, appear*
> *Primordial buddha Samantabhadra,*
> *Buddhas of the five families and consorts, and emanations in retinue—*
> *Lamas of the mind direct-transmission lineage, shower down your blessings!*

The dharmadhatu is the unborn **palace of the dharmakaya, free from** the eight **conceptual elaborations**, the pure field of the spontaneously perfect great equality. Out of this palace **comes the primordial buddha,** or "eternal protector," the dharmakaya **Samantabhadra,** and his retinue that is no different from the teacher; they have the same wisdom-mind, pervading equally. The five aggregates are the male deities of the five families such as Vajrasattva, when transmuted into their pure form. The five primary elements are the female deities of the five families such as Mamaki in their pure form. So, the emanations of the buddhas of the five families **in union, together with their retinues of emanations,** arise from the basic space of the dharmadhatu in the form of deities while in their wisdom-mind they are one taste with the dharmadhatu. They are the lamas of the wisdom-mind-transmission lineage. We invoke their wisdom-mind and remind them of their aspirations: "**Please shower down your** great **blessings,** both ordinary and supreme, right now—all your blessings and empowerments, and all your qualities of wisdom, love, and power." They send out the blessings of their enlightened bodies as tiny deities, the blessings of their enlightened speech as seed syllables, and the blessings of their enlightened mind as hand implements in lights of the five colors, like a gathering of rainbows.

Invocation of the Lamas of the Sign-Transmission Lineage

From the palace of magical vajra display emerge
Garab Dorje, Manjushrimitra,
Shri Singha, Jnanasutra, and the rest—
Lamas of the sign-transmission lineage, shower down your
blessings!

Similarly, the great half-nirmanakaya half-sambhogakaya **palace** comes from the **magical vajra display,** the dynamic energy of primordial wisdom. Emerging from this palace are the masters **Garab Dorje, Manjushrimitra, Shri Singha, Jnanasutra, and so on.** They are the **lamas of the sign-transmission lineage,** who didn't need to train progressively in stages; instead the signs of the treasury of the space of dharmata were naturally released.[20] We invoke their wisdom-mind and remind them of their aspirations and pledges. And in the way just explained, we request them to **shower down** their great **blessings,** so that the siddhis and blessings of their three secrets (body, speech, and mind) become inseparable from ourselves, our place, and our practice articles.

Invocation of the Lamas of the Oral Transmission Lineage

From the palace of the nirmanakayas who train beings,
The eight vidyadharas and the Lotus-Born,
The twenty-five king and subjects, and the rest—
Lamas of the oral-transmission lineage, please shower down your
blessings!

Furthermore, **from the** great **palace of the nirmanakayas** (who bring vast benefit to all the limitless **beings** wandering throughout the six realms of existence, **training** them by benefiting each according to their needs in activities spontaneously accomplished, everlasting, and all-pervasive) **come the eight** great **vidyadharas**, holders of the Kagyé transmissions; the **Lotus-Born** Guru and his retinue of the mahasiddhas of Tibet; **his twenty-five** chief disciples, "**the king and subjects**"; the eighty mahasiddhas of Yerpa; the hundred realized masters of Chuwori; **and so on.** These are the **lamas of the oral-transmission lineage.** They have received instructions not from ordinary human beings, but from teachers manifesting naturally to their perception; that is, teachers who are simply the appearance aspect that is the magical display of primordial wisdom, and who transmitted the teachings to them orally like filling vases to the brim. Since their entrance to the path has been hearing the teachings, they form what is called the oral lineage. We invoke the wisdom-mind of these masters and remind them of their aspirations and pledges in the way that has been described.

The Blessings Descend

Make this mandala glow in vivid splendour!
Make the practice articles glisten and sparkle!
Ignite the great bliss in our body, speech, and mind!
Grant us the siddhis, supreme and ordinary!
OH AH HUNG   VIDYADHARA E A RA LI PEM PEM   HUNG
   HUNG HUNG HUNG HUNG HUNG HUNG HUNG HUNG

In this way, all the blessings of the enlightened body, speech, mind, qualities, and activity of the lamas of the mind, sign, and oral-transmission lineages descend in the form of deities, seed syllables, hand implements, and so on. Through this, your entire surroundings are blessed and transformed into the great self-manifesting pure land of absolute Akanishtha, and your retreat house is transformed into a vast, heavenly palace made of the five wisdoms.

In **this mandala**, within its perfect and extraordinary magical array, all symbols, their meaning, and the correspondences are perfectly complete and naturally and spontaneously present within the essence of infinite purity in which the deity and realization are inseparable. The mandala is vivid, magnificent, full of splendor, and so on. So with these blessings, this mandala is a perfect, wondrous, magical display.

"Bless **the practice articles** so that their nature becomes wisdom nectar, enriched with the most perfect color and fragrance, abundant taste, and potency—**make them glisten and sparkle!**"

"Bless the **body, speech, and mind** of the practitioners (ourselves and our vajra brothers and sisters) so that they are transformed into the three vajras, and **ignite** in our being the indestructible **great bliss** of primordial wisdom. Grant us, right now, all the siddhis—the supreme siddhi, which is the attainment of the level of the gathering of all the sugata lama vidyadharas, and the ordinary siddhis, which are the four activities, eight great accomplishments, and so on."

The Mantra

> OM is enlightened body;
> AH is enlightened speech;
> HUNG is enlightened mind;
> VIDYADHARA, awareness holder;
> E is here;
> A RA LI, display;
> PEM PEM, rein in;
> HUNG HUNG, shower down the great blessings.

"Rein in here the displays of enlightened body, speech, and mind of the vidyadharas and shower down these great blessings."

g) Blessing the Offerings

(1) The Absolute Blessing of the Offerings

The primordial display of offering substances which has never been arranged is all the phenomena of samsara and nirvana, all that appears and exists, which, without any notion of rejecting, accepting, leaving anything out, or adding anything in, has always been appearing by itself, unimpededly and primordially. Therefore, among these offerings that have always been displayed and do not need to be deliberately arranged, every single offering is sealed by the great wisdom of equality, free of conceptual elaboration. That is why the absolute, inexpressible blessings of the offerings is to recognize the nature as it is and to rest in this state.

(2) Blessing of the Offerings in the Rigdzin Düpa Text

Our text follows the elaborate Vajrayana approach.

> *OM AH HUNG*
> *Offering clouds of all that appears and exists*
> *Are blessed in the amrita of wisdom,*
> *And all outer, inner, and secret offerings*
> *Become the great, miraculous display of Samantabhadra's*
> *offerings.*

Visualize yourself as the deity.[21] From your heart streams out a white syllable OM, the essence of the vajra body of all the victorious ones. It radiates rays of light that purify the impure perception of a real universe and beings within it. Then the essence of vajra speech comes out in the form of the red syllable AH emanating rays of light that multiply all the offering substances so that they become as vast as the treasury of space. Then you send out the essence of the vajra mind, the dark-blue syllable HUNG. It emanates rays of light that bless the offering substances, and they become the great wisdom of bliss and emptiness, the wisdom-mind of the buddhas. **The offering clouds of all that appears** (the whole universe) **and all that exists** (all sentient beings within it) **are blessed in the** great **nectar of primordial wisdom**, and, in particular, in the eight auspicious substances, the seven emblems of royalty, the tsok articles, chants, dances, music, and so on—all sorts of offerings defying imagination. Also offered are the seven **outer** offerings, the **inner** offerings of the five sensual stimulants, the **secret offerings** of amrita, torma, and rakta, and the most secret innermost offerings of union, liberation, and suchness. In short, every offering is presented without anything missing. "May they **become the immense** clouds of **offerings** arising as the **miraculous display of** the noble **Samantabhadra!**"

The Offering Mantra

OM, the essence of the five kayas;
VAJRA, vajra;
ARGAM, water to rinse the mouth;
PADAM, water for the hands and feet;
PUPE, flowers;

DUPE, incense;

ALOKE, light;

GHENDE, scented water;

NEWITE, food;

SHABTA, music;

SARWA, all;

PENTSA, five nectars;

RAKTA, blood;

BALINGTA, torma;

MAHA, great;

SUKHA, bliss;

PUDZA, offer;

AH, unborn;

HUNG, the offering of the five wisdoms.

2. The Main Part

The main section of the Gathering of the Sugata Vidyadharas has seven sections.

a) Generating the Deity

(1) How to Generate the Support and the Supported

The Atiyoga Approach to Kyerim

Generally speaking, all paths come down to the vajra path of union. It is called vajra path of union because it brings together skillful means and wisdom. We need to understand that skillful means and wisdom refer also to kyerim and dzogrim; kyerim is known as the "skillful means generation stage," while dzogrim is known as the "wisdom completion stage." The life-force of all skillful means generation stage practices is contained within "the four nails that bind the life-force of the practice." Therefore, Patrul Rinpoche said that every aspect of kyerim is included within these four nails, with nothing missing; so to ignore them amounts to not knowing kyerim.[22]

So, the means by which we purify our ordinary body, speech, mind, and actions into enlightened body, speech, mind, and activity are deity, mantra, and the emanation and reabsorption of the dharmata.[23] As it is said,

The samadhi that purifies the ordinary body and matures it into the
  enlightened body is the path of vajra;
By purifying the obscurations of speech, recitation brings
  enlightened speech;
Unchanging wisdom liberates the mind, and is the secret to realizing
  the enlightened mind;
The supreme way to transmute actions into the accomplishment of
  supreme activity is emanation and reabsorption.

We have already mentioned the Mahayoga and Anuyoga approaches to
kyerim. These practices are meant to purify the four modes of birth (the
object of purification) by relying on the generation stage practice (the agent
of purification). The Atiyoga approach to kyerim is based on killing the
three types of rudra—outer, inner, and secret.

The rudra of the outer view of self is our clinging to outer phenomena
as real. "Outer phenomena" here refers to the vast world of the universe
that contains sentient beings. This outer appearance of the earth, water,
fire, wind, and space arises when, under the influence of ignorance, we do
not recognize the face of the space-like all- pervading environment of the
ground, kayas, and wisdoms. Instead we solidify things and take them to
be real. This approach teaches us to purify the appearance of this world into
pure fields as an antidote to clinging to outer phenomena as real.

The rudra of the inner view of self is our unending experience of attachment and desire for our house or retreat place, and for our possessions. The
method taught as the antidote to this is to visualize our dwelling place as a
celestial palace.

The rudra of the secret view of self is our constant cherishing, at all times
and in all circumstances, of what we call our "self" or "I," which we think
is indestructible. The method taught as the antidote to this is to visualize
ourselves as the deity.

The practice of skillful means generation stage is also a means to bring
forth enlightened body, speech, and mind in our ordinary body, speech, and
mind. You must know that all this is also included in the deity, mantra, and
the emanation and reabsorption of the dharmata: the body must be generated
as the deity, speech purified as mantra, and all thoughts and concepts turned
into the emanation and reabsorption of the dharmata. To summarize, if
appearances, sound, and awareness become ordinary, the approach and recitation practice becomes ineffective. That is why Jigme Lingpa wrote down,[24]

All sights and grasping at them are the perfect mudra of the deity's
forms,
All sounds are pure as the great bliss of mantra,
All thoughts mature as clear light dharmakaya...

This quote is the important summary presenting the three aspects of purification, perfection, and maturation of approach practice according to our
tradition. Patrul Rinpoche has also said,[25]

Looking "below," all kyerim practices correspond to the way
samsara is. That is why samsaric and delusional habitual patterns
that need to be eliminated can be purified using kyerim practice.
So kyerim *purifies.*

All kyerim practices also correspond "above" to the nature of
nirvana. So kyerim induces the perfect presence of all fruition
appearances—buddhas' activities, qualities, the mudras of the
forms of the deities, and so on—in the essence of the present
rigpa of the ground. In this way, kyerim *perfects.*

All the practices of kyerim conform to the key points of dzogrim. Therefore, they mature for the second stage of the path, the
practice of dzogrim, or great clear light dharmakaya. Hence, they
mature.

This is why kyerim practice is said to purify, perfect, and
mature.

Hence, all skillful means generation phase practices are contained in the
four nails that bind the life-force of the practice. The four nails are:

The nail of deity samadhi,
The nail of mantra recitation,
The nail of dharmata,
The nail of the activity of emanation and reabsorption.

The Nail of Samadhi[26]

There are three samadhis:

1. The **vajra-like samadhi of suchness** in which we rest in the all-

pervading space of great emptiness, the great equality, and our own rigpa, free of conceptual elaboration.

2. In the **samadhi of the illusory universal manifestation,** we meditate on illusion-like compassion for all beings who have not realized emptiness and wander in samsara.

3. **The causal samadhi of heroic gait,** which is the meditation on the deity's seed syllable, the expression of the first two samadhis.

In this way, we lay these three samadhis as the foundation for the practice. Then, in order to purify, the habitual tendency for any of the four types of birth, in our present experience, we visualize the outer universe as a celestial palace and its inner inhabitants as deities. Your body appears in the form of the deity that is like an illusion, appearing yet lacking inherent existence, just as a reflection appears in a mirror. These clearly appearing forms shouldn't be the object of grasping, just as when objects appear in a dream, but we know we are dreaming. Concerning the appearance aspect, the visualized forms are clear and complete, distinct right down to the black and white parts of the eyes. Concerning emptiness, the visualized forms are without even an atom of concrete existence, not like some inanimate matter, but rather as the great union of appearance and emptiness. Visualize in this way with vivid clarity as described in the Rigdzin Düpa text, as I will explain now.

(2) Generating the Deity in the Rigdzin Düpa Text

> *HUNG! Unaltered rigpa, empty yet luminously clear!*
> *There, the panoramic awareness of vipashyana reveals all plays of interdependence,*
> *Spontaneously perfect and infinitely pure*
> *In a great mandala spontaneously complete.*

Generation of the Mandala

The text does not follow the Mahayoga approach to generating the mandala via the three samadhis. Rather, it is the Anuyoga approach emphasizing the great dharmata that is the inseparable unity of all-pervading space and primordial wisdom.

As we say HUNG, all appearances arising through your deluded perception are destroyed, there and then. Settle naturally in the state of rigpa, free of any specific focus in space-like dharmata. Within this great primordial purity in which rigpa and emptiness are indivisibly united, the **rigpa** of the ground, which is **unaltered** by deluded thoughts or destructive emotions, is experienced as the great **empty** equality of samsara and nirvana. Yet, as rigpa's radiance is unobstructed, while empty, its nature is luminous **clarity,** or self-cognizance. So in the great wisdom of rigpa, clarity and emptiness are inseparable. There **the panoramic awareness of vipashyana** sees the nature of things clearly and vividly. The expression or play of this vipashyana is the appearance aspect, every single appearance of environmental phenomena and beings that arises interdependently. You visualize the universe and its inhabitants as the great mandala of the **spontaneously-perfect, infinitely pure** reality. Concerning "mandala," (*kyil khor*) its meaning has been clarified by Jigme Lingpa in *The Casket of Siddhis*, the retreat manual for the Rigdzin Düpa.[27] "Center" (*kyil*) refers to the supported deities, and "periphery" (*khor*) refers to the supporting palace.

Visualization of the Environment—the Pure Field

The ground has no impure features such as undulations, outcrops, holes, or ravines; nor is it rugged, stony, or thorny. It is soft and even everywhere, like the palm of a young girl's hand. It is vast and wide, as limitless as space. It is supple and yielding underfoot. There are medicinal meadows where sweet fragrances waft through the air. The ground is checkered with squares of the five colors of the rainbow and dotted with ravishing lotus flowers of white, yellow, red, and blue. There are stretches of golden sand, turquoise pastures and, in the intermediate areas, lakes and ponds of all sizes, full of water that possesses the eight qualities. Everywhere there are wish-fulfilling trees that rain down whatever is wished for. There are all kinds of bird and animal emanations who sing the melodious tunes of the Dharma. Brilliant rays of light in the five colors of the rainbow fill the sky in the ten directions. Dakas and dakinis beyond the imagination, who are the magical display of wisdom, dart about, dancing beautifully, singing melodious songs, and playing music. Many kinds of flowers of the gods shower down in a delicate rain. In the center of this immense, wonderful, pure field is the **great mandala,** which is like the pure field of the Copper-Colored Mountain. It is primordially and **spontaneously** present, with all the qualities of the fruition **perfectly complete.**

The Palace

Its inconceivable, delightful palace—
Square, with four doors and all its characteristics,
With symbols, meanings, and correspondence all perfectly
*   complete*
In great unimpeded clarity with no outside and inside. In the
*   center...*

This **palace**, or **inconceivable** mansion, is the great Palace of Lotus Light. Its three stories represent the three kayas. The moment we see it, we are naturally filled with joy—it is **delightful**. This is the generated palace. It is **square** in shape. In the east, the floor is made of precious white crystal, signifying the mirror-like wisdom. In the south it is made of lapis lazuli, the dark-blue jewel signifying the wisdom of all-pervading space. In the west it is made of ruby, the red jewel signifying the wisdom of discernment. In the north it is made of emerald, the green jewel signifying the all accomplishing wisdom.

The ceiling is gold, signifying the wisdom of equality. In the four outer walls of this palace are **four doors**, symbolizing the four immeasurables. On these four walls there are bells, garlands made of precious substances, rising jewels, sun and moon pendants, tiny bell ornaments, bejeweled tail fans, and many kinds of jewels of the gods, nagas, and humans. The upper part of the palace is ornamented with gargoyles made of precious substances, and at the summit is a crowning ornament formed from a vajra and jewel. The outer walls, courtyards, entrance corridors, torana, and all the features of this inconceivable palace are made of many precious substances and bathed in rainbow light. These most excellent **characteristics** ornament the palace. All the **symbols, meaning, and their correspondences** are perfectly present; in other words, all the aspects of enlightenment (from the four applications of mindfulness up to the most excellent qualities) are fully contained within the visual forms. Furthermore, the correspondence between symbols and meaning shows the qualities at the time of the ground, the symbols point to the qualities at the time of the path, and the meanings relate to the qualities at the time of the fruition. In brief, the full set of symbolic images, meanings, and their correspondence present on just one side of a single palace contains the complete array of enlightened qualities, for example. None of these features, whether **outside or inside**, are solid or tangible like the things pertaining to the truth of suffering. This inconceivable palace is made of self-appearing primordial wisdom. It is the **great unimpeded clarity**; the outside appearing clearly from the inside, and the inside appearing clearly from the outside.

The Seats

> *On a multicolored lotus, a sun and a moon,*
> *HUNG transforms instantly, perfect the very moment I think of*
>   *it...*

In the center of this inconceivable palace, on a very large and broad octagonal throne, is a **multicolored lotus**: It has three layers of a thousand petals each, white at the bottom, red in the middle, and blue on top. On top of the lotus are radiant **sun and moon** seats. Above them rests the causal syllable HUNG, the essence of rigpa, radiating bright and clear rays of white, yellow, red, green, and blue light.

Guru Rinpoche

> *I am the Lotus-Born, Prevailing Over All That Appears and*
>   *Exists*
> *In whom all the buddhas are actually present,*
> *One face, two hands, white tinged with red.*
> *As a sign of my complete mastery over the three yanas,*
> *I wear monastic robes, gown, and cloak.*
> *My right hand wields the five-spoked vajra in the threatening*
>   *mudra,*
> *My left holds the skull-cup containing the long-life vase,*
> *Cradled in my left arm is the beautiful goddess, Mandarava.*
> *On my head I wear the lotus hat,*
> *And I am seated in the graceful posture of royal poise.*

The seed syllable HUNG **transforms** into you in the form of Guru Rinpoche, **instantly, the moment you think of it**. The features of his body are **perfect**ly complete with the major and minor marks, and all the ornaments and robes. He is the universal embodiment in whom all the love, compassion, and power, all body, speech, mind, qualities, and activities of every **buddha** manifest. The king of Oddiyana, the master **Prevailing Over All That Appears and Exists** (Nangsi Zilnön), **the lotus-born** guru, Pema Jungne. He is white with a tinge of red, smiling, and his eyes are semi-peaceful and semiwrathful. He is adorned with the thirty-two major and the eighty minor marks. His hair partly covers his back.

He has **one face**, signifying the one taste of all phenomena in the state of suchness, the dharmata; **two hands**, signifying the interconnection of skillful means and wisdom; his complexion is **white like a** conch shell, **with a tinge of red,** as if he wore vermillion make-up, signifying the union of bliss and emptiness. His three robes, which he wears one on top of the other, show his perfect mastery over the three vehicles. The blue brocade **gown** shows his perfect mastery over the Secret Mantra Vehicle, the three **monastic robes** show his perfect mastery over the shravaka vehicle, the red **cloak** shows his perfect mastery over the bodhisattva vehicle, and the great brocade cloak with a tiger-skin trim indicates that he is a universal monarch. He also wears the white, secret vajra garment and earrings and rings made of precious substances.

The **five-spoked,** golden **vajra in his right hand** shows that he has attained the level of the five kayas. He wields it, threatening the negative influences (*dön*), which are dualistic thoughts.

In his left hand he has a skull-cup with a long-life vase. The skull-cup shows that he ripens and liberates sentient beings through the vehicle of the result, and the vase of longevity shows that he takes care of students through his great attainment of the level of vidyadhara with power over life.

In his left arm he cradles the beautiful goddess Mandarava, who is ravishing and captivating. This shows that he is the embodiment of the three kayas, with their seven attributes, who remains neither in samsara nor in nirvana.

On his head, on top of the crown protuberance, **he wears the Lotus Hat,** signifying that he is the master of the five buddha families. In this regard, Guru Rinpoche has three kinds of hats. This second buddha was himself born on Lake Dhanakosha, "Milky Lake," not from the cause of a father and the circumstance of a mother, but instantaneously born from rigpa, on the pistil of a lotus flower. Upon his realization of appearance and existence arising as the ground, the dakinis enthroned him as the chief of the family and gave him the hat called Lotus Bud. When the king of Zahor,[28] Vihardhara, tried to burn Guru Rinpoche alive, the fire element could not harm him because his body is a vajra body. Instead, he remained seated, naked and fresh in the middle of an extraordinary lotus. At this point the king was awestruck and great faith arose in him. He opened for Guru Rinpoche the door to his treasure of brand-new silks and garments and said, "Take all my hats and clothes!" He offered him his kingdom, servants, and court. The hat offered on this occasion is called Lotus That Liberates Upon Seeing. When he went to the eight charnel grounds to accomplish specific ascetic practices that go beyond the empty extremes of good and bad actions, the dakinis gave him, as a mark of honor, the Deer Hat, also called the Lotus Hat. This is the one he wears here. In another instruction manual[29] this lotus hat has been identified as the Lotus That Liberates Upon Seeing, but I don't think this is the case.

Even though he has actualized for himself the level of the dharmakaya, still he is accomplishing with nonreferential compassion the eternal, all-pervasive activities for all others, the sentient beings who roam in samsara and particularly beings of these times of degeneration. The way he sits, **the graceful posture of the royal poise,** shows that he is doing this continuously without any interruption.

The Lineage Masters

> *Above his head, in an expanse of shimmering spheres of rainbow*
> *lights,*
> *Sits Garab Dorje in sambhogakaya ornaments,*
> *Brilliant white, holding a vajra and a bell crossed at his heart.*
> *Above his head is the primordial protector*
> *Samantabhadra in union, the color of the sky.*

The teacher of the supreme vehicle, the vidyadhara **Garab Dorje**, sits **above his head in an expanse of shimmering spheres of rainbow lights.** This indicates that Guru Rinpoche leads students on the path of Atiyoga, the pinnacle of the nine yanas. Garab Dorje wears the thirteen **sambhogakaya ornaments.** He is **brilliant white** in color and sits **holding** in his two hands **a vajra and a bell** crossed at **his heart. Above** Garab Dorje's **head is the primordial protector,** the dharmakaya **Samantabhadra, in union** with his consort Samantabhadri. They are both the **color of the sky.** Their forms are empty, yet luminously clear.

The Eight Vidyadharas

Around Guru Rinpoche, on each of the eight lotus petals
In the midst of five-colored spheres of light
Are the eight vidyadharas who accomplished the sadhanas of the
    Glorious Heruka.
All in heruka costume,
Each playing damaru and bell with their two hands,
They delight in dance with their consorts.
In the color of their respective direction, or dark blue in the inter-
    mediate directions.
In essence they are the deities of the eight Kagyé sadhanas.

Around Guru Rinpoche's seat, **on** each of the **eight petals** of a **lotus**, encased **in** concentric **spheres of light of the five colors,** like chests, stand the eight bodhisattvas on seats of lotus, sun, and moon. They are the pure aspect of the eight consciousnesses at the time of the ground. They are **the eight vidyadharas who accomplished the sadhanas of the Glorious Heruka:** Manjushrimitra, who received the transmission of Jampel Ku (Manjushri, enlightened body); Nagarjunagarbha, who received the transmission of Pema Sung (Hayagriva, lotus speech); Hungchenkara, who received the transmission of Yangdak Tuk (Yandak Heruka, enlightened mind); Prabhahasti, who received the transmission of Purba Trinlé (Kilaya, enlightened activity); Rambuguhya, who received the transmission of Jikten Chötö (mundane worship); Vimalamitra, who received the transmission of Dudtsi Yonten (Amritakundali, enlightened activity); Dhanasamkrita, who received the transmission of Möpa Drangak (maledictory fierce mantra); and Shantigarbha, who received the transmission of Mamo Bötong (Mamo, calling and dispatching).

As a sign that they adopt the particular ascetic practice of the yogis, the secret conduct of great bliss, the eight vidyadharas, holders of the eight transmissions of Palchen Heruka, are **all** adorned with **the costume** and ornaments **of Palchen Heruka,** with their hair in a topknot, wearing bone ornaments, tiger-skin skirt, and so on. **They play the damaru with their right hand, and with their left** the silver white **bell** that resonate the Dharma sound of the union of wisdom and skillful means, of bliss and emptiness. They are enjoying themselves, **dancing** in union **with their consorts.** Their bearing is majestic and they assume the postures of dance. **They** appear in the color of the main direction they stand in, which means white in the east, dark blue in the south, red in the west, and green in the north. Those in the intermediate directions radiate dark blue light. We visualize them clearly and completely as the eight vidyadharas, while knowing that in essence they are the eight Kagyé deities, and the eight bodhisattvas as a sign that they have revealed samsara's natural purity.

The Other Vidyadharas and the Deities of the Tantras

All around are the vidyadharas of India and Tibet, and
The great incarnations: the twenty-five disciples—king and
*   subjects—*
In their various appearances and garments,
Moving with vajra dance gestures.
Above, the yidams, dakas, and dakinis
Of the four or six classes of tantra
Are assembled like seeds in a sesame pod.

All around, the space is filled with all the deities of the four or six classes of tantras, such as the three inner tantras. All the learned and accomplished vidyadharas of India and Tibet are there in a huge crowd. In particular, the twenty-five disciples—the king and his subjects—are present, wearing their various visages and garments that show the signs of their accomplishments in their appearance. They are moving about in all kinds of vajra dance gestures and appear like optical illusions. Above, yidams, dakas, and five family dakinis of the four or six classes of tantras fill the space with all the dakas and dakinis of the sacred lands and places, assembled like sesame seeds in open pods. They all appear clearly without jumbling the details; the deities' bodies are like illusions, but appear vivid and clear with every detail precise, right down to the black and white parts of their eyes. At the same time they are empty, so they don't have even a speck of inherent existence; they appear clearly as the great union of appearance and emptiness.

The Protectors

The outer pathway is populated by the seventy-five glorious protectors,
The twenty-eight ishvaris, and so on—

All the samaya-bound guardians who abide by the command—
who swirl like the wind.
At the four gates are the four great gings.

Outside, along **the outer pathways** and all around are **the seventy-five glorious protectors, the twenty-eight ishvaris, and so on.** They display the nine dances of the wrathful deities. These nine dance expressions are:

- The three expressions of the body: the expression of desire, which makes them look seductive; the expression of anger, which makes them look strong; and the expression of ignorance, which makes them look repulsive.
- The three expressions of speech: sounds of laughter, such as "ha ha" and "hee hee"; roaring fearsomely like a lion and verbally attacking with words such as "Grab him! Throw him down!"; and sounds that are incredibly loud and unbearable, full of fury, like a thousand dragons booming all together.
- The three expressions of mind: the expression of compassion, taking care of all beings who are deluded; the expression of fury, taming with wrath sentient beings who are difficult to train; the expression of the peace of the one taste of all things in the dharmata.

In this way, all the protectors of the Dharma **who** pledged to **abide by the command** and are bound by their samaya commitments, headed by the twenty-eight ishvaris, **swirl like the wind.**

At each of **the gates** in the **four** directions stand the factions of the **four** classes of **great gings** appointed to guard the entrances. Visualize them all clearly, protecting practitioners from outer and inner obstacles and keeping watch over the samayas by keeping an eye on good actions and transgressions.

They are all the play of appearance and emptiness,
Yet they are clear, distinct, and spontaneously present.

All the deities **appear yet are empty;** they are empty yet appearing. Their appearance does not obscure their empty nature, and their empty nature does not prevent them from appearing. In the natural state in which everything arises as a play of indivisible emptiness and appearance, the forms of the deities are **clear,** precise, **distinct,** vivid, self-arising, and **spontaneously present.**

In brief, as Jigme Lingpa said,[30] we need to know that all the features of the environment and the deities of the mandala that arise are nothing other than the one who emanates and reabsorbs—the Lotus-Born Guru.

The Invitation

> *Their three centers are marked with the three syllables,*
> *Which are the three vajras in nature.*
> *They send out powerful rays of light to invite*
> *From the supreme land of dharmadhatu nature,*
> *From the nirmanakaya field of Orgyen in the west,*
> *From the sacred places and lands, from the eight charnel-grounds,*
>   *and*
> *Especially from Ngayab Langké Ling and*
> *The Glorious Copper-Colored Mountain,*
> *The deities of the Rigdzin Düpa mandala—*
> *I invite you to this place,* SAMADZA!

The three centers—forehead, throat, and heart—of the deities of the mandala are marked with the three syllables OM, AH, and HUNG, respectively. The nature of these three syllables are the three vajras: the vajra body, speech, and mind. Intense rays of light emanate from the three syllables and, as they reach the supreme land of dharmadhatu, the natural, all-pervading space of phenomena, the rupakayas arise. The rays of light also reach pure fields such as the nirmanakaya field of Orgyen in the west, and so on, the twenty-four sacred places, the thirty-two sacred lands, the eight great charnel grounds, and so on, and reaching especially Ngayab Langké Ling, the land of the rakshasas, and the Palace of Lotus Light on the Glorious Copper-Colored Mountain in the southwest.

The rays of light invite all the deities of the mandala gathering of vidyadhara sugatas, saying, "I invite you to come to this place, at this very instant, SAMADZA!" You invoke them by chanting the seven-line prayer longingly and in a powerful voice.

b) Invocation

> HUNG! *In the past, during the first kalpa,*
> *In the northwest of the land of Oddiyana,*
> *In the heart of a blossoming lotus flower,*

You have attained the marvelous supreme siddhi,
And are renowned as the Lotus-Born,
Surrounded by your retinue of many dakinis
And ocean-like hosts of realized vidyadharas,
Following in your footsteps, we practice.
Please come to shower your blessings on us—

As you say HUNG, the sound that is the self-arising seed of enlightened mind, invokes the buddhas and reminds them of their aspirations and pledges. Then the Lotus King Guru ("Guru Pema Gyalpo," in other words, Guru Rinpoche) arises, embodying in one person all the qualities of the body, speech, and mind of all the buddhas, and manifesting as the most supreme being to ever grace the three realms of existence.

"**In the past, during the first kalpa**" refers to Guru Rinpoche appearing at a time that was like a golden age, a springtime for the teachings and sentient beings, during which both were maturing.

The perfect place is in the country of the dakinis on the **northwestern** border of **Oddiyana**, the land of the vidyadharas to the west, a beautiful island with many excellent riches, on the perfect Lake Danakosha, clear and limpid with the eight qualities of pure water.

There **blossomed** a large **lotus** stem topped by a thousand exquisite **flowers** in the colors of the five families, where the victorious Amitabha appeared with a five-colored syllable HRIH at his heart. Suddenly, the syllable HRIH lands on the anthers of the udumbara flower, and HRIH turns into the peerless protector of the three realms of existence, who has attained the truly **marvelous, supreme siddhi**, the **attain**ment of the level of union of Vajradhara, who is **renowned as "Lotus-Born,"** who is the embodied concentration of the qualities of the three secrets, the enlightened body, speech, and mind of infinite victorious buddhas entirely—in other words, the perfect teacher.

He is **surrounded by** the special beings who are receptive to and can be tamed by the Secret Mantra Vehicle. Dakas and **dakinis** throng around him; they are like sesame seeds in an open pod. They form the perfect assembly.

At all times, the main deity and his retinue are never anything but the illusory display of primordial wisdom taming beings. This is the perfect time.

We think, "All sentient beings, myself included, take you as a teacher and will **follow in your footsteps. We** will **practice** your teachings of the two stages of the path, kyerim and dzogrim, and so on, and all your profound

Dharma instructions that ripen and liberate, exactly as you teach them, and realize them in our stream of being." This indicates the perfect teaching.

"**Please come** to this place so that we may rely on the blessings of your wisdom, your love, and your power; like alchemy transmuting iron into gold, bless our body, speech, and mind. For that, please come from wherever you dwell, the pure field of the Copper-Colored Mountain in Ngayab Ling or any other place. Let the great power of your compassion transport you here to this place!"

> *Shower them down on this supreme place!*
> *Confer the four empowerments on us supreme practitioners!*
> *Remove any negativity, obstructing force, and disturbance to our*
>   *practice!*
> *Grant us supreme and ordinary siddhis!*
> **OM AH HUNG VAJRA GURU PEMA TÖ TRENG TSAL   VAJRA**
>   **SAMAYA DZA DZA**

Now that Guru Rinpoche and his retinue have come, we formulate our request: "Bless this **supreme place,** adorned with a multitude of positive and auspicious features, with an abundance of qualities of enlightened body, speech, and mind, wisdom, love, and power. Let **them** rain **down** in the form of small deities for the body, seed syllables for speech, and hand implements for the mind. Swiftly shower them down in this very place, right now. And to **us supreme practitioners** who have entered the door of the profound group-assembly practice—the ocean-like gathering composed of the vajra master and vajra brothers and sisters—please grant right now all **four empowerments,** including the empowerments of the inconceivable secret body, speech, and mind, and so on. **Remove** all outer **obstacles,** the **negative forces** and **disturbances to our practice;** all inner obstacles, such as the thoughts akin to the five poisonous, destructive emotions; and all secret obstacles, the deluded dualistic appearances, and so on, into basic space. **Grant us** right now all **ordinary and supreme siddhis!**"

c) Requesting the Wisdom Deities to Take Their Seats

(1) The Absolute Request

The wisdom of rigpa is a wisdom that is free of change or alteration at any point in the past, present, or future. Therefore, when resting in the natural state in which this wisdom is manifest, we are beyond request and requester—realizing this is the absolute request to remain. If we turn to our text:

> HUNG! *In this mandala generated through skillful means,*
> *All of you deities invited from the basic space of wisdom—*
> *Deities of the mandala of Lama Rigdzin—*
> *Stay contently in the absence of duality.*
> VAJRA SAMADZA TISHTA LHAN

Now that I have entered the door of the Secret Mantra Vajrayana, the profound path of skillful means that ripens and liberates, and I am **in the** great **mandala** of all the deities of the three seats that I have **generated through** kyerim (**skillful means**), **the basic space** of emptiness (**wisdom**) manifests unimpededly as the deities we've invited. These **deities of the mandala** gathering the sugata **lama vidyadharas** (that includes the support, the palace and environment, and the supported, the deities) are the great indivisibility of the deity and realization manifesting; in other words, the indivisibility of the higher two truths, or the state of equality without duality. We are asking these deities to sit with great **contentment in** this **absence of duality**.

(2) The Elaborate Approach

In the elaborate approach, we offer to the deities of the mandala seats corresponding to their family, such as a lion throne, lotus flowers, and so on. Then, we visualize that they come and sit on them. This is on the conventional relative level.

d) Prostration

(1) The Absolute Prostration

The lama endowed with the three kindnesses introduces us instantly to the face of rigpa itself, relying on the path of profound pith-instructions. We decide upon one thing and one thing only, and we rest in the natural display of self-appearing primordial wisdom. Confidence and joy in this is the supreme prostration of meeting the view.

HUNG! The deity is oneself, oneself is the deity,
A self-manifesting mandala
With no good to adopt nor bad to reject,
Still I offer the symbolic prostration of interdependence.
A TI PU HO PRA TI TSA HO

The **deities** visualized clearly in this mandala of the deities of the three seats are the three-kaya wisdom of our own rigpa. Deities and wisdom are inseparable—they cannot even be brought together or taken apart. Self-aware dharmakaya appears in a display of rupakaya **deities**. So in this great **mandala** that is a **manifestation** arising from the magical display of self-existing wisdom—its own dynamic energy—there **is nothing good to** hold on to nor anything **bad to** eliminate; in short, nothing to **adopt** or **reject** since such characteristics do not exist. Still, all phenomena, which arise **interdependently**, are but an unimpeded, **symbolic** display that is self-arising and self-manifesting. To rest in this realization is the **prostration** of meeting the view.

(2) Elaborate Relative Approach

ATI PU HO means prostration. As we say **PRA TI TSA HO**, the deities bow their heads, responding to our prostration. Visualizing this is the relative practice.

e) Offering

(1) The Absolute Offering

To realize that all objects appearing to the six consciousnesses arise as ornaments of great primordial purity, the union of rigpa and emptiness, in offering clouds of indivisible bliss and emptiness, constitutes the unelaborate, ultimate way of making offerings.

(2) Offering in the Rigdzin Düpa Text

OM AH HUNG! Vessel and content all arise as offering clouds,
Desirable objects and five sensual stimulants,
Auspicious objects, auspicious symbols, and seven emblems of
    royalty,

Amrita, torma, and rakta, purely and joyfully offered,
Laughing and singing dancing girls,
Hundreds of thousands of consorts in great-bliss union,
Offerings, offerers, recipients all
Utterly pure within the space of wisdom.
This great mudra of offering and all offerings,
I offer to you, deities of the vidyadhara gathering—
Accept them, and grant us empowerments and siddhis!

OM VAJRA ARGHAM PADAM PUPE DUPE ALOKE GHENDE
NEWITE SHABTA RUPA SHABTA GHENDE RASA PARSE AH
HUNG
SARWA PENTSA BHALINGTA RAKTA MAHA SUKHA DHARMA-
DHATU AH HUNG

As you say **OM AH HUNG**, recognize that the offering substances are in essence the body, speech, and mind of all the victorious buddhas. In that state of recognition, the seven **outer** offerings, the **inner** offerings of visual objects, sounds, odors, tastes, and textures, and the secret offerings of the three realms are transformed into a nectar of enlightened body, speech, and mind that we offer, as well as offering the whole of appearance (the **vessel**-like world) and existence (the **content**-like sentient beings) and so on. In brief, everything **arises** in a complete display of offerings made of the most **desirable** things. The essence of these offerings is the enlightened mind, primordial wisdom and empty bliss, while they appear **as** great **clouds of offerings** that please and satisfy the deities of the mandala.

The offerings consist of:

- the outer offerings of the seven **kinds of offerings,**
- the inner offerings of the **five kinds of sensual stimulants,**[31]
- **the eight auspicious substances,**
- **the eight auspicious symbols,**
- **the seven emblems of royalty,**
- the offering of union, or offering of **amrita,** which is the medicinal nectar into which white and red bodhichittas have been transformed, and whose union is bodhichitta, the union of the empty aspect and appearances,
- the **torma** that gathers the essence of the three realms,
- and the **rakta** enjoyment of the three realms as blood,
- the liberation offering in which we offer the liberation into self-

lessness of all the rudras of the view of self in all three realms, and so on.

In short, the amount of things that we offer is immeasurable.

Also we make offerings that delight the five senses. We offer the sixteen and thirty-two offering goddesses and so on, beautiful and laughing in the flowing movements of dance, with hundreds of thousands of spiritual consorts, the union with whom arouse the great bliss that is wisdom and skillful means indivisible. Ultimately all attachment at the reality of the three spheres[32] (grasping at something to offer) someone who offers, and someone to receive all the offerings are completely purified within the basic space of great primordial wisdom that sees the lack of reality of all these appearances—this is the **great mudra of offering**. Finally, you say to the deities: "All of **you deities of** the mandala **gathering of** the sugata **vidyadharas**, who manifest everywhere throughout the whole expanse of space in the ten directions, please **accept these offerings** in the state of great nondual rejoicing, **and grant us** all the **empowerments and siddhis** this very instant."

f) Offering Praise

(1) The Absolute Approach to Offering Praise

Ultimately, the supreme praise is the wonder, trust, confidence, and joy that comes from seeing the way rigpa abides as the dharmakaya ground, and from seeing its qualities.

(2) Offering Praise in the Rigdzin Düpa Text

Alternatively, our text says:
> Praises to the Lama

> *HRIH! Unaltered great simplicity—Lama Dharmakaya,*
> *Sambhogakaya experiencing great bliss, Lama Lord of Dharma,*
> *Born from a lotus stem, Lama Nirmanakaya—*
> *To the three kaya Lama Vajradhara, I prostrate and offer praises!*

"HRIH!" The letter HRIH is the seed syllable of unimpeded enlightened speech. Its sound invokes the deities of the mandala and reminds them of their aspirations and pledges.

The **lama** is the primordially **unaltered,** self-arisen, natural state: the absolute bodhichitta free of all conceptual elaboration. As the dharmakaya mind of all the victorious ones, non-conceptual wisdom, this natural absolute deity is free of characteristics such as faces or hands. The empty essence of this great emptiness is taught to be the **dharmakaya.**

This dharmakaya is empty in the way we just explained, yet its luminous radiance arises unobstructedly as **sambhogakayas,** who perfectly **experience** (*sambhoga*) **great bliss**—the lama endowed with the five perfections. He is **the "Lord of the Dharma."** It is taught that the cognizant nature is the sambhogakaya. The dynamic energy of this dharmakaya rigpa abiding as the ground is compassion that arises without obstruction—the **nirmanakaya lama born** miraculously and instantaneously from a self-arisen **lotus.** He is a nirmanakaya of diverse and unimpeded manifestations. In brief, you **offer praises and prostrate to** the deity who is the indivisible unity of **the three kayas,** the ultimate natural **Vajradhara**; in other words, the union of rigpa and emptiness.

Praises to His Retinue of Eight Vidyadharas

> *At Enchanting Mound you ripened the siddhis of the profound*
> *and vast path,*
> *In the eight charnel grounds you seized the stronghold of*
> *realization,*
> *Masters of an infinite ocean of mandalas,*
> *Eight great vidyadharas, I offer praise and prostrate to you!*

Furthermore, in the grove by the great **Enchanting Mound** Stupa, you received many transmissions, such as the various teachings of the Eight Sections of Sadhana (the Kagyé), and **ripened the siddhis of** many **profound and vast** Dharma teachings. You exerted yourselves in practice **in the eight** great **charnel grounds.** Meditating in this way **you seized the stronghold of** the fruition, the **realization** of the view as limitless as space, and **mastered** all the teachings **of an infinite ocean of mandalas,** particularly of the eight Kagyé. In short, to the **eight great vidyadharas** who received transmission of the supreme accomplishment, you **offer praise and prostrate.**

Praises to the Disciples of the Great Master of Orgyen

You soar in the vast expanse of realization
And guide beings manifesting all manner of appearances and
  deeds;
You hold the life-force of the extraordinary vajra-essence wisdom,
Twenty-five heart sons, king and subjects—I offer praise and
  prostrate to you!

Guru Rinpoche's twenty-five disciples, known as the king and subjects, were accomplished masters from Tibet who opened the Dharma treasury of the **vast expanse of realization** of the mind of all the buddhas, space-like and free of conceptual elaboration. So they **soar** above all expressions of primordial wisdom in the great purity and equality of samsara and nirvana. They **manifest all manner of appearances**, showing diverse signs of accomplishment, such as travelling without obstruction through mountains and rocks, riding the rays of the sun, flying in the sky like a bird, and so on. They use these and many other **activities** and appearances to train **beings** on the path, since they are very skilled in means. Also, they **hold the life-force of** the wisdom intent of the treasury of Dharma, **the extraordinary Vajra-Essence** teachings.[33] In this way **I offer praise and pay homage to you,** Guru Rinpoche's **heart sons, the twenty-five disciples, king and subjects.**

Praises to the Deities of the Mandala

Also, the three root deities present in the emanation mandala of
  vidyadharas,
Because of samaya and compassion,
Messengers who manifest from the wisdom-space,
Deities of the entire mandala, be the recipient of my praises and
  prostrations!

In this great **emanation mandala** gathering **of vidyadhara** sugatas, with the support and the supported, I am the samayasattva whose faith and strong devotion invokes the wisdom-mind of the deities and reminds them of their pledges and aspirations. So at that moment, they all arise as rupa-kayas from the basic space of phenomena: To **the three root deities** of the lama, yidam, and dakini **present** in this mandala through the power of nonreferential great **compassion**, and all the deities of the Kagyé **who manifest from the** all-pervading **wisdom-space**, yidams, dakas, dakinis, and Dharma protectors who abide by the command and their **messengers** who accomplish their activities; in brief, to all the **deities of the entire mandala**, the magical display of primordial wisdom, **you offer praises and prostrations.**

g) The Mantra Recitation

Next, you "open the mansion of mantra recitation," which means a front-visualization of jnanasattvas identical to the mandala you've been visualizing with the support and supported, separates from the self-visualization like bubbles rising from water, instantly clear and vivid.

(1) Rigdzin Düpa Text of the Mantra Recitation

> *At my heart, upon lotus, sun, and moon,*
> *Is the blue letter HUNG. Around that*
> *The mantra-garland turns, with letters as fine as if written by a*
> *   single hair.*
> *It emanates rays of light that purify environment and beings,*
> *So everything is now pure; meditate on the mandala of the deities.*
> *Until this is actualized, I will not let go of the practice!*
> OM AH HUNG VAJRA GURU PEMA SIDDHI HUNG

First, when you practice the approach alone, you need to concentrate on and actualize the meaning of the lines that start, "At my heart, upon lotus, sun, and moon . . ." However, at the beginning, and until the deities appear clearly, you don't need to do the emanation and reabsorption of light rays.

(2) The Four Nails

Remainder of the Nail of All Appearance as the Deity

So the four nails that bind the life-force are the root of kyerim practice, and I have already explained the first one, the "nail of deity samadhi" in the generating the deity section.[34] But we still have to identify the three crucial aspects of purification, maturation, and perfection for this first nail of deity samadhi, the generation of the deity.

The generation of the deity addresses "below" samsara, which we have been experiencing from beginningless time. It does so by bringing the crucial points of purification and elimination of the habitual patterns of bodies born in samsara through the four types of birth.

Similarly, since dzogrim is presently the life-force of kyerim, "above" deity generation perfects within the expanse of the great dharmakaya, or rigpa of the ground, all inconceivable secrets of the buddha kayas; based on the magical display of kayas, we fully perfect all activities, such as training all sentient beings who need to be trained, wherever they are, and in whichever way is appropriate. This is how kyerim practice perfects.

Also, now at the point of training on the path, we purify the net of channels in our body into the deities' kayas. Through the strength of pressing the vital points of the vajra body, deity generation practices mature for all dzogrim practices.

(a) The Nail of the Mantra Recitation

Here, since we need to know this when we practice the approach, let's go through the root text.[35]

> *In Nangsi Zilnön's heart,*
> *The king of vidyadharas, Vajradharma,*
> *Is the color of coral who, as if anointed with oil,*
> *Is glistening and radiant, with a glowing complexion.*
> *He has one face and two hands, semipeaceful and semiwrathful,*
> *Naked, with bone ornaments and topknot.*
> *He holds vajra and bell intertwined. On his thigh,*
> *The blue yogini holds her hooked knife and skull-cup,*
> *Adornments the same as her consort.*
> *Both show intense desire*
> *Joined in undefiling great bliss.*

You visualize yourself clearly as Guru Rinpoche in his **Nangsi Zilnön** form—Prevailing Over All That Appears and Exists. You are the samayasattva. **At** your **heart** is the jnanasattva, **the king of vidyadharas, Vajradharma.** His body is **the color of coral** and it **is glistening and radiant, as if anointed with oil, and has a glowing complexion. He has one face and two hands,** and is **semipeaceful and semiwrathful, naked** and in union with **the blue yogini**. At his heart is the mantra-garland which is like a chain arranged in a circle around the core seed syllable BAM. This seed syllable BAM is the samadhisattva. Thus, samayasattva, jnanasattva, and samadhi-sattva constitute what is called the "three nested sattvas." Focus your mind one-pointedly in this way on the garland of syllables of the essence-mantra as you recite the mantra.

In the case of the approach practice measured by numbers, recite the mantra one hundred thousand times for each syllable.[36] Otherwise, the approach practice can be measured by duration, in which case you would count the number of months you would spend on the recitation, for example. To measure the approach practice by signs, you practice until you meet face to face with the deity. These are the different methods to determine the length of a retreat.

In particular, it is said that it is important to exert ourselves in mantra recitation that involves knowing the in-breath to be OM, the out-breath to be HUNG, and holding the out-breath to be AH.

The Vajra Guru Mantra

OM AH HUNG are the seed syllables of the three kayas.

VAJRA refers to rigpa endowed with the seven vajra qualities, the dharma-kaya great equality free of conceptual elaboration.

GURU is lama. "Gu" stands for the Sanskrit word *guna*, which means "quality," while *ru* means heavy. So the lama is "heavily loaded with quali-ties," refering to the sambhogakaya endowed with the five certainties.

PEMA means lotus, indicating that the particular deity here is of the Lotus speech family. Also, he is called Lotus-Born because he was born from a lotus, on an island in Lake Dhanakosha. What is the meaning of this image? A lotus flower grows in mud without being stained by it, the supreme nirmanakaya subduer of beings acts for the benefit of sentient beings in the six realms of samsara while remaining untainted by samsaric negativities and faults. So PEMA refers to the nirmanakaya.

SIDDHI means "accomplishment," and refers to the supreme accom-plishment of attaining the level of the Lama Vidyadhara, and the ordinary accomplishments—the four activities, the eight great accomplishments, and so on.

With HUNG we request, "Please grant them to us, in our mind-stream, right now!"

In brief, the three syllables OM AH HUNG are the three kayas; VAJRA is the dharmakaya free of characteristic and thought; GURU is the sambhoga-kaya endowed with the five certainties; PEMA refers to the nirmanakaya in his various manifestations to train beings; SIDDHI refers to the supreme and ordinary siddhis; and HUNG is the request to grant them, immediately.

Purification, Perfection, and Maturation in the Nail of the Essence-Mantra

It is also important here that we hold the three crucial points of purification, perfection, and maturation, based on the nail of the essence-mantra. It must purify "below" the habitual patterns of speech of sentient beings, the nature of sounds expressed when in samsara. The practice is perfecting by bringing to perfection in the expanse of rigpa of the ground in which all the inconceivable secret qualities of fruition at the time of buddhahood "above" are perfect. In the "middle," all the present aspects of speech and wind-energy while practicing the path are purified into the nature of the essence-mantra; the practice must be endowed with this crucial point of maturing for all dzogrim practices based on wind-energy as in the Mahayoga father tantras.

(b) The Nail of the Unchanging Wisdom-Mind

The nail of the unchanging wisdom-mind is the name given to embracing the view of dharmata. As explained, we visualize all that appears and exists, the universe and beings, as the spontaneously present deity, mantra, and palace. They are nothing other than the mandala of all that appears and exists, arising as the ground, and not an arrangement produced by the compounded mind; this would be an improper way to think.

So, the nail of unchanging wisdom-mind is, when you've had dualistic thoughts (self-other, samadhisattva-jnanasattva, pure-impure, practice-result), to avoid grasping onto them individually while being aware that they are just spontaneously present within the expanse of nondual great equality, the mandala of the primordial enlightened state of samsara and nirvana.

Therefore, our own mind and the great wisdom of the enlightened mind of the deity have always been present and inseparable. This is what "mandala of the vajra space of equality" refers to.

Next, the nail of the unchanging wisdom-mind must bring forth the crucial points of purification, perfection, and maturation as follows: "Below," the crucial point is to purify the deluded mind, negative thoughts, and all the habitual patterns of samsara in the expanse of the empty cognizance of our own rigpa. "Above," the crucial point is to perfect within the expanse of the nail of unchanging wisdom, in other words, the rigpa of the ground, the inconceivable secret of the enlightened mind at the time of buddhahood's omniscient primordial wisdom. And in the "middle," now, at the moment of the path, it matures dzogrim, the empty yet appearing primordial wisdom of the nondual great equality.

(c) The Nail of the Activity of Emanation and Absorption

The nail of activity through emanation and reabsorption of light rays is an exceptional method to accomplish the four types of ordinary and supreme activities for any deity, and is very important.

The Practice of Emanation and Absorption

So, you visualize the universe and beings within it as the mandala of deities, and every aspect is always and ever the enlightened mind, the dharmata wisdom. All sounds of the enlightened speech essence-mantra become the invincible voice of the Buddha endowed with sixty melodious tones. In terms of the body, if the deity is peaceful, it displays the nine ways of a peaceful deity, and if it is wrathful, it displays the nine dances of a wrathful deity. From the mantra-garland at the heart, masses of rays of light spread out.

Emanation 1: Accomplishing the Four Activities

When accomplishing the four types of activity, to practice simply, visualize the rays of light as follows: brilliant white rays of light shine out from the mantra-garland, and as they emanate, they accomplish the activities of pacifying sickness and negative forces; shining rays of yellow light emanate and accomplish the activities of enriching, expanding life, merit, and wealth; resplendent red rays of light emanate and accomplish the activities of magnetizing, bringing the three realms under your control; and dark-green rays of light emanate and accomplish the activities of destroying harm doers, enemies, and obstructing forces.

Emanation 2: Making Offerings To and Satisfying the Buddhas

Again, rays of light shoot up from the mantra-garland. All the buddhas of the ten directions and three times together with their bodhisattva heirs are present in a front-visualization mandala. And, even though on the absolute level the one who offers and the one who receives the offerings are not different, from the perspective of appearances the deities in the front-visualization enjoy the offerings we manifest for them. In this way, imagine that they are all satisfied with the taste of the great primordial wisdom of bliss and emptiness.

Emanation 3: Stirring the Three Realms of Samsara From Their Depths

Again from the mantra-garland, rays of light of skillful means emanate down to all sentient beings in the six realms in inconceivable number. The light rays touch all beings, who, instantly, see all aspects of ignorance being wiped away, while their bodies are transformed into deity bodies, all their speech into essence-mantra, all their thoughts into the wisdom of the dharmakaya—the essence of buddhahood which is without change or transformation. In brief, imagine that the three realms of samsara are stirred up from their depths.

Purifying, Perfecting, and Maturing in the Nail of Emanation and Reabsorption

The nail of emanation and reabsorption also contains the crucial points of purification, perfection, and maturation. It is purifying since "below," it purifies the appearance aspect of impure activities of body, speech, and mind when in samsara, such as warding off enemies, protecting loved ones, business, agriculture, and so on. It is perfecting, because "above" it perfects the ground, the fruition, and the inconceivable activities of all aspects of enlightened body, speech, and mind at the time of perfect buddhahood. It is maturing, because in the middle at the time of practice on the path, it matures for both aspects of dzogrim, the training on the path, the pure exertion that spontaneously accomplish the benefit of oneself and others, composed of (1) the ordinary path with focus on the activities of body, speech, and mind, and (2) the extraordinary path without focus, the direct perception of wisdom, which is the clear light yoga, also called the union of appearance and existence in the body of light.

(3) The Significance of the Four Nails

In this context, these four nails that bind the life-force of the practice have all the crucial points of ground, path, and fruition, as well as those of view, meditation, fruition, and action. Patrul Rinpoche said,

> The view is the nail of unchanging wisdom, and the ground;
> The path, which is meditation, is the nail of deity and the nail of
>   mantra, while the nail of mantra is implicitly action;
> The nail of activity is both supreme and ordinary fruitions;
> This is called the "path of primordial union."

This means that since the nail of unchanging wisdom is the view, it is also the ground. The path corresponds to the nail of deity samadhi that is meditation, and the nail of essence-mantra that is not only meditation, but also action. Since the nail of activity through the emanation and reabsorption of rays of light brings about the accomplishment of the ordinary and supreme siddhis right now, it is the fruition. Thus, do not consider that the four nails that bind the life-force of the practice, and view, meditation, action and fruition, or ground, path and fruition are different, practiced separately, or are a progression. In fact, they have always been a single path from the beginning and never different, a path of indivisible unity. You must keep this in mind.

In brief, the nail of unchanging wisdom is the view. It is the wisdom of the present rigpa of the ground, the great dharmakaya, which is indivisible primordial wisdom and basic space. Its self-manifestation is called the "relative mandala of vajra space." This is the union of kyerim and dzogrim. In this state, sounds, which are audible yet empty, are transformed into the natural sound of the mantras. Then, we carry out the visualization called "the play of activities through emanation and reabsorption." When we do this, the enlightened body, speech, and mind, and the great primordial wisdom of fruition, the spontaneous accomplishment of the two benefits with no elaboration or effort, is accomplished that very moment in our mindstream. That is why we talk about Secret Mantra Vajrayana, or fruition vehicle.

Furthermore, if we know these crucial points on the meaning of the four nails that bind the life-force of the practice, we can gain control over the life-force of everything. At the level of the ground, in the mandala of the wisdom of the view, we gain control over the life-force of both existence and peace by realizing the equality of samsara and nirvana. At the level of the path, meditation that masters the mandala of deity and mantra gives control over the life-force of both kyerim and dzogrim. The conduct of the fruition that spontaneously accomplishes the two benefits gives control over great skillful means beyond imagining. It is like when Rahula swallowed the moon in the sky: by making only this one moon disappear, he also got hold of every single of its reflections in water, everywhere in the world. In the same way, with the knowledge of this sole pith-instruction of the four nails that bind the life-force of the practice, we simultaneously practice all the crucial points of the intent of the inconceivable sutra and tantra teachings.

The Forty Major Key Points of the Four Nails

On top of that, there are various key points that relate specifically to each of the four nails.

The Eighteen Major Key Points of the Nail of Unchanging Wisdom

To know the equality of samsara and nirvana is the key point to utterly purify attitudes of accepting and rejecting.

To know the one taste in emptiness is the key point that destroys clinging to reality and attachment to true existence.

To know that appearing and being empty are indivisible is the key point to perfect the two accumulations simultaneously.

To embrace the view is the key point to prevent kyerim and dzogrim from parting.

Not wavering from the state of realization is the key point to arriving at meditation instantly upon the view.

Free from clinging to the extraordinary deity, you have the key point of avoiding the pitfall in the development stage.

The perfection of all that appears and exists arising as the ground is the key point to eliminate dualistic fixation on self and other.

The realization of primordial liberation perfect in the ground is the key point to eliminating the pitfalls of the five poisons.

To realize the wisdom of dharmakaya is the key point to perfecting the three kayas in oneself.

With the key point of knowing the ground and the fruition to be of one taste, we don't need to make efforts to practice on the paths and bhumis.

To realize the all-pervasive lord of the one hundred families is the key point of accomplishing all the deities by practicing one.

Meditation arriving at the fruition is the key point of not searching for enlightenment elsewhere.

Fruition arriving at the ground is the key point to liberating fixation and attachment to the idea that there is something to attain.

Oneness in the expanse of the dharmata is the key point that purifies clinging to the samayasattva and jnanasattva.

Achieving the supreme accomplishment is the key point to spontaneously accomplishing the two benefits of self and others.

Being beyond good and bad, accepting and rejecting, is the key point for not having to rely on ritual purity or righteous conduct.

To know that all things are primordially present, without anything to do, is the key point for not needing complex rituals.

To purify attachment to philosophical systems is the key point to reaching the peak of all vehicles.

These are the eighteen main key points and there are many more than this. However, these are the "life-force of the life-force." Since the nail of unchanging wisdom binds also the life-force of the other three nails, it is indispensable.

The Six Major Key Points of the Nail of Concentration on the Deity

To see clearly the appearance aspect as the deity is the key point that keeps the practice from straying into emptiness alone.

To take the relative as the path is the key point for uniting the two truths.

Purifying the solidification of things is the key point to eliminating clinging at the true existence of ordinary things.

To perfect the aspects of the ritual is the key point for perfecting the great accumulation of merit.

To visualize clearly the body of the deity is a key point, as it will be the cause of the rupakaya.

To be in harmony with the way the fruition abides is the key point to spontaneously accomplish the three kayas.

The Ten Major Key Points for the Nail of the Essence-Mantra

To take vajra speech as the path is the key point that purifies the obscurations of speech.

To meditate on the three nested sattvas is the key point to liberating body, speech, and mind simultaneously.

To focus on the visualization of the mantra-garland is the key point for abandoning ordinary thoughts.

The recitation that is like a moon with a garland of stars is the key point for resting in meditative concentration through which mind finds its natural resting place.

The recitation that is like a whirling firebrand is the key point to giving rise to the wisdom of bliss and emptiness.

The recitation that is like bees swarming around a broken hive is the key point for liberating words and sounds as mantra.

To accumulate the necessary number of life-force essence-mantra is the key point for receiving the blessings from the deities.

Developing the power of speech is the key point for making everything we say of benefit to others.

Accomplishing the true speech of vidya-mantras is the key point for accomplishing whatever aspiration we make.

With the key point of mastering the speech of the victorious ones, worldly gods and spirits will follow our command.

The Six Major Key Points of the Nail of Emanation and Reabsorption

The accomplishment of the supreme accomplishment is the key point that naturally brings forth the mundane accomplishments.

To be able to direct the visualization is the key point for not being dependent on other actions.

To perfect enlightened activity is the key point for effortlessly benefiting others.

Spontaneously accomplishing the benefit of others is the key point for accomplishing the deeds of the buddhas.

Being inspired by the impetus of bodhichitta is the key point for not straying into lower yanas.

Ripening and liberating beings to be trained is the key point for maintaining the lineage, generation after generation.

As outlined here, since the four nails that bind the life-force of the practice contain these forty key points, they include all the crucial points of the Secret Mantra Vajrayana path. Without them, practice has no life-force, and it is like a lifeless corpse. This is why they are called "nails that bind the life-force." They are called nails that bind the life-force also because they bind all duality into the oneness of nondual wisdom.

3. Conclusion

a) Blessing of the Offerings

The ganachakra tsok is the method for quickly perfecting the two accumulations of merit and wisdom based on the profound skillful means of the Secret Mantra Vajrayana. As our text says:[37]

> Of all the ways of accumulating merit, the ganachakra is supreme,
> With the samaya substances gathered by the dakinis,
> The inner offerings are excellently arranged . . .

So, we arrange as many offerings as we can gather, including the different kinds of edible and drinkable offering substances, meat and alcohol, and so on.

> *HUNG! My heart emanates RAM YAM KHAM;*
> *They purify any fault and defect in the tsok offerings.*
> *Now OM AH HUNG transform them into nectar*
> *In a proliferation of offerings of sensual stimulants as vast as*
> *space.*

You've been visualizing yourself clearly as the deity. Now you emanate **from your heart** a syllable **RAM**. Fire bursts out of it and burns away all grasping at reality, all thoughts and concepts, and habitual tendencies. Then a syllable **YAM** emerges from your heart. Wind blows from it that scatters all obscuring habitual tendencies. Finally, a syllable **KHAM** comes out; water streams out from it that dissolves everything into emptiness, and the whole universe and sentient beings within it merge with all-pervading space. This **purifies all fault and defect in the tsok offerings.**

Then, even though this is not mentioned in the practice text, a syllable AH now emerges from all-pervading space and transforms into the immense kapala of wisdom, as vast as the dharmadhatu. The skull-cup is white on the outside, red on the inside. It stands on a tripod of skulls, above RAM, the seed syllable of fire, itself above YAM, the seed syllable of wind. The inside of the kapala is divided into five sections, one in each of the four directions and a central part. The sections contain the five meats and the five nectars, which are endowed with the power of perfect nourishment.

Now as you say OM AH HUNG, YAM at the bottom below the kapala blows wind, so RAM above it blazes with fire. As a result, the nectar in the kapala boils and steam rises up. The steam touches the three syllables OM AH HUNG that are arranged one above the other inside the hub of the five-spoked vajra topping the moon-lid of the kapala. The three syllables then emanate rays of light that radiate to the pure fields in the ten directions and invoke the wisdom nectar in these pure fields. The wisdom nectar returns and melts into the nectar inside the kapala. The offerings inside the kapala transform: they are now primordial wisdom in essence, while they appear as **nectar**. The nectar completely suffuses the realms of the three kayas of the victorious ones in the form of beautiful rays of rainbow light. Steam rises from the nectar and forms clouds of rainbow colors from which all manner of pleasing and delightful things and **sensual stimulants proliferate** and spread throughout the whole of **space**, like the offering clouds of noble Samantabhadra, or the offerings of the Sky Treasury, for example.

b) Inviting the Deities to the Tsok

Inviting the Guests to Come from Their Abodes

> *HUNG! From Akanistha, the realm of great bliss,*
> *The nirmanakaya land of Orgyen to the west,*
> *And especially the glorious mountain of Ngayab,*
> *The sacred places and lands, and the eight charnel grounds, and*
> *   so on,*
> *All you deities of the Rigdzin Düpa,*
> *Pray honor our invitation to the tsok and come!*

We invite all the deities to come to the tsok from the dharmakaya **Akanishtha**, the Akanishtha of absolute reality; the **realm of great bliss**, the sambhogakaya Akanishtha, the Great Lord's supreme abodes,[38] such as Gandavyuha; the terrestrial Akanishtha realm of the nirmanakaya, which is the highest of the five pure abodes of the gods in the Form Realm; also from the celestial realms of nirmanakaya; the **nirmanakaya land of Orgyen in the West**; and especially from the Palace of Lotus Light on the **Glorious**

Copper-Colored **Mountain** in Chamara (**Ngayab**), the twenty-four **sacred places** and the thirty-two sacred **lands**, the eight great charnel grounds, and so on.

We invite all the deities of the Gathering of the Lama Sugata Vidyadharas to come from these places to where we are turning the great wheel of the ganachakra feast. We implore them to come this very instant, unimpededly.

The Place of the Tsok Practice

> *The tsok shrine in the charnel ground is so full of joy!*
> *The gathering of dakinis so heartwarming and inviting!*
> *The yogins and yoginis so very pure in their samaya!*
> *The delightful tsok offerings are so bright and pleasing!*
> *Please come! Shower down your great blessings on this tsok feast!*
> *Grant us supreme and ordinary siddhis!*

The **tsok shrine** within **the charnel ground** where the tsok feast is taking place has all the qualities of the interdependent symbols, meanings, and their correspondences with nothing missing, so it **is** a perfect place **full of joy**. It is **so heartwarming and inviting** because it **gathers** all the dakas and **dakinis**, abundant offerings, gods, samaya-bound deities, and others. **Yogins and yoginis** (the vajra master and vajra brothers and sisters) are **so pure in their samaya** as they have never caused disharmony among themselves. The vast **tsok offerings** gathering **delightful** sensual stimulants of the five kinds glow with **bright and pleasing** color, odor, taste, and potency. "In this place, ornamented with these glorious qualities, guests of the tsok: lamas, yidams, buddhas, bodhisattvas, dakas, dakinis, Dharma protectors and guardians, **please come** and **shower down your great blessings on** these offerings with your enlightened body, speech, and mind. **Grant us** at this very moment the **supreme** siddhi—the level of the vidyadhara lama—and the ordinary siddhis—all the qualities of the eight great accomplishments, and the rest!"

c) Offering the First Portion

> *HUNG! Three roots deities, ocean of vidyadharas,*
> *Dakinis and Dharma protectors who keep samayas,*
> *Accept these tsok offerings of sensual enjoyments we give you;*

Grant us the supreme and ordinary siddhis!
GANA CHAKRA PUJA KHAHI

All the **deities** of the **three roots** have come and are now gathered here for the tsok, together with the **ocean of** deities of the lama **vidyadharas**, the buddhas and bodhisattvas of the ten directions and four times who are the lama, and the oceans of dakas, **dakinis, and Dharma protectors who keep samayas.** You emanate offering goddesses from your heart, who multiply like a butter lamp lighting a second, which lights a third, and so on. They offer to all these deities clouds of **sensual enjoyments** similar to the manifestation of offerings of the noble Samantabhadra. These offerings satisfy the guests of the tsok, so then we request them to **grant us** all the **supreme and ordinary siddhis.**

The Mantra

GANA means "tsok" or "gathering";
CHAKRA means "wheel";
PUJA means "offer";
KHAHI means "accept."

As you recite this mantra, consider that the offerings fill the hearts and minds of all the guests with great bliss.

d) Confession

HUNG! In all my lives without beginning,
Every violation of root and branch samayas I have committed
Since I passed the door of Secret Mantra,
Offering the sensual stimulants of the tsok, I now confess!
VAJRA SAMAYA AH

In all my lives, through time **without beginning**, I have been circling in samsara. Whenever I have entered the Mahayana path of Secret Mantra Vajrayana, **whatever violations of the root and branch samayas I may have committed**, such as the fourteen root downfalls, through the power of this vast **offering of sensual stimulants, I confess** them within the pure and immaculate dharmadhatu.

e) Annihilation and Offering

(1) The Crucial Points of the Practice of Annihilation and Offering

The Three Crucial Points of Fortress, Ravine, and Life-Force

When practicing annihilation it is very important that the three crucial points of fortress, ravine, and life-force be present:

- The "great fortress of the view" is the realization that all phenomena that appear and exist within samsara and nirvana are nothing other than our own perception.
- The crucial point of meditation is to bring forth the rigpa of the ground and to bring all appearance and existence under your control. This is called the "great ravine of meditation."
- The "life-force of focus" means seeing all deluded appearances as the *la*, life, and life-force[39] of the enemies and liberating them into the expanse of undeluded primordial purity.

Visualization of the Three Objects

In the practice of annihilation, the three visualizations, or visualization of the three objects, are necessary. They are:

- The visualization of outer objects as rudras;
- The visualization of inner objects, the sense faculties, as the symbolic weapon, the supreme son; and
- The visualization of secret objects, the thoughts appearing to the deluded mind, as the appearance of the deity.

To perform the annihilation, you need:

- Irreversibility, which you generate by visualizing yourself as Palchen Heruka.
- Repulsiveness, which comes from visualizing Vajrakilaya's Supreme Son.
- And to be without sympathy, which comes from bringing to mind the specificities of the targets of our practice and seeing them as enemies.

The Three Supports of Life, Cleansing, and Place

In the middle of the heart-center of the object to be liberated is the subtle essence of blood, which is barely the size of a small bird's head. In its center, visualize a white syllable A, as the support for the rudra's life, merit, and physical appearance. The A dissolves into the three HUNGs at the tip of the phurba to be absorbed into the core seed syllable in your heart. This is called "the support of life."

Together with the syllable A, in the heart-center of the object of annihilation, you visualize either a syllable NRI or a syllable TRI as the support for the defiled consciousness (the seventh consciousness). When the phurba hits this syllable, the rudra faints and all his thoughts dissolve into dharmata while the seed syllable transforms into a tiklé of light. This is called "the support of cleansing."

This tiklé then dissolves into the three HUNGs at the tip of the phurba. Uttering "PHAT" three times ejects it from the phurba and it dissolves into the heart of the heruka. The tiklé then travels downward, is channeled through the vajra of this male deity, and becomes a son taking birth from the secret place of the consort. This is called the "support of the place."

The practice of guiding the consciousness of the dead, for example, and the practice of liberating enemies through annihilation (with the three essential supports of life, cleansing, and place) are two different methods with a similar purpose. They are called the "Buddhas' Instructions from the Mantrika's Triangular Ritual Fire Pit."

(2) The Rigdzin Düpa Text

> *HUNG! Ignorance, karma, negative emotions, and dualistic*
>   *grasping*
> *Breed ego-clinging and its rudras;*
> *I strike down their body—NRI TRI DZA!*
> *I send their consciousness into the expanse of dharmadhatu with*
>   *a PHAT!*
> *Enjoy the tsok offering of their body!*
> *RUDRA SARWA HALA PENTSA PUTSA KHAHI*

Dualistic grasping, destructive emotions, and **ignorant** actions or **karma** are the root of the three realms of existence of samsara. They **breed**

the **self-grasping mind** that is the source of all outer, inner, and secret **rudras** of the view of self. Here it is this self-grasping that we identify as the real enemies called the "seven types of violators to be liberated." You visualize yourself clearly as Palchen Heruka.[40] You hold the phurba in your hands. It lets out sparks of fire from its flaming tip. See the phurba as the Supreme Son, and say, "**I strike down** the aggregates in the **physical form** of the rudra of self-grasping!" Visualize at the heart of the target of annihilation the syllables **NRI** and **TRI**, which are the support of their defiled consciousness. As you say **DZA**, the rudras are repressed and overwhelmed, and faint. All their thoughts and concepts dissolve in dharmata; in other words, **PHAT sends the consciousness up into the expanse of the dharmadhatu** that knows no delusion. Then, with the rudras' **physical form** having been transformed into untainted tsok offerings, say, "Deities of the ocean-like mandala, please accept and **enjoy** these **offerings!**"

> **RUDRA HALA** is all the flesh and blood of the liberated rudras of
>   dualistic grasping;
> With **PENTSA**, they are transformed into the five wisdom nectars.
> **PUTSA KHAHI** means "enjoy this untainted offering!"

Then, as you share the tsok, consider that you receive fully all the compassion, empowerments, and blessings of the qualities of body, speech, and mind, as well as the wisdom, love, and power of the deities in the front-visualization. They come to you in the form of the four empowerments, for example, and dissolve into you. At that point realize the indivisibility of samayasattva and jnanasattva, and rest in the unaltered natural state.

f) Remainder

> *HUNG! On the edge of the great mandala*
> *Dwell ishvaris, gings, and langkas.*
> *Accept this remainder torma*
> *And protect us yogins from obstacles to accomplishment!*
> *UTSITA BHALINGTA KHAHI*

Around **the edge of this great mandala,** a natural manifestation of primordial wisdom, are the **ishvaris;** the eighteen great **gings,** who are the nine husband ging and the nine vajra-spouse ging, Vajra Trulmoche and the rest;

the gathering of rakshasas with their king, Ravana, the master of **Langka**; the thirty-two dakinis; the 360 messengers, and so on. They are the guests to whom we offer the remainder. Although in essence they are but the magical display of the great Palchen Heruka's compassion, they appear in the form of worldly demons. They cannot lay claim to the main offering portion of the great mandala, but they can partake of the remainder offering, so we offer them the **remainder torma**. As **they accept this** great wisdom-nectar, we request them to **protect us practitioners**—the vajra master and students—from any **obstacles to** our **accomplishment** of great enlightenment, and to provide us with all favorable circumstances.

> **UTSITA** means "remainder,"
> **BALINGTA** means "torma," and
> **KHAHI** means "accept, enjoy!"

As we recite this, we make the offerings, and imagine that the guests who receive the remainder offering are satisfied, and accomplish the activities we request of them.

g) Summoning—Invoking and Reminding of the Pledges

> *HUNG! Rise up Rigdzin Düpa deities!*
> *Reveal your form out of dharmadhatu!*
> *Crush any obstacle to enlightenment!*
> *Halt the degeneration of the elements in the environment and*
> * beings!*
> *Heal any deterioration to channels, wind-energy, and wang tang!*
> *Take us to the fruition of practice!*

Make your invocation following the words of the text. Who is **rising up?** The deities of the Gathering of the Lama Sugata Vidyadharas. Where do they rise from? They arise as rupakaya **from** the expanse of great primordial wisdom, **the space of dharmadhatu** that is beyond dwelling in any extreme. Once they have arisen, what do they do? Through wrathful activities, they **crush** the **obstacles** to our realization of great **enlightenment;** they **heal** any degeneration related to **the elements**—earth, water, fire, wind, and so on—of the outer **universe and sentient beings** it contains; they restore our vajra body that is the special support we need to attain enlightenment, by healing **any deterioration in the channels and wind-energy, and wang tang,** or strength, and so on; and they **take us** that very instant **to the fruition of the practice** of this great mandala of Rigdzin Düpa; in other words, they give us all the siddhis, ordinary and supreme.

h) Cheto (Covenant)

Here again, who are we offering to? To the protectors who obey commands and remain at the edge of the great mandala.

As it is said:

> Since we hold the lineage of the vidyadharas,
> And you all are gods and demons of this family...

First we say these or similar words. This is to remind them of the samaya they pledged to keep. To encourage them to accomplish what they have promised, we offer them a torma. This is why this practice is called cheto, or "covenant."

> *HUNG! Long ago, in the Akanishtha heaven of great bliss,*
> *In pleasant places such as the three god realms,*
> *When the great secret tantras were revealed,*
> *The protectors of the Vajrayana teachings*
> *Were given a seat in accordance with their solemn samaya vow.*

Long ago, in pleasant pure fields—such as **the Akanishtha heaven of great bliss** of Gandavyuha, **in the three celestial realms** of Akanishtha from among the five pure abodes of the Form Realm, Tushita and the Thirty-Three in the Desire Realm, and so on—teachers such as Vajradhara **taught the** general **tantra** teachings of **Secret** Mantra Vajrayana and the specific tantra sections of Dzogchen. At that time, those who had been given **the protect**ion of the Secret Mantra **teachings** were appointed, such as the Protectress of Mantra (Ekadzati), who has power over creation and destruction in the world, and they received empowerments and pledged to keep their **solemn samaya vows** strictly. They were entrusted with watching over and taking care of these teachings. So these deities of the edge of the great mandala **were given a seat corresponding** to their rank and their appointment.

Then, in Tibet, the land of snows,
When the master Padma Tötreng
Turned the Secret Mantra wheel of Dharma,
He seized the heart and life-force of the great gods and spirits,
And they joined the ranks of guardians of the teachings.

Then in Tibet, the land of snows and of the red-faced people, **the master Padma Tötreng**tsal built the immutable, spontaneously present temple of Samyé in accord with the traditions of India, China, and Nepal, before he **turned the wheel of Dharma** of the unsurpassed **Secret Mantra**, giving teachings such as the Heart Essence of Clear Light (Ösel Nyingtik)[41] for beings to be trained who were endowed with great fortune resulting from their karma and aspiration prayers. At this time, **he seized the heart and life-force of the great gods and spirits** of Tibet, such as Nyenchen Tanglha, so they all took an oath to guard the teachings and he placed them under his command.

Finally, in the pure field of clear light
In the Palace of Great Bliss,
The vidyadhara Pema Wangchen
Was entrusted by the Lotus-Born and Drime Özer
With the vast and profound expanse of Longchen Nyingtik.
When the dakini of the all-pervading space of wisdom
Gave him the symbolic script of Clear Expanse[42]
Life-Force Razor of Wild Rahus and others
Took a solemn oath to be fierce protectors of this teaching.

That **final** occasion is recounted by Jigme Lingpa in his biographical account called *A Dancer like the Moon in Water,*[43]

In the pure state of clear light, I met the king of Dharma from Orgyen, Manjushrimitra, and others, in the sky before me . . .

Likewise, here, **clear light,** which is completely free from any sort of existence in essence, basic space pure without adventitious stain, is however clear and cognizant in nature. This clear and cognizant aspect is what **pure field** and **Palace of Great Bliss** refer to. In the sadhana, the words "**vidyadhara Pema Wangchen**" stand for Jigme Lingpa. This is explained in *The Words of the Vidyadhara That Bestow the Majesty of Great Bliss.*[44]

So, within the Palace of Great Bliss in the pure field of clear light, Pema Wangchen, or Jigme Lingpa, beheld the joyful faces of **the Lotus-Born Guru Padmasambhava** and the omniscient **Drime Özer** (Longchenpa), who offered him the gift of an ocean of pith-instructions. They **entrusted** to him the ultimate pith-instructions of **the profound and vast** teaching of the **Longchen Nyingtik.** With their speech, they spoke to him words of encouragement and inspiration. With their wisdom-mind, they blessed him. On the walkway of the Boudhanath Stupa in Nepal, Jigme Lingpa met face to face with **the dakini of the** dharmakaya **space of wisdom.** She **gave him the symbolic script** and the yellow scroll of the Heart Essence of the **Clear Expanse**—in other words, the Longchen Nyingtik—and opened the seal of the space treasury for this mind terma. At the time of this incredibly auspicious event, **fierce** protectors of the Dharma bound under **oath,** such as the great rishi Rahula, who is also known as "**Life-Force Razor of Wild Rahus,**" gathered to keep watch over the terma.

> *So, accept this offering torma with all its ornaments,*
> *And carry out the four activities!*

According to your pledge, now again **accept this offering torma with all its ornaments,** help us by **carrying out** without hindrance **the four** types of **activities** as requested of you.

i) Preserving the Relationship with the Tenma Sisters

> *HUNG! You who obey the command of the glorious one and pro-*
> *tect Tibet,*
> *Twelve mother and sisters Tenma*
> *Come! Accept the rinsing water of the torma,*
> *And carry out the activities we demand of you!*
> *MA MA HRING HRING BHALINGTA KHA HI*

In the past, in the Asura Cave at the border of India and Nepal, the great master from Orgyen, Padmasambhava, with Langchen Palgyi Senge, one of his main disciples, opened the mandala of the great and glorious Drekpa Kundul,[45] and gave a Vajrayana empowerment. At that time, he bound the recipients under oath to **obey his command.** When the twelve Tenma made their pledge **and** promised to **protect Tibet,** he poured samaya water on the tongues of the Tenmas, placed a symbolic crown corresponding to their particular buddha family on each of their heads, placed the unchanging vajra in their hands, and entrusted them to protect Tibet, and particularly to prevent the *tirthikas* from entering. These twelve Tenma sisters are also known as the twelve mamos of supreme bliss. They are the four female demons, the four *menmos*, and the four *yakshinis*. The Palchen Düpa sadhana lists them as follows[46]:

> At the border of Nepal and Tibet, Tseringma,
> Latö Dorje Yamakyong,
> Nöjin Gang La Kunzangmo,
> Drokchen Khordul Gekkyi Tso,
>
> Jomo Gangrar Chenchikma,
> Changna Khading Lumo Gyal,
> Kharak Dorje Khyung Tsunma,
> Machen Pomrar Drakmogyal,
>
> Gongtsun Demo Bökham Kyong,
> Dragtsen Dorje Menchikma,
> Jomo Nakgyal Yarmo Sil,
> Wuna Dorje Zulemen.

"You the **twelve mother and sister Tenmas** with your legions of a hundred thousand female assistants, please approach. We offer you **the rinsing water of the torma** and this torma blessed into nectar. **Accept** them with great joy and **accomplish all the various activities** that we practitioners **request of you.**"

The Mantra

> **MAMA** is the essence of the twelve mamos.
> **HRING HRING** means "gather here."
> **BALINGTA** means "torma" and
> **KHAHI** means "accomplish!"

j) Horse Dance

> *HUNG! In this mandala of the vidyadhara victors,*
> *All damsi demons who pervert and lead astray*

Are suppressed beneath the seal of the nine yanas—
Let them never rise again!
TAM BHA YA NEN

A *damsi* demon is someone with whom we have shared samayas, a vajra brother or sister with whom we received empowerments and commitments, but who has stained them and became a demon. So the vajra tent does not stop them from entering the mandala. At this point we summon them and suppress them under the torma receptacle. For that we say to them: "All those who are now creating obstacles to the correct practice of the profound **mandala of the victorious ones** of the Lama **Rigdzin** and to the accomplishment of the siddhis ordinary and supreme—**the damsi demons** of dualistic deluded thinking **who pervert and lead us astray**—are **all suppressed beneath** the torma receptacle symbolizing the absolute nature free from delusion and appears clearly as an iron Mount Meru." As we say this, we banish them to the city of Yama beneath the earth. We hold them there with **the seal of the nine yanas**—the three yanas of the outer vehicle leading from the origin of suffering, the three yanas of the inner vehicle of Vedic asceticism, and the three yanas of the secret vehicle of powerful transformative methods—saying, "Until the three realms of samsara are completely empty, you will **never rise again!**"

k) Receiving the Siddhis

> HO! *Deities of the mandala of vidyadharas,*
> *The samayas of approach and accomplishment are fulfilled.*
> *The dawn of Vajrasattva is breaking:*
> *The time has come to grant us the siddhis!*
> *Send from the mandalas of your body, speech, and mind*
> *The blessings of supreme, secret, nondwelling wisdom*
> *Of vajra body, speech, and mind!*
> *Grant us all the siddhis, supreme and ordinary,*
> *This very instant!*
> OM AH HUNG VAJRA GURU PEMA TÖ TRENG TSAL VAJRA
>   SAMAYA DZA
> KAYA WAKKA TSITTA A LA LA SIDDHI PALA HUNG

"HO!" is an expression of joy: we rejoice at the perspective of receiving the ordinary and supreme siddhis. We are happy to have now perfectly **ful-**

filled the commitments measured in signs, number of recitations, or duration of practice. These siddhis are the result of practicing **approach and accomplishment** according to the **samayas of the deities of the mandala of Rigdzin** Düpa, through the practice of the main deity alone, the practice of the gathering of the deities of the mandala, and so on. Therefore, we say: "Now **the dawn of Vajrasattva is breaking** in the east." At this first moment of dawn, as the day is breaking, **the time has come to grant us**—the vajra master and vajra brothers and sisters—**the** supreme and ordinary **siddhis.** So, you ask the lama vidyadharas to send the blessings from the **mandalas of** their enlightened **body, speech, and mind** of the **supreme secret wisdom,** ultimate and definitive, which is the inseparable unity of appearance and emptiness and does **not dwell** or fall into either of the two extremes of samsara and nirvana, and is the essence of the three **vajras**—enlightened **body, speech,** and **mind.** We ask them to **grant us** this **supreme siddhi,** which is the direct experience of the state of the Lama Rigdzin Düpa. We also ask them to give us the eight **ordinary** siddhis.

The eight ordinary siddhis are, as it is said:

> Celestial realm, sword, pill,
> Fleet-footedness, vase, *yaksha* servants,
> Elixir, and balm of magic sight.

1. The siddhi of celestial realm is the ability to go to celestial realms without having to die.
2. The siddhi of sword gives the ability to overcome any hostile army.
3. The siddhi of pill gives the ability to bless pills made of different medicinal substances that will make you invisible when holding them in your hand;
4. With the siddhi of fleet-footedness, by wearing boots you have blessed, you can walk around a lake in an instant;
5. With the vase siddhi you can create a vessel that makes anything you put inside it, food or money, for example, inexhaustible.
6. The siddhi of yaksha is the power to make yakshas your servants. They then follow your orders and accomplish the work of a million people in a single night.
7. The siddhi of elixir gives you a lifespan as long as that of the sun and the moon, the strength of an elephant, the beauty of a lotus, and gives you the youthful sensation of feeling as light as a cotton ball whenever you get up from your seat.

LIGHT OF THE SUN AND THE MOON — 163

8. With the siddhi of the balm of magic sight, you can see things beneath the surface, such as treasures hidden in the ground and the like, when you apply the balm to your eyes.

You request the siddhis saying, "This very instant, please grant us all these ordinary and supreme siddhis!" The meaning of the mantra is as follows:

KAYA means "body";
WAKA means "speech";
TSITTA means "mind";
SARWA means "all";
A LA LA is an expression of joy;
SIDDHI means "accomplishment";
PALA means "good"; and
HUNG is the request "grant them to us!"

l) Confession

HUNG! In the mandala of the gathering of vidyadharas,
Incomplete offerings, inattentive practice,
Drowsy, dull, and lifeless meditation,
All such confusion and mistakes I confess—forgive me I pray!

To whom do you confess? To all the deities of **the mandala of the** Gathering of Lama Sugata **Vidyadharas,** who are in front of you. What do you confess? You confess having made **incomplete offerings.** You also confess falling prey to **distraction** during the practice of approach and accomplishment. You confess the times when your **meditation** was without clarity and was obscured by **dullness, drowsiness, and lifelessness.** In short, **you confess all confusion and mistakes,** and you ask all the deities to **forgive** you in their wisdom. Then you recite the hundred-syllable mantra, which purifies all impairments of samaya. Now, purified and free of obscuration, you actualize that you receive the supreme siddhi.

m) Dzogrim Dissolution

(1) Dissolution in General

Generally, in Mahayoga, the dzogrim dissolution is as follows: the pure wisdom deities, who appeared from the causal mantra syllable HUNG, dissolve back at this point into the state of suchness, the dharmata, in a reverse of the way they appeared. The entire arrangement of the pure field dissolves into the palace. Then the palace dissolves into the deities, the deities into the principal deity, the principal deity into the jnanasattva and the jnanasattva into the mantra-garland surrounding the seed syllable. The mantra-garland dissolves into the samadhisattva (the core seed syllable). The core seed syllable then dissolves into the dharmadhatu, and you rest for a moment free of reference point. This is the crucial point for eliminating the extreme of eternalism.

From this state of clear light, the illusory, postmeditation form of the deity—that is just the same as the one generated earlier in the practice—arises again, instantly like a fish jumping out of water. The universe and the beings within it all arise as the mandala of deities. This is the crucial point for eliminating the extreme of nihilism.

Then in the postmeditation session you go about your activities seeing everything as an illusion, as generally expressed in the texts on this subject.

(2) In the Rigdzin Düpa Text

> HO! Like bubbles dissolving on water,
> The self-manifesting deity mandala
> Reabsorbs into the expanse of primordial wisdom—VAJRA MU!
> In postmeditation, everything arises as the illusory body of the
> deity.

The text uses the example of **bubbles** that **dissolve** back into the water they arose from. Just so, the **deities** and palace of the Rigdzin Düpa **mandala** that **manifested** from the appearance aspect or magical display of the great dharmakaya wisdom, our **own** rigpa, **reabsorb** back **into the** unaltered **expanse of primordial wisdom** free of conceptual elaboration and without reference point—VAJRA MU! As we say this, the mandala dissolves back into the all-pervading space of equality of inseparable empty awareness. Rest in equipoise as long as you can. Then **in postmeditation,** the deities of the mandala-gathering of the vidyadhara sugatas **arise** instantly, like fish jumping out of water, or like the **illusions** of a conjurer. You see the whole universe and every being within it as the display of the body, speech, and mind of the vidyadhara lama. Place the three syllables at your three centers while knowing that their essence is the body, speech, and mind of all the victorious buddhas, to wear "the armor equivalent to the deity." Then resume your usual activities.

n) Dedication and Aspiration Prayers

HO! I dedicate all virtues of the three times
To be the cause for all to realize primordial omniscience;
May I and all those gathered here
Attain enlightenment together, in one mandala!

We dedicate **all** roots of **virtue** accumulated in **the three times**—past, present, and future—by all sentient beings who pervade the whole of space, and in particular the merit of the present assembly, vajra master and vajra brothers and sisters. We **dedicate** it all **to be the cause for every being** in the three realms to attain the level of the universal lord and **primordial** protector Samantabhadra—the unsurpassable state of **omniscience**. Through this, may everyone gathered here, practicing together as a group—master and vajra brothers and sisters—**attain enlightenment together in one mandala** without ever separating!

o) Prayer for Auspiciousness

(1) In General

Every buddha of the ten directions along with his bodhisattva offspring manifest as rupakayas in the sky before us out of the dharmadhatu. They dance gracefully with myriad beautiful, attractive, auspicious expressions. They play every kind of musical instrument and chant melodiously in the voice of Brahma, their speech resounding words of auspiciousness. Their minds remain in the unchanging equality of the all-pervading dharmadhatu.

They let flowers of auspiciousness fall from their hands, which cascade down in a refreshing shower that triumphs over all adversity and harmful circumstances, and causes virtues and positive qualities to increase just like a waxing moon. As you recite the mantra of the essence of interdependent origination, consider with delight that you enjoy the glory of this new golden age.

(2) In the Rigdzin Düpa Text

> *HO! Through the blessing of the lineage of vidyadharas,*
> *The truth of the Three Jewels, and*
> *The circumstances created by the profound Secret Mantrayana,*
> *May all be auspicious to quell the eight fears!*
> *May all be auspicious for increasing longevity and merit!*
> *May all be auspicious to bring appearances under our control!*
> *May all be auspicious to annihilate negative forces!*
> *All sights and grasping at them are the perfect mudra of the deity's*
>   *forms,*
> *All sounds are pure as the great bliss of mantra,*
> *All thoughts mature as clear light dharmakaya—*
> *May all be auspicious, so that we attain the unimpeding rainbow*
>   *body!*

Through the blessing and compassion of all the lamas **of the** unbroken **lineage of vidyadharas**—from Samantabhadra and the lamas of the mind-transmission lineage, through the vidyadharas of the sign-transmission lineage and the great individuals of the oral-transmission lineage, right up until the present day; by the power of **the** great **truth** of the words of the **three** precious **jewels**, the Buddha, Dharma, and Sangha; through the powerful **circumstances created** by practicing correctly the mandala of **profound Secret Mantra**,

- **May all be auspicious to quell the eight fears** of lions, elephants, fire, snakes, thieves, captivity, flesh-eating demons, and drowning.
- **May all be auspicious** to see **increase** in the six wealths of **long life, merit**, fame, and so on!⁴⁷
- **May all be auspicious** for us to gain the capacity **to bring under control all appearances** manifesting as the universe and beings, without hindrance, such as attaining the four stages of aspirational practice!⁴⁸
- **May all be auspicious** for us to have the power **to annihilate** all **negative** influences and obstructing **forces**!

The aspect of present **sights**, our impure, deluded perceptions of this world, as well as our **grasping** onto them as real, are **all** ultimately **perfect** in the display of the **mudra of** buddha **forms—the deities** who appear as the magical net of wisdom of the lama-gathering of vidyadharas. In the same way, **all** various aspects of **sound** in this world arise ultimately **as** the utterly **pure** self-radiance of **mantra,** the indestructible **great bliss of** enlightened speech. And **all** rising **thoughts,** which are the magical display of dualistic mind, are purified in the great equality, the unity of primordial wisdom and basic space free of conceptual elaboration; they are **matured as the clear light** primordial wisdom of the great **dharmakaya. May all be auspicious so that** when all this is actualized **we** may discover in this very life the body of great transference, the **unimpeding** great **rainbow body;** we may realize the level of dharmakaya for ourselves, and for others stir the three realms of samsara from their depths, as we accomplish the everlasting, ubiquitous, and spontaneous enlightened activities. For all this, may all be auspicious!

This was taught by the dull mantrika of these degenerate times called Peyak Tulku at Kadak Trödral Ling as was requisite for a vase consecration with the vajra guru mantra.

A Clearly Reflecting Mirror

Chöpön Activities for the Rigdzin Düpa,
the Inner Sadhana of the Longchen Nyingtik Cycle

By Patrul Rinpoche

Homage to the lama!

A. Arrangement for a Rigdzin Düpa Drupchö[1]

1. Mandala

Generally, we would use a sand mandala, or a drawing of the mandala. The practice supports and empowerment substances are placed on top, and then the seven offerings[2] around. Tormas and other offerings must be placed in front of the mandala, when there is one. You can dispense with the mandala only when you practice simply with meditation on self-visualization alone. In all other cases, you must have a physical mandala, in which case, the arrangement in front of the mandala is the following:

2. Top Offering Shelf

a) The Rigdzin Düpa Torma

First, in the middle of the top offering shelf place the Rigdzin Düpa torma. The torma's lowest level holds the general gathering of the retinue represented by as many *tepkyus* as possible. On the middle level are the twenty-five disciples in the form of twenty-five butter jewels (*norbu*). Above is the eight-faceted jewel representing the eight vidyadharas. Above the jewel are a sun and a moon symbolizing indivisible means and wisdom. Above this is the round lama torma ornamented with a four-petaled lotus.

b) Fulfillment-and-Confession Torma

The fulfillment-and-confession torma[3] goes to the left of the Rigdzin Düpa torma, and is similar in form. Alternatively, you can just have the Emptying the Lower Realms from Their Very Depth (*Narak Kong Shak*) tormas. They should be placed as follows: the round white four-petaled peaceful fulfillment torma with forty-two tepkyus to the right; and the four-petaled wrathful fulfillment torma (*paltor*)[4] with fifty-eight tepkyus to the left.

To the right and left of both tormas,[5] place kapalas of amrita and rakta, with alcohol and water added to their respective substances, together with their individual spoons. If you have gathered several hundreds of amrita, rakta, and butter lamp offerings, arrange them according to space like when arranging the shrine for the practice of the Peaceful and Wrathful Deities.

3. Second Offering Shelf: the Dharmapala Tormas

In the middle of the second offering shelf place the protector tormas of The Protectress of the Sacred Command and Her Brother and Sisters (*Kasung Magön Chamdral*). In the center is Ekadzati (a red *paltor*); to her right is the Gönpo Maning torma with triangular *triri* torma; to her left is the triangular Damchen Dorje Lekpa torma, characterized by a goat's head; behind is the triangular Rishi Rahula torma that is twisting to the right; and in front the triangular female protector torma of Durtrö Lhamo, all surrounded with seventy-five tepkyu for the seventy-five glorious protectors.

To the left of this, a separate Rahula torma called "the chief and the eight-fold assembly"[6] is placed with the "human corpses of flesh and mountains of flames."[7]

To their right is the "permanent"[8] triangular Tenma torma set,[9] from left to right: white, black, and red, each with three tepkyus at the front in the respective color.

To the left of Magön is the Tseringma torma: round, white, with a vase-like belly, and four round white tormas in the four directions.

To its left is the cheto torma. It is a red, triangular triri type torma, with three tepkyus on each of its three sides.

And if you want to place separate amrita and rakta for the Dharma protectors, then put them to the right and left of these tormas, just as before.

If Lekden, Tsimara, and so on are to be practiced, add specific tormas here.

4. Third Offering Shelf

On the third offering shelf, the lowest one, put the peaceful offerings, from drinking water to music, common to both the self and front mandalas. Arrange also the wrathful offerings to the Dharmapalas: blood of *argam*; five organs of *pupe*; great fat of *dupe*; great grease lamp (*aloké*); bile for *gendé*; and the wrathful *zhalzé* torma for food offering.[10]

In front of these, place the required offerings, such as the offerings to the eight classes of gods and spirits, tsok, Tenma, daily dharmapalas offerings, the four-petaled kator with a *chang tri* ornament, and round pellets (*tepril*).

If you have a table big enough, you can place the mandala and tormas and offerings in front. It is not wrong to prepare the arrangement in this way. However, you can also make a fourth level, using the table where the mandala—whether a drawing or made of heaps—is arranged as the upper level, according to what the chöpön can manage. So on the three lower levels you would arrange the offerings as mentioned above; that is easy. If you have as many *phukong* as there are protector tormas, then place a phukong for each of them. Protector tormas should also be ornamented with colored ribbon and small pieces of meat to make them beautiful.

B. Activities During the Recitation Practice

After the preliminaries, whether elaborate or short, bless the outer offering bowls, the offerings to the eight classes of gods and spirits, and the phukongs. Then at the beginning offer them out onto a high place.[11]

Place the gektor low. Sprinkle it with purifying water and at the end of expelling the negative forces section, hold it below the knees and go throw it out. It can also be taken outside at the descent of blessing section, with incense, and while wearing the hat.

At the descent of blessings in the Rigdzin Düpa sadhana text, you need to remove the lids of amrita and rakta.

At blessing of the offerings, it is not necessary for the lama to sprinkle the activity water himself. But, if he doesn't, the chöpön must sprinkle clean water over the outer offerings. Amrita and rakta are each simply raised, and sprinkled on the torma. But no droplet of amrita and rakta should touch the outer offerings.

At the invitation, light some incense also. Then, customarily, there is nothing else to do.

At the end of the mantra recitation, the torma offerings are made full by adding more food offerings to them.[12] The offerings are increased by adding more water and should also be blessed again. When saying the words of offering,[13] sprinkle amrita and rakta over the tormas.

When the sadhana is repeated in a second session,[14] then it's not necessary to offer kator and gektor again for the second session. Add more to the tormas and the offerings to make them complete, but though the prayers recited are the same as in the earlier practice section, there is no chöpön activity in the second one. Generally, whether it is for a drupchen or for a drupchö, the tradition is to chant the prayers in these two practices differently. In any case the practice leading to the mantra recitation should be of equal length, so the number of mantra recitations should be the same in both sessions.

In the afternoon session, at *Emptying the Lower Realms from Their Very Depths*, hold the amrita kapala in the right hand and sprinkle in accordance with the words of fulfillment, simply raising the spoon each time. At the rakta offering, take the container in the left hand and like before raise the rakta spoon in your right hand each time.

At the torma fulfillment, sprinkle amrita and rakta over the torma at the end of the section.

At the lamp fulfillment, light the butter lamp and place it near the tsok.

Tsok

The place where the tsok offering is arranged should be covered with tiger skin[15] and so on, in front of the mandala. The tsok tormas and so on are placed to the right, and the kapala containing *tsok chang* to the left.

The chöpön enters the central aisle of the temple, makes three prostrations, and requests the tsok. The chöpön blesses the offerings by sprinkling inner water and activity water. He cuts out the three tsok portions and arranges them. Then he offers each portion at the appropriate section of the text, sprinkles them with the tsok chang, and places them with the offerings. At this point he also needs to cut out one portion of the pure remainder offering, and place it on a plate.

Tsok Distribution

The first offering to be distributed is the offering to the lama. Then start distributing the food on the right aisle, and the liquids on the left. Go around the assembly, offering them the long-life knot to touch.[16] Walk in a composed manner without rushing around as is often done during empowerments.[17]

Remainder

Once the tsok has been enjoyed, collect the remainder offering. Take the remainder container to the back of the assembly to start collecting the offerings and finish by placing the vajra master's remainder offering on the top. Then, in front of the mandala house, put the clean remainder that was prepared earlier on a tripod set on a human skin or on the "remainder mandala"[18] and next to it the unclean remainder. Then you need to see if the two remainders need to be mixed[19] (here we don't have the time to go into this). So, you mix the two remainders, and then present them to the lama, who blesses them with the inner offering through the garuda mudra. In the Gemang tradition it is tsok chang that is poured through the mudra. The remainder torma is placed in the middle of the remainder mandala in the middle of the tripod. If it is still daylight, just put incense in it. But if it is already dark, then add the glorious flames (*palbar*).[20] Holding the offering with the samaya mudra of Heruka, empty it in one pile on the ground seventy steps outside the practice hall, and return.

Dharmapalas

Bless the torma offering to the protectors by sprinkling clean water and so on. At the invocation of *The Protectress of the Sacred Command and Her Brother and Sisters*, light incense. At the offering and request, put the phukong in the lower round metal basin, and when you say, "We invoke you! We give you! We offer you!"[21] raise up the upper part containing the tea offering.

Then after Za, Tseringma, Yüdrönma, etc., put the hat on for the Tenmas, hold the torma in the right hand and the tea offering phukong in the left. Hold and lift them upward. Keep them held high up at the end of the hall. Even if you practice in a house, you should make sure to stand at the proper place. During the break in chanting, the torma is carried outside and offered in a high place. Come back before the end of the music. Increase the dharmapala offerings by adding more to them. Then from the offering praise section, put on the hat. Offer the cheto torma outside with incense if it is daytime, and glorious flames if it is night. Then sprinkle the Tenma offering with the water used to rinse the recipient of the cheto torma, and offer it outside. Cheto and Tenma offerings can also be carried out together, in which case the use of rinsing water may not be so easy, so do whichever is easier.[22]

Horse Dance

Again the torma receptacle is placed at the end of the hall. While wearing the hat, after the lama has raised the vajra, go up in the central alley between the front rows and take the vajra from his hand. Hold it up and take it to the torma receptacle. Suppress with the double-vajra mudra, placing the vajra first to the east-west direction and then the north-south direction. Go back from the end of the hall, bringing the vajra, and offer it back into the lama's hand. Turn the torma receptacle over, lift it upward, and throw flowers.

Offerings

Increase the torma and outer offerings by adding more to them, sprinkling water onto them, and so on. Make sure to do this before the offering of praise. At the end, sprinkle the torma with amrita and rakta also.

Tashi Prayer

At the prayers for auspiciousness, there is nothing to do apart from distributing flowers and so on.

In general, those who go outside to offer the tormas should wear their zen and hat, and should take their hat off before reentering. Do not wear hats for the serkyem and gektor.

The day the practice is over, the large cheto, Tenma, and preliminary tormas present in the practice hall should be offered. After, you need to offer the daily tormas (*gyun tor*). Make sure to always offer the daily dharmapala tormas during their petition offering practice. The tormas of dharmapalas can either be offered on the last evening after the practice, or in the *sang* the next day. If you do it this way, even if you do not do the full practice, detailing all the torma offerings to the protectors, the best is to recite, "The teachings of the Buddha, a precious, blazing vessel..."[23] at the end of the sang and offer all the tormas at that point into the fire of the sang.

There is nothing more than this.

I, Patrul Rinpoche, wrote this according to the tradition and the definitive, authentic instructions of the omniscient father and son without adding anything of my own making, at the request of some new shrine servers. Virtue! Virtue! Sarva mangalam!

The Lotus Garland Adornment

A Practice Arrangement Easy to Implement
That Links the Different Elements of the
"Empowerment Conferring Majesty,"
the Root Empowerment of the Rigdzin Düpa from
the Longchen Nyingtik Cycle

───────

By Jamgön Kongtrul Lödro Tayé

NAMO GURU PADMAKARAYA!
Kaya embodying the victorious ones of the three times,
Treasury of the great secret definitive Dharma,
You are like space, yet imbued with enlightened activity,
Jetsün Padma, to your feet I bow!

This empowerment is to ripen students
Who wish to experience the very essence of the space treasury of the vast
   expanse
With the ultimate means of accomplishing
The sadhana of the vidyadhara who has mastered the nine expanses of
primordial wisdom.

The outer benefiting empowerment to ripen students will be given by fol-
lowing the way it is presented in other great mandalas. For the inner enabling
empowerment, I use the clear instructions for this specific empowerment that
are found in the root text. So this ritual has three sections:

   1. The preparation: arranging the articles and substances,
   2. The main part: the sadhana practice and the conferring of the empow-
      erment, and
   3. The concluding steps.

A. The Preparation: Arranging the Articles and Substances

In an isolated and pleasant place, arrange the peaceful mandala on a clean table. You can either draw it according to the text, with all the doors and characteristics of the deities, or place down nine heaps of flowers to represent the main deity and the eight deities in the retinue. In its center, place a vase filled with liquid on a three-legged stand, with an aperture ornament and a ribbon tied around it. To the right of the mandala, place the text of this practice. If you do not have one, wrap various sections of the scriptures, such as sadhanas and other texts, in silk, and place them on the right. On the left, put a skull-cup with the perfect characteristics, filled with a preparation of alcohol, Dharma medicinal nectar (chömen), and the three sweets. On top of the skull-cup put a melong *coated in sindhura powder and marked with tiklés.[1] Place a crystal on top. Along the side put the tsakli card of the consort, and then place a silken canopy above the arrangement. Set out the amrita, rakta, and torma, and lay out the outer offerings around the arrangement. Gather the necessary practice substances and articles, such as the protector tormas, the preliminary tormas, tsok articles, and so on, as usual.*

B. Establishing the Foundation with the Sadhana Practice, and Conferring the Empowerment

1. Accomplishing the Sadhana to Give the Empowerment

First, you need to accomplish the sadhana before you can give the empowerment. Follow the text of the inner sadhana of Rigdzin Düpa, starting with refuge and bodhichitta, and guiding you through the sequence of practice. Meditate with self- and front-visualizations indivisible. If your realization is not very high, divide the "house of the mantra." For the mantra recitation, visualize as indicated in The Concealed Instructions *(Gabjang), and recite the mantra of approach, the vajra guru mantra, and the mantra of accomplishment, the mahaguru mantra. Then say:*

Instantly, in the immeasurable palace of the self-arisen vase, appears the mandala-assembly of vidyadharas, vivid and clear like stars reflecting on the surface of a pure lake. I appear clearly in the form of the deity; the core seed syllable and the mantra at my heart emanate rays of light. The mantra-garland at my heart emanates mantra-garlands that go out and follow the mantra thread (*zungtak*), and invoke the wisdom-mind of the vase deities. Emanating and reabsorbing rays of light, the two purposes are accomplished, and the nectar of untainted great bliss descends in a great flow from the body of the deity into the vase, filling it completely.

As you visualize these lines, hold the mantra thread and recite at least one hundred approach mantras and one hundred accomplishment mantras.

Inside the activity vase, on a lotus and a sun,
Stands Pema Wangchen, red in color,
Holding a lotus club and a lasso,
Amid a vast expanse of wisdom fire.
The vajra amrita flows out of his body
And fills the vase completely.
OM VAJRA KRODHA HAYAGRIVA HUNG PHAT

Recite the mantra about one hundred times. At the end, chant the prayers of offering and praise, and recite the hundred-syllable mantra.

With OM AH HUNG, offer the water from the conch into the vase. Think that the deities of the vase of complete victory melt into great bliss and become one taste with the vase water.

Offer the torma to the terma protectors, throw the flower of awareness, and request the authorization to grant the empowerment.

2. Actual Empowerment

a) Preparing the Students

For the actual empowerment, first you need to cleanse the students and give the gektor in the usual way. Issue the command and meditate on the protection spheres as indicated in the sadhana text. Guide students in generating bodhichitta, explain the Dharma, and introduce this teaching; in particular, you may say as follows:

(1) Background to the Teaching

All the tantras, *agamas*, and pith-instructions are indications in the form of words and symbols pointing to the ultimate, "the self-arisen, great secret pith-instructions." They are wisdom treasures hidden in the wisdom-mind of the victorious ones. Dakinis, through the power of their realization, hid them as treasures in space; the vidyadharas also hid them in the earth inside caskets that cannot be affected by the elements. When they are required for training beings on the path, great beings with the right karma break open the seals and reveal these treasures fully. Here we are concerned with one such individual with good karma, who was foretold in *The Seal of Prophecies from Lama Gongdü*[2] in the following way:

> In the south will appear a tulku named Özer,
> Who will liberate beings through the profound teachings of the Nyingtik.
> He will lead whoever is connected to him to the pure land of the vidyadharas.

And Orgyen Chöje Lingpa's prophecies say:

> In the district of Yor in central Tibet, will come someone called Changsem Pema,
> A protector of the Kagyü and Nyingma teachings; he will train beings through skillful means.

There are many passages in the Sarma and the Nyingma teachings in which Guru Rinpoche's vajra breath praises the tertön who revealed these teachings. This treasure revealer is someone who devoted his entire life to raising the victory banner of practice, and who, as a result, became an accomplished master, a mahasiddha. He is also regarded, without the slightest question, as an embodiment of both king Trisong Detsen and prince Gyalse Lharje together. I am talking about the great vidyadhara Jigme Khyentse Özer, also known as Wangchen Yeshe Dorje Tsal, or Jigme Lingpa, to whom the dakinis handed the symbolic letters of the five expanses. He was blessed by repeated direct encounters with the precious Guru of Oddiyana and the omniscient Longchenpa Drime Özer, and his mind merged indivisibly with the vast expanse of their realization. It is based on this that he set down in writing the great wisdom treasury of the space of the vast expanse—the Longchen Nyingtik. A continuous flow of enlightened activities springing from these teachings has been liberating previously unfreed sentient beings beyond counting, both in the central land and at the borders of Tibet and Kham, and even as far away as China and Mongolia. It is for such a teaching, the Rigdzin Düpa, the Inner Sadhana for the Longchen Nyingtik Cycle, that I am going give the root empowerment called Royal Anointment Empowerment. *And so on.*

To that end, I have accomplished all the preparations and initial practices. Now each of you should offer the mandala.

Say this to introduce the students to these teachings. Then ask the students to offer the mandala and request the empowerment.

(2) Empowerment Request

Repeat the following prayer to the lama, who is indivisible from the main deity of the mandala, with a mind filled with heartfelt devotion:

> HO! Please accept us in your great compassion,
> The fortunate sons and daughters of noble family.
> Grant us entry into this mandala of great samaya,
> And bring us to maturation!

The request is repeated three times. Then instruct and give permission in the following way:

> HO! Entrance to this mandala of the supreme secret
> Is difficult, and there is great risk involved.
> Impaired samayas will bring ruin.
> So if you can keep the samaya, I will grant you the empowerment!

(3) Refuge

Visualize in front of you the entire host of the three roots deities and all the samaya-bound Dharma protectors of the Lama Rigdzin Düpa mandala, with the confidence that they are sitting right here. In their presence, give rise to the thought that you are now taking refuge in them until you and all sentient beings, as limitless as space, reach complete enlightenment. Repeat after me:

> Homage!
> I and all infinite beings
> Take refuge in the lama, the essence of the Three Jewels,
> And in the mandala of the multitude of vidyadharas,
> With devotion and from the depths of our hearts!

(4) Bodhichitta

Generate bodhichitta in aspiration by giving rise to the wish to lead all sentient beings, who are as limitless as space and have all been extraordinarily kind parents to us, to the state of complete enlightenment. Also generate bodhichitta in aspiration by thinking, "To be able to act upon this, I will enter the mandala of the Lama Rigdzin Düpa and follow the swift path of the vajra pinnacle." With this in mind repeat after me:

> HO! I have entered this mandala of vidyadharas and
> I recall all sentient beings in the six realms, my parents;
> Moved by immeasurable compassion that aches for their
> liberation,
> Aspiration, action, and absolute bodhichitta: fill my heart!

(5) Seven-Branch Offering

Then perform the special seven-branch offering specific to this practice, which is for gathering the accumulations, purifying all negativity, and increasing everything positive. Out of the unborn state, the miracle of birth manifests like bubbles arising from water: the lamp of naturally arising wisdom, clear light dharmadhatu wisdom beyond thought and description, abides as the primordial, utterly pure mandala of the naturally arising three kayas. Within the expanse of the lamp of pure basic space marked by the lamp of empty spheres that forms the support, the supported radiance of rigpa manifests as the deities of the vajra chain of awareness. The vajra chains of awareness are seen directly by the senses, the far-reaching water lamp, which thus connects with the lamp of naturally arising wisdom. Meeting the deities in this manner is the prostration.

Offer in an ocean of offering clouds the increased experience of rainbow-light spheres that arise from this.

By resting in the state of the great full-measure of rigpa, in which all appearances arise naturally as kayas and wisdoms, you confess the negativity and faults of holding onto a perceiving subject and perceived objects by relating to subject, object, and action.

Rejoice in the complete perfection of the great accumulation of untainted wisdom, in the exhaustion into the expanse of dharmata nature of all appearing phenomena, the fruition endowed with twofold purity.

Request the outward radiance of great transference wisdom kayas to turn unceasingly, with the continuous flow of vajra speech, the Dharma wheel of Dzogchen within the eternal expanse.

Pray and request that the great reflection-like vajra rainbow bodies remain as long as samsara endures.

Dedicate the virtuous accumulation of such untainted wisdom to the complete purification of both obscurations in the expanse of the youthful vase body; do this dedication while being fully aware that there is no dedication in the basic space of dharmadhatu.

In other words, repeat three times the following, keeping in mind the crucial points of the extraordinary view and meditation just explained:

> HO! Like bubbles bubbling out of water,
> The wisdom expanse emanates deities;
> The direct experience of rigpa is my prostration.
> Increase of experience is my offering.
> In the full maturity of rigpa, I confess!
> In the exhaustion of phenomena, I rejoice!
> Out of the expanse of great transference, please turn the Dharma
>   wheels!
> In the great rainbow body remain, we pray!
> I dedicate all merit gathered toward the youthful vase body!

(6) Descent of Blessings

In order to establish the foundation for the empowerment, we are going to invoke the descent of wisdom. So concentrate on the key points of body, speech, and mind, and direct your practice in the following way:

Rest in clear light emptiness, the nature of all phenomena, the great simplicity free from any conceptual elaboration. Its natural radiance is the spontaneously present, infinite purity of the great mandala that now appears. In the center of the mandala there are lotus seats below, a sun seat above it, and a moon seat on top. On these seats, you appear instantly in the form of the great master who embodies all families; you wear the cloths and ornaments of the Great Guru Prevailing Over All That Appears and Exists, Mahaguru Nangsi Zilnön. Your complexion is white with a tinge of red. You wield in the air a golden vajra with your right hand that forms the menacing mudra, and with your left hand in the mudra of meditative equipoise you hold a kapala with a long-life vase full of longevity nectar. On your head, you wear the lotus hat. You wear the gown, the Dharma robe, and the cloak, one on top of the other. In the cradle of your left arm you hold the wisdom dakini, who is your own radiance. You sit with grace and majesty, your legs in the posture of royal ease, amid an expanse of rainbow spheres of light. On the crown of your head there is a white syllable OM, at your throat a red syllable AH, and a blue syllable HUNG at your heart.

Infinite rays of light shoot out from the heart of the lama and the deities in the mandala, and from the seed syllables at the three centers of each of you. They reach all the deities of the three roots and all buddhas and bodhisattvas in the buddha fields of the ten directions, and, in particular, the pure fields of the three-kaya lamas where they abide, invoking their wisdom-mind. The deities of the three roots and the buddhas and bodhisattvas gather in droves. They all have the appearance of Guru Padma Tötrengtsal, and fill the whole of space. They dissolve into you and bless you. Actualize this very strongly.

Light some incense. Playing damaru and bell, chant the invocation from the sadhana text, the prayer starting with "HUNG! *In the past, during the first kalpa...*" ("*ngön gyi kalpé dangpo la...*"). *At the end, add* HUNG HUNG HUNG AH RALLI PHENG PHENG *after the Tötrengtsal mantra.*

May the flow of blessings from the wisdom deities fully imbue your body, speech, and mind. *Say* TISHTA BENZA HUNG *while sealing with the vajra.*

This concludes the preliminary practices that make you recipients who can receive the empowerment.

b) Main Part

Next comes the main part, the actual conferring of the empowerment. It has five sections: the vase, secret, wisdom, and word empowerments, and entrustment with all empowerments.

(1) Vase Empowerment

First, for the vase empowerment, visualize rays of light emanating from the heart of the vajra master; they invite the mandala of victorious vidyadharas who arrive and fill the expanse of space; then they pour a continuous flow of vajra nectar with all manner of auspicious marks into the vase and fill it completely; finally, the empowerment ritual that scatters away (students' stains in body, speech, mind, and of the three combined) and pours (the capacity to give rise to the wisdom that ripens these four into the four vajras)³ is granted. Actualize this.

Hold the victorious vase and say:

> HUNG! The deity's palace of the auspicious vase
> Is filled with the water that is nectar indivisible from the deities.
> By granting this empowerment to you, fortunate disciple,
> May your clinging to appearances be exhausted in the mudra of the deity,
> So that you swiftly attain the level of a completely matured vidyadhara,
> And reach the bhumi of Universal Radiance!

Recite the root mantra and add at the end KAYA ABSHIKINTSA OM.
Place the vase on the head of the students and give them some water from the vase.

In this way, the vase empowerment has been bestowed upon you. As a result, the obscurations of the body and the channels are purified; you are empowered to practice kyerim, the generation phase; and the seed for the transformation of the aggregates, elements, sense sources, eight consciousnesses, and senses and their objects into kayas and wisdoms is sown; the ability to accomplish the nirmanakaya is implanted into your stream of being.

(2) Secret Empowerment

For the secret empowerment, consider the vajra master to be the embodiment of all buddha families, and that he appears as Tötrengtsal in union with the wisdom dakini, his own self-radiance; from their union white bodhichitta and red bodhichitta—the nectars that contain all the buddhas—merge with the nectar of the kapala in one taste; experience this at your throat. This is what you need to actualize.

Give the secret substance and say,

> HUNG! The bodhichittas from the union of the consorts
> Swirl, red and white, inside the skull-cup.
> Through granting this empowerment to you, fortunate disciple,
> May the subtle elements within your channels mature into mantra syllables,

So that you swiftly attain the level of a vidyadhara with power over
  life,
And reach the bhumi of Lotus of Nonattachment!

Say the root mantra and add at the end WAKA ABHIKINTSA AH.

In connection with this, you will now receive the transmission for the
mantra recitation. Direct the practice in the following way:

From the heart of the vajra master, garlands of the root mantra emerge in
a continuous string; they enter the students' throats and descend to circle
around your hearts; all the elements of inner air responsible for movement
are now perfected as the empty resounding wheel of mantra. Actualize this
and repeat after me . . .

*Recite the approach mantra and the accomplishment mantra three times
each, with the students repeating after you.*

By receiving the secret empowerment in this manner, the obscurations
of your speech and inner air are purified; you are empowered to use the
unsurpassable, extraordinary samaya substances to recite the mantra, and
to do the inner heat practice of tummo; you have gained the quality of some
mastery over the ten inner airs; and you now have the ability to accomplish
the sambhogakaya.

(3) Wisdom Empowerment

For the wisdom empowerment, consider that the consort—the embodiment of wisdom, who is of the finest beauty with her attractive body and
her youthfulness, and is of most excellent family and disposition—is given
into your hand.

Giving the image of the consort, say:

HUNG! The source of all phenomena
Is the secret consort of great bliss.
I grant her to you, fortunate disciple—
May you actualize the wisdoms of the four joys,
And swiftly attain the level of a mahamudra vidyadhara
And reach the bhumi of the Great Gatherings of Rotating Syllables.

Recite the root mantra and add at the end TSITTA ABHIKINTSA HUNG.

Think that the wisdom consort, who was given to you in this manner,
now says, PADMA BHANDZA MOKSHA HO, acknowledging she was called

upon to help you attain liberation. So she places herself on your lap, you give rise to intense desire with the three considerations and you enjoy her, leading you to experience the wisdoms of the four joys.

By granting the third empowerment in this way, the obscurations of your mind and tiklés are purified; the accumulation of the eighty innate thought patterns has ceased; you are empowered to bring forth the direct experience of the primordial wisdom of unchanging great bliss through the path of someone else's body—the consort's body; and the ability to accomplish the dharmakaya is implanted within you.

(4) Symbolic Word Empowerment

Fourth, the symbolic word empowerment. The clear and faultless mirror represents the view of primordial purity, the ground. The path, the meditation of spontaneous presence, is illustrated by the rainbow crystal. Now bring together symbolic objects and what they represent, and rest in that clear light that recognizes itself.

Show the crystal and the mirror, and say:

> HO! On the surface of the clean mirror of primordial purity
> Shines stainlessly the radiant crystal of spontaneous presence—
> This empowerment of symbols and meaning in perfect
>   correspondence
> Makes you realize the natural state of stainless awareness;
> You will swiftly attain the level of a spontaneously accomplished
>   vidyadhara,
> And reach the bhumi of Great Bliss!

Say the root mantra and add at the end DHARMADHATU ABHIKINTSA AH.

Now sit straight, applying the crucial points of the body, and rest in simplicity, the state of freedom from all extremes and mental elaboration.

Sit for a while. In that state, utter a fierce PHAT, followed by, "What is mind?" As a result,

Transfixed, with no thought whatsoever (*hede che*), words are left as they are, perceptions lead to no thought, nothing, so you are abiding by primordial wisdom. Recognize this!

Moreover, as this view is said to relate to scripture and reasoning, here is a quotation from the scriptures that expresses it perfectly:

Free from words, thoughts, or descriptions,
Unborn, unceasing, the very essence of space,
The wisdom of our own rigpa
Is the Great Perfection, the mother of the buddhas of the three times.[4]

Then, if you are a vajra master with great realization, visualize an AH syllable at your heart and ask the students to concentrate on it; as you and the students rest in meditation, say AH twenty-one times.

Having received the fourth empowerment in this manner, the karma of the ground of all and the cognitive obscurations are purified; you are empowered to meditate on primordial wisdom, the inconceivable Great Perfection; and the ability to accomplish the svabhavikakaya is implanted within you.

(5) Entrustment With All Empowerments

Since you have been completely entrusted with this transmission, now generate strong and powerful devotion for all the root and lineage masters. As a result, they transfer all the blessings of their mind direct-transmission lineage to your own stream of being. Think that you have now received the great empowerment in all secret words and meaning of the Dzogchen Longchen Nyingtik.

Place the volume on the heads of the students, and say,

> HO! Dharmakaya Samantabhadra,
> Sambhogakaya buddhas of the five families,
> Nirmanakaya Garab Dorje,
> Great master Manjushrimitra,
> Vidyadhara Shri Singha,
> Great pandita Vimalamitra,
> Padma Tötreng of Orgyen,
> Dakini Yeshe Tsogyal,
> Sovereign ruler Trisong Detsen,
> Son of the buddhas Drime Özer Longchenpa,
> Jigme Lingpa Longchen Namkhe Naljor, and the rest—
> Glorious protector vidyadhara masters who are the root and lineage
>   lamas of the Natural Great Perfection—and
> Yidam deities and dakinis in your multitudes,

Together with the ocean-like, vast gatherings of Dharma protectors
and guardians,
Grant your empowerments here and now to these fortunate
disciples.
Bless them,
Set their realization alight,
Bring forth their yogic practice,
Lead them to the stronghold of ultimate realization within the
expanse of Dzogchen, beyond action and thinking. Let them
attain the rainbow body of great transference within a single
lifetime and a single body, and establish them at the very level of
Glorious Samantabhadra himself!

*Recite this three times and rest in the state free of any object of focus, while
they receive the realization of the lineage masters. Say prayers of auspiciousness.*
The root empowerment for the mind terma of the great vidyadhara Jigme
Lingpa, the Longchen Nyingtik inner sadhana Rigdzin Düpa, a transmission called the "Royal Anointment Empowerment" has been performed
well. So now think, "I must do my best to maintain root and branch samayas," and repeat after me:

All the root samayas of body, speech, and mind,
The twenty-five branch samayas,
And the Dzogchen samayas such as absence, oneness, and
suffusion—
I promise to maintain them in the proper way.

Repeat this three times. Then the students offer the thanksgiving mandala.
Once again, completely give up your body and all your possessions and
offer them to the universal lord, the lama himself. Keep that in mind and
repeat after me:

Lord of the mandala, whatever your commands,
I will carry out each and every one;
To you I also offer everything—
Hold us as your students and accomplish your activities, we pray!

Say this three times, and dedicate the merit. Then the students can leave.

3. Conclusion

To conclude the practice, the vajra master offers tsok by following the Rigdzin Düpa sadhana as usual until the end of the prayers of auspiciousness. If you can, do the Kasung Magön Chamdral and so on, and Kongshak Dorje Tollu and so on, each at their respective place in the practice.

More elaborate practice based on the Utterly Clear Essence, A Presentation of the General Meaning of Empowerment[5] *can be performed, and the way to add the deity empowerment can be learned from the powerful siddha Kunzang Shenpen's teachings.*

A treasure cherished by the ocean of accomplished masters—
Make it the basis to pursue the accomplishment!
May you reach the kaya of spontaneously accomplished vidyadhara
In manifest enlightenment, and awaken in this life!

I, Chimé Tenyi Yungdrung Lingpa, wrote this according to the intent of the root text, at Dzongsar Tashi Lhatse's monastery. May virtue abound!

Appendix 1: The Thirty-Seven Factors of Enlightenment

The thirty-seven factors of enlightenment are thirty-seven practices undertaken and perfected at specific stages of the paths of accumulation, joining, seeing, and meditation (the first four of the five paths) and are present thereafter as qualities of enlightenment, the fifth path, or path of no more learning. They are:

- the four applications of mindfulness,
- the four genuine restraints,
- the four legs of miraculous powers,
- the five powers,
- the five strengths,
- the seven elements for enlightenment, and
- the noble eightfold path.

1–4) THE FOUR APPLICATIONS OF MINDFULNESS

The four applications, or foundations, of mindfulness refers to the close application of mindfulness to:

1. the body,
2. feelings,
3. the mind, and
4. phenomena.

The Buddha's most detailed teaching on mindfulness is found in the *Satipatthana Sutta* (Pali sutra). *Sati* means "mindfulness" and *patthana* means "application," or "foundation."

Training in the four applications of mindfulness enjoys a special place in the Shravakayana tradition, and also forms part of the thirty-seven factors of enlightenment on the Mahayana path.

To practice these four applications of mindfulness according to the Shravakayana, meditate on:

· the impurity of the body,
· the feelings of suffering,
· the impermanence of consciousness, and
· the fact that mental objects are ownerless (there is no self to which they belong).

To practice according to the Mahayana, during the meditation session meditate on the same objects as being space-like and beyond all conceptual constructs. In the postmeditation period, consider them to be illusory and dreamlike.

There is a threefold distinction between the Shravakayana and the Mahayana approach to this meditation:

· In the Basic Yana, the focus is on our own body, feelings, and so on, while in the Mahayana, the focus is on the bodies, feelings, and so on of others.
· Again, in the Basic Yana, the focus is on the impurity aspect and so on, while in the Mahayana the meditator concentrates on emptiness.
· Finally, with regard to the purpose of this meditation, in the Basic Yana the practice is performed with a view to liberation from the impure body and so on, while in the Mahayana this meditation is performed in order to attain complete enlightenment.

Khenpo Namdrol says:

When the shravakas practice the application of mindfulness of the body, they meditate on their body in the form of a skeleton, and concentrate on its impermanence, impurity, and suffering nature. In contrast, the bodhisattvas meditate on their own bodies and the bodies of others, focusing on their insubstantiality, their emptiness, and their selflessness.

This meditation is termed close mindfulness, because the practitioner discerns the general and particular characteristics of the body and so on with uninterrupted attention.[1]

5–8) THE FOUR GENUINE RESTRAINTS

The four genuine restraints are practiced at the middle level of the path of accumulation. They are:

1. To avoid generating any negative state that has not arisen,
2. To abandon negative state that has arisen,
3. To generate virtuous states that have not arisen, and
4. To not allow any virtuous states that have arisen to deteriorate, and to develop them further.

The Sutra of the Ten Bhumis says:

> To avoid generating unvirtuous dharmas that have not yet arisen, we develop the intention, apply effort, are diligent, and take hold of the mind and settle it correctly. We do the same in order to abandon unvirtuous dharmas that have arisen, and to generate virtuous dharmas that have not yet arisen. To maintain whatever virtuous dharmas have arisen without allowing them to deteriorate, to expand them, to develop them further, and to bring them to completion, we develop the intention, apply effort, and so on.

9–12) THE FOUR LEGS OF MIRACULOUS POWERS

The four legs of miraculous powers are the third group of practices in the thirty-seven factors of enlightenment, practiced at the greater level of the path of accumulation. They are called "legs" of miraculous powers because they are like legs that will carry you to the subsequent attainment of the six clear perceptions and so on:

1. intention,
2. diligence,
3. attention, and
4. discernment.

Khenpo Namdrol says:

> These four legs of miraculous powers are related to the four noble truths. Remaining in isolation means isolation from suffering. Free from attachment means freedom from the origin of

suffering. Remaining in cessation denotes the cessation of suffering, and the meditation on complete transformation is the path.

13–17) THE FIVE POWERS

The five powers are the fourth group of practices in the thirty-seven factors of enlightenment. They are practiced on the first two stages of the path of joining. They are:

1. faith,
2. diligence,
3. mindfulness,
4. concentration, and
5. wisdom.

Khenpo Namdrol says:

> The powers occur during the stages of warmth and summit on the path of joining. They are called powers since they control the phenomena of total purity. Of course, the bodhisattvas on the path of accumulation have faith, diligence, and so on, but they have not yet become powers. When the bodhisattva reaches the path of joining they become powers, but they are still susceptible to their opposing factors.

18–22) THE FIVE STRENGTHS

The five strengths are the fifth group of practices in the thirty-seven factors of enlightenment, and are practiced on the final two stages of the path of joining. They are:

1. faith,
2. diligence,
3. mindfulness,
4. concentration, and
5. wisdom.

The Sutra of the Ten Bhumis says:

The five strengths are the same as the above [i.e., the five powers], once they have become capable of overcoming their opposing factors.

23–29) THE SEVEN ELEMENTS FOR ENLIGHTENMENT

The seven elements for enlightenment are practiced on the path of seeing. They are:

1. mindfulness,
2. discernment of phenomena,
3. diligence,
4. joy,
5. pliancy,
6. samadhi, and
7. equanimity.

Khenpo Namdrol explains:

> Mindfulness is the branch of remaining, since it prevents us from forgetting the other factors, thereby ensuring that they remain. The discernment of phenomena, or wisdom, is the essential branch, because the essence of the awakening of the path of seeing is wisdom. Diligence is the branch of renunciation, because through diligence the dharmas of ordinary beings are abandoned or renounced on the path of seeing. Joy is the branch of benefiting. Pliancy, samadhi, and equanimity are the branches of freedom from negative emotions. Pliancy is the main branch of freedom from negative emotions. Samadhi is the branch that supports the absence of negative emotions. Equanimity is the branch of the nature of freedom from negative emotions.

30–37) THE NOBLE EIGHTFOLD PATH

The noble eightfold path is practiced on the path of meditation. It consists of:

1. correct view,
2. correct intention, or thought,

3. correct speech,
4. correct action or conduct,
5. correct livelihood,
6. correct effort,
7. correct mindfulness, and
8. correct concentration.

Khenpo Namdrol explains:

> The noble eightfold path pertains to the postmeditation of the path of meditation.
>
> Correct view is the fully eliminating branch because it eliminates all the opposing factors. Correct thinking is the branch that enables understanding of the view. Correct speech, action, and livelihood are the branches that inspire faith in others. Correct speech is the means through which we communicate our own understanding to others and inspire them with faith. Correct action, which refers to the forsaking of negative actions, such as killing, is a means to inspire others through diligence. Correct livelihood means inspiring others through having few desires. Correct effort, mindfulness, and samadhi are antidotes. Correct effort is the antidote to the root emotional obscurations to be abandoned through the path of meditation. Correct mindfulness is the antidote to the subsidiary emotional obscurations to be abandoned through the path of meditation. Correct samadhi is the antidote to samadhi's opposing factors.

APPENDIX 2: *A Short Gyalto Practice for the Altars of the Four Kings*

By Jamyang Khyentse Wangpo

Ritual for Putting Up the Altars

Arrange the offering torma in front of the kings' posts.

Offering

RAM YAM KHAM
Utterly pure dharmadhatu—from this natural state
Mountains of offerings arise naturally.
They are like the clouds of offerings of Samantabhadra
And fill infinite space.
OM BENZA ARGHAM PADYAM PUPE DHUPE ALOKE GHENDE
NEWITE SHABTA AH HUNG
Bless the torma following the text of your practice.

[RAM YAM KHAM
In the natural state of emptiness appears DROOM, which transforms into
an enormous, spacious vessel. Within the vessel appears the tormas of the
most excellent color, fragrance, taste, and potency.
OM AH HUNG HO (three times)]

Invitation

Invite the deities: From my heart, rays of light stream out. They invite the
four great kings with their retinue from the four sides of Mount Meru—
BENZA SAMADZA.

   Actualize this saying, DZA HUNG BAM HO: *the deities are now here, indivisible from their supports.*

Torma Offering

OM DHRITA RASHTA YA SOHA
OM BIRU DHAKA YA SOHA
OM BIRU PAKSHA YA SOHA
OM BAISHRA MANA YA SOHA
SAPARIWARA IDAM BALINGTA KHA KHA KHAHI KHAHI
(3 times)

Offering

Make the offering with OM TSA TUR MAHA RADZA SAPARIWARA ARGHAM PADYAM PUPE DHUPE ALOKE GHENDE NEWITE SHABTA PRATITSA SOHA

Praises

You whose sight is vast and profound,
Dhritarashta and Virudhaka,
Virupaksha and Vaishravana,
Four great kings of the four directions,
East, south, west, and north—I prostrate and offer praises to you.

Entrusting the Activities

Please enjoy this torma offered in generosity
And give us practitioners and people around us
Good health, long life, and power,
Glory, renown, and good fortune,
And the whole of the vast resources and pleasure.
Please grant the accomplishments of the different activities—
Pacifying, enriching, and so on.
Protect me who keeps his samaya!
Accompany me on the journey to the accomplishments!
Keep me from untimely death, and eliminate all sicknesses,
Demons, and obstacles makers!
Clear away all bad dreams, inauspicious signs,
And negative activities!

May the world be in peace, and harvests plentiful!
May crops multiply, and herds grow!
Source of all good and virtue,
Let everything we wish for be accomplished!

Recite the four mantras as above:
OM DHRITA RASHTA YA SOHA
OM BIRU DHAKA YA SOHA
OM BIRU PAKSHA YA SOHA
OM BAISHRA MANA YA SOHA
And then to ensure that the four kings and their retinue remain for a long time,
SUPRA TISHTA BENZAYÉ SOHA

Prayer of Auspiciousness

May there be happiness here in the day, happiness in the night,
Happiness even in the middle of the night,
Happiness all the time, day and night!
May the Three Jewels make everything auspicious!

RITUAL FOR TAKING DOWN THE ALTARS

When taking down the altars, place offering tormas that you bless as before. Skip the invitation section, but do the offering torma, offerings, praises, and entrusting the activities as before. Then do the following.

Confession

If anything was incomplete, missing
And without any efficiency,
Whatever mistakes I have made,
Please bear and forgive them all!

Request to Come Back

OM! Since you accomplish the benefit of all sentient beings,
Please grant us the accomplishments.

Return to your buddha field,
But please make sure to come back again.
BENZA MU

Recite appropriate prayers of auspiciousness, before bringing the offering torma to a clean place. After you have taken down the altars, take the tormas to an empty land. By Khyentse Wangpo. Virtue!

Appendix 3: Book Outline by Chapters

I. *Prayer to Rigdzin Jigme Lingpa Invoking His Previous Incarnations*

II. *The Casket of Siddhis: A Recitation Manual for the Rigdzin Düpa*

III. *The Crucial Points of Visualization for the Rigdzin Düpa Long-Life Practice*

IV. *The Words of the Vidyadhara That Bestow the Majesty of Great Bliss: Notations on the Rigdzin Düpa, the Inner Sadhana for the Longchen Nyingtik Cycle*
  A. Preliminaries
    1. Preparation
      a) A Brief Presentation on the Ngöndro
        (1) The Four Thoughts
        (2) How to Follow a Spiritual Friend
        (3) Taking Refuge
        (4) Bodhichitta
        (5) Vajrasattva
        (6) Mandala Offering
        (7) Kusali Accumulation
        (8) Guru Yoga
      b) The Way to Practice the Guru Yoga Approach Retreat
        (1) Before the Retreat
        (2) The Guru Yoga Practice
    2. The Rigdzin Düpa Recitation Retreat
      a) Introductory Comments on the Rigdzin Düpa Recitation Retreat
        (1) The Significance of Rigdzin Düpa
          (a) Lama Rigdzin
          (b) Lama Kagyé

(2) The Way to Practice the Sadhanas of the Longchen
    Nyingtik
(3) Developing Confidence
    (a) Confidence in the Teachings
    (b) Confidence in the Lineage
    (c) Confidence in Ourselves
  b) Arranging the Shrine
B. The Actual Practice of Approach and Accomplishment
  1. The Stages of the Practice
    a) Lineage Prayers
    b) Blessing the Vajra and Bell
    c) The Seven Preliminary Sections
      (1) Invoking the Field of Merit
      (2) Taking Refuge
      (3) Bodhichitta
      (4) The Accumulation of Merit and Wisdom—The Seven
          Aspects of Devotional Practice
        (a) Prostration
        (b) Offering
        (c) Confession
        (d) Rejoicing
        (e) The Request to Turn the Wheel of Dharma
        (f) The Request to Remain
        (g) Dedication
      (5) Dissolution
      (6) Torma to the Obstructing Forces
        (a) Self-Visualization
        (b) The Offerings
        (c) Issuing the Command
        (d) The Absolute Approach
      (7) The Protection Spheres
        (a) The Relative Protection Spheres
          i) Formation
          ii) The Ground
          iii) The Inner Layer
          iv) The Outer Layer
          v) The Vajra Canopy
          vi) The Intermediate Layer

iv) The Gates

v) The Surroundings

(b) Symbols, Meaning, and Correspondence in the Palace

i) Symbols

ii) Meaning

iii) Correspondence

(c) The Seats and the Seed Syllable

(d) The Deities

i) Guru Rinpoche

ii) The Lineage Masters

iii) The Eight Vidyadharas, Twenty-Five Disciples, and So Forth

iv) The Protectors

(e) The View of the Visualization

(f) The Extent of the Mandala

(g) The Jnanasattva in Guru Rinpoche's Heart

i) The Bone Ornaments

a. The Bone Wheel

b. The Earrings

c. The Necklace

d. The Bracelets

e. The Brahmin's Bone Thread

f. The Bone Belt

(h) Invoking the Deities of the Mandala

ii) Vajradharma

(3) The Invitation

(4) Requesting the Deities to Be Seated and Remain

(5) Symbolic Prostration

(a) The Importance of Paying Homage and Making Offerings

(b) Prostration

(6) Offerings

(a) Outer and Inner Offerings

(b) Secret Offerings

(7) Offering Praise

(a) Praise to Guru Rinpoche

(b) Praise to the Eight Vidyadharas

(c) Praise to the King and Subjects
(d) Praise to the Protectors of the Dharma
(8) The Mantra Recitation
  (a) Approach
    i) The Mantra
      a. The Mala
      b. The Nature of the Mantra
    ii) The Visualization
    iii) How to Recite Mantras
    iv) The Vajra Guru Mantra
    v) The Song of HUNG
    vi) Lama Guru Rinpoche
    vii) The Vajra Chain
    viii) The Benefits of This Practice
    ix) The Duration of the Practice
    x) Concluding a Session of Approach Practice
    xi) Dividing Your Day into Sessions
    xii) What Not to Do on Retreat
  (b) Accomplishment
  (c) How to Practice According to the Extraordinary Path of the Nyingtik
e) Conclusion: The Stages of the Tsok Practice
  (1) Tsok
    (a) Confession
    (b) The Tsok Offering Itself
      i) Blessing the Offering
      ii) Inviting the Field of Merit
      iii) Offering the First Portion of the Tsok
      iv) Confession
      v) Annihilation
        a. Liberation Through Annihilation
        b. The Actual Practice
      vi) Enjoying the Offering Substances
      vii) Remainder Offering
        a. The Preparation of the Remainder Offering
        b. The Recipients of the Offering
        c. The Mantra
  (2) Summoning

(3) Covenant (Cheto)
(4) Offering to the Tenma
(5) Horse Dance—Suppression
(6) Receiving the Siddhis
    (a) The Day Before
    (b) The Actual Day of Receiving the Siddhis
(7) Confession of Mistakes in Practice
(8) Dissolution
    (a) Dissolution Itself
    (b) General Postmeditation Advice
    (c) Concluding the Retreat
(9) Prayers of Dedication and Aspiration
    (a) Dedication
    (b) Aspiration
(10) Prayer for Auspiciousness

2. Afterword

V. *The Light of the Sun and the Moon—Generation and Perfection Stages: Notes Explaining the Words of the Rigdzin Düpa, the Inner Sadhana for the Longchen Nyingtik Cycle*
A. Introduction
The Four Reasonings
    1. The Reasoning of Same Basis
    2. The Reasoning Based on the Way Seed Syllables Are Formed
    3. The Reasoning of Blessing
    4. The Reasoning of Direct Experience
The Four Kinds of Kyerim Practice
    1. The Very Elaborate Practices of Kyerim
    2. The Elaborate Practices of Kyerim
    3. The Simple Path of Kyerim
    4. The Extremely Simple Path of Kyerim
B. The Practice Text of Rigdzin Düpa
    1. Preliminaries
      a) Refuge
        (1) The Absolute Approach to Refuge
        (2) Refuge in the Rigdzin Düpa Text
        (3) The Crucial Point of Refuge
      b) Bodhichitta

(1) The Absolute Approach to Bodhichitta
(2) Bodhichitta in the Rigzdin Düpa Text
c) The Seven Branches of Devotional Practice
    (1) The Absolute Approach
    (2) The Seven Branches in Rigdzin Düpa
        (a) Prostration
        (b) Offering
        (c) Confession
        (d) Rejoicing
        (e) Imploring the Buddhas to Turn the Wheel of Dharma
        (f) Requesting the Buddhas and Teachers to Remain
        (g) Dedication of Merit
d) Expelling Negative Forces
    (1) The Absolute Expelling of Negative Forces
    (2) Expelling Negative Forces in the Rigdzin Düpa Text
e) The Protection Spheres
    (1) The Absolute Approach
    (2) Protection Spheres in the Rigdzin Düpa Text
f) The Descent of Blessings
    (1) The Absolute Descent of Blessings
    (2) The Elaborate Approach
g) Blessing the Offerings
    (1) The Absolute Blessing of the Offerings
    (2) Blessing of the Offerings in the Rigdzin Düpa Text
2. The Main Part
  a) Generating the Deity
    (1) How to Generate the Support and the Supported
    (2) Generating the Deity in the Rigdzin Düpa Text
  b) Invocation
  c) Requesting the Wisdom Deities to Take Their Seats
    (1) The Absolute Request
    (2) The Elaborate Approach
  d) Prostration
    (1) The Absolute Prostration
    (2) Elaborate Relative Approach
  e) Offering
    (1) The Absolute Offering

VI. *A Clearly Reflecting Mirror: Chöpön Activities for the Inner Sadhana Rigdzin Düpa, the Inner Sadhana of the Longchen Nyingtik Cycle*

A. Arrangement for a Rigdzin Düpa Drupchö
  1. Mandala
  2. Top Offering Shelf
      a) The Rigdzin Düpa Torma
      b) Fulfillment-and-Confession Torma
  3. Second Offering Shelf: the Dharmapala Tormas
  4. Third Offering Shelf
B. Activities During the Recitation Practice

VII. *The Lotus Garland Adornment*
A. The Preparation: Arranging the Articles and Substances
B. Establishing the Foundation with the Sadhana Practice, and Conferring the Empowerment
  1. Accomplishing the Sadhana to Give the Empowerment
  2. Actual Empowerment
      a) Preparing the Students
          (1) Background to the Teaching
          (2) Empowerment Request
          (3) Refuge
          (4) Bodhichitta
          (5) Seven-Branch Offering
          (6) Descent of Blessings
      b) Main Part
          (1) Vase Empowerment
          (2) Secret Empowerment
          (3) Wisdom Empowerment
          (4) Symbolic Word Empowerment
          (5) Entrustment With All Empowerments
  3. Conclusion

GLOSSARY

Activity Vase: Ritual practices generally involve two vases with a similar appearance containing sacred water: the main vase, and the activity vase. Through the power of deity, mantra, mudra, and samadhi, the main vase is transformed into the palace and its water into the mandala of deities for the duration of the practice, and is generally placed in the center of the mandala. The activity vase is used for water purification during the different stages of the ritual for ceremonies such as empowerments. The activity vase, used by the chöpon, is usually placed on the vajra master's table.

Agama: Vajrayana teachings are divided into three categories of teachings: tantras, agamas or compendiums, and the *upadeshas* or pith-instructions. Tantras are always accompanied by the agamas, presenting the same teachings but in a shorter, more accessible way than the tantras, which are very extensive teachings. Pith-instructions are simple, direct, practical instructions.

Asura Cave: Also known as the "Upper Cave of Yangleshö," a cave sacred to Guru Rinpoche and located above the village of Pharping, near Kathmandu, Nepal, where Guru Rinpoche reached awakening before going to Tibet. Guru Rinpoche reached the ultimate accomplishment there through the practice of Visuddha (Yandak Heruka), but he had to overcome obstacles beforehand through the practice of Vajrakilaya. So, for Nyingmapas, visiting this site is the same as going to Bodhgaya, since it is the place where Padmasambhava manifested the state of complete enlightenment. Tulku Urgyen Rinpoche restored the cave in the late 1980s/early 1990s, and built a monastery and three-year retreat center that surrounds the cave.

Chimpu: The mountain above the monastery of Samyé where there are many retreat caves and huts. Even to this day there are practitioners in long-term retreat there. At the time of the founding of the monastery of Samyé, at King Trisong Detsen's request, Padmasambhava opened the mandala of the Vajrayana teachings in the caves of Chimpu to the twenty-five disciples. Nine of the twenty-five attained siddhis through practicing the sadhanas he transmitted to them.

Chuwori: One of the main mountains of Tibet. The Chuwori region is situated in central Tibet about thirty miles southwest of Lhasa. This is the place where Thangtong Gyalpo had his main seat.

The deities of the three seats: The forty-two peaceful deities are present in the three seats as follows:

- The aggregates (*skandhas*) and elements (*dhatu*) are the seats of the five male and five female buddhas respectively, and together they are called "the seat of the buddhas."
- The sense faculties and their objects are the seats of the eight male and eight female bodhisattvas together with the six *munis*, and are called "the seat of the bodhisattvas."
- The limbs are the seats of the male and female wrathful deities, which here are the four male and the four female gatekeepers. So the limbs are called "the seat of the wrathful deities."

Drodül Lingpa: See Trengpo Tertön.

Drupchen: Literally "vast accomplishment." It is a form of intensive group practice that epitomizes the depth, power, and precision of the Vajrayana, drawing together the entire range of its skillful methods and including: the creation of the mandala house; the complete sadhana practice with visualizations, mudras, chants, and music; continuous day and night practice of mantra recitation; the creation of tormas and offerings, with sacred substances and precious relics; the tsok feast; the sacred dance of *cham*; as well as the construction of the sand mandala. Guru Rinpoche said that several days participating in a drupchen can yield the same results as years of solitary retreat, and great contemporary masters such as Kyabje Dilgo Khyentse Rinpoche have made a point of encouraging and reviving the practice of drupchen, because of its power of transformation in this degenerate age.

Drupchö: An elaborate way of doing a particular Vajrayana practice over several days (three to eight days) in a group. Unlike a drupchen, which is also practiced over several days, this is not a twenty-four-hour practice; it is only done during the day.

The eight auspicious substances: The mirror, gorocana (*giwang*) medicine, yogurt, durva grass, bilva fruit, a conch shell that spirals to the right, cinnabar, and mustard seeds.

The eight auspicious symbols: (1) The most precious parasol that protects from suffering, destructive emotions, illness, harm, and obstacles; (2) the auspicious golden fish, symbolizing fearlessness, freedom and liberation, happiness, fertility, and abundance; (3) the wish-fulfilling vase of treasure, an inexhaustible source of long life, wealth, and prosperity that fulfills all our spiritual and material wishes; (4) the exquisite lotus blossom that stands for purity of mind and heart, and transformation, as well as compassion and all perfect qualities; (5) the conch shell of far renown, symbolizing the far-reaching melodious sound of the spiritual teachings; (6) the glorious endless knot, the sign of interdependence; (7) the ever-flying banner of victory, which means victory over all disagreement, disharmony, or obstacles, and the attainment of happiness, both temporary and ultimate; and (8) the all-powerful wheel, symbolizing the teachings of Buddha, and is the source of spiritual values, wealth, love, and liberation.

The eight conceptual elaborations: Cessation, arising, nonexistence, permanence, coming, going, being multiple, and being single.

The eight great charnel grounds: On the ordinary level, charnel grounds are the sites for corpse disposal around a city to accommodate the rituals of the different Indian castes. These eight great charnel grounds are the places where the dismembered parts of Rudra's body came to rest, after they were scattered from the top of Mount Malaya. The energy centers of his body—the head, heart, naval, and genitals—fell in the four cardinal directions; his four limbs fell in the four intermediate directions. From these parts, eight great trees arose, and around these trees developed the eight great charnel grounds. They are:

1. The Cool Grove in the east
2. Perfected in Body in the south
3. Lotus Mound in the west
4. Lanka Mound in the north
5. Spontaneous Mound in the southeast
6. Display of Great Mystery in the southwest
7. All-Pervading Utter Joy in the northwest
8. Mound of the World in the northeast

The eight great ordinary accomplishments: The accomplishments of the celestial land, the sword, the pill, swift feet, the vase, enslaving *yakshas*, the elixir, and the eye lotion. For Khangsar Tenpe Wangchuk's explanation, see pages 155–56.

The eight jeweled ornaments: The crown, earrings, short necklace, armlets, two long necklaces (one longer than the other), bracelets, anklets, and rings.

The eight perfect freedoms: (1) The perfect freedom of form observing form; (2) the perfect freedom of the formless observing form; (3) the perfect freedom of observing beauty; (4) the perfect freedom of infinite space; (5) the perfect freedom of infinite consciousness; (6) the perfect freedom of nothing whatsoever; (7) the perfect freedom of neither presence nor absence of perception; and (8) the perfect freedom of cessation.

The eight vehicles of the gradual path: Also known as "the eight vehicles of cause and result," these are the first eight of the nine yanas. Their approach is to rely on different stages, which are causes that will eventually bring the result of enlightenment. They stand in distinction to the final vehicle of Dzogpachenpo, in which the final result is taught directly.

The eighteen unshared qualities of a buddha: Among the twenty-one sets of immaculate qualities of the Buddha's dharmakaya, as explained in Mipham Rinpoche's *Gateway to Knowledge*. These are eighteen qualities that are unique to the buddhas and are not possessed by the shravakas and pratyekabuddhas:

1. Their physical conduct is without error;
2. Their speech is without impediment or imprecision;
3. Their minds are never lacking mindfulness;

4. Their minds are only ever resting in meditative equipoise;
5. They do not entertain varied ideas about their perceptions;
6. They never experience neutral states lacking full discernment;
7. They never lack the willingness to uphold the lineage of the Three Jewels and to benefit beings;
8. They never lack the enthusiastic diligence to work for others' welfare;
9. They are never without the mindfulness that ensures they never forget to see all things and events exactly as they are;
10. They are never without the wisdom that discerns precisely all things and events;
11. They never lack total freedom from the two obscurations;
12. They never lack the wisdom of complete liberation;
13. All the actions of their body are preceded by and undertaken with wisdom;
14. All the actions of their speech are preceded by and undertaken with wisdom;
15. All the actions of their mind are preceded by and undertaken with wisdom;
16. They see into the past with wisdom vision that is without attachment and without impediment;
17. They see into the present with wisdom vision that is without attachment and without impediment;
18. They see into the future with wisdom vision that is without attachment and without impediment.

The eighty innate thought patterns: The various emotional and cognitive states are divided into three groups: (1) the first group, states resulting from anger, has thirty-three categories; (2) the second, states resulting from desire, has forty; and (3) the third, states resulting from ignorance, has seven types of conceptualization.

The Enchanting Mound Stupa: Shankarakuta Stupa/Dechetsekpa Stupa is located in the Cool Grove (Shitavana) charnel ground, one of the eight great charnel grounds. This is a place of the revelation of the Kagyé.

The five aggregates: The five skandhas are the five mental and physical components of our existence, and are the basis for self-grasping. They are: (1) form, (2) feeling, (3) perception, (4) formation, and (5) consciousness.

The five pure abodes: They are the five highest abodes among the seventeen abodes of the Form Realm and are part of the eight abodes of the fourth *dhyana* level of the Form Realm. They are so called because they are exclusively the dwelling places of noble beings. These five are: Not as Great, Without Distress, Great Vision, Sublime Light, and above them all, Akanishtha, the Unsurpassed.

The five silk adornments: The headband, upper garment, long scarf, belt, and lower garment.

The **five wisdoms**: They are five aspects of primordial wisdom: (1) wisdom of dharmadhatu, (2) mirror-like wisdom, (3) wisdom of equality, (4) wisdom of discernment, and (5) all-accomplishing wisdom.

The **four activities**: (1) *Pacifying* conflict, sickness, and famine; (2) *enriching* which is increasing longevity and merit; (3) *magnetizing* the three realms; and (4) *subjugating* hostile forces.

The **four or six classes of tantra**: The Sarma tradition, or New Translation schools, recognizes four classes of tantra, the three outer classes—(1) Kriya Tantra, (2) Charya Tantra, and (3) Yoga Tantra—and one inner class of tantra called (4) Anuttarayoga Tantra, or Highest Yoga Tantra. The latter is divided into three: father tantras, such as the *Guhyasamaja Tantra*, the so-called "king of tantras"; Mother Tantras, such as the *Chakrasamvara Tantra*; and nondual tantras, such as the *Kalachakra Tantra*. In the Nyingma school of Tibetan Buddhism, the tantras are divided into six classes: the three outer classes of tantra (which are common to both the Sarma and Nyingma traditions): (1) Kriya Tantra, (2) Charya Tantra, and (3) Yoga Tantra; and the three inner classes of tantra (specific to the Nyingma school): (4) the Mahayoga tantras, (5) the Anuyoga tantras, and (6) the Atiyoga tantras.

The **four fearlessnesses**: (1) fearlessness in asserting their own perfect realization; (2) fearlessness in asserting their own perfect abandonment; (3) fearlessness for the sake of others in revealing the path to liberation; and (4) fearlessness for the sake of others in revealing potential hindrances on the path.

The **four levels of a vidyadhara**: Specific to the Dzogchen and Nyingma tradition, in general: (1) matured vidyadhara; (2) vidyadhara with power over life; (3) mahamudra vidyadhara; and (4) spontaneously accomplished vidyadhara. Khenpo Ngakchung explains:

> Those who have the ability to purify the ordinary body with the fire of concentration and transform it into a subtle body acquire the power of immortal life and are called Vidyadharas with power over life. Those who have not been able to purify their bodies but whose minds have ripened into the deity's body are known as matured vidyadharas. Those who are on the second to the ninth bhumis are Mahamudra Vidyadharas. Then, at the end of the path, at the moment buddhahood is reached, they are spontaneously accomplished Vidyadharas.[1]

The **four modes of birth**: The sutras teach that all forms of birth fall into one of four categories: (1) womb birth (concerning humans and certain classes of animals and *pretas*); (2) egg birth (concerning only certain animals); (3) spontaneous generation from warmth and moisture, or heat-moisture birth (concerning certain "inferior" types of animals); and (4) miraculous birth or manifestation (concerning all gods, hell beings, and beings in the intermediate state, as well as certain classes of preta and humans, such as bodhisattva emanations).

The four perfect knowledges: (1) Perfect knowledge of meaning, (2) perfect knowledge of Dharma, (3) perfect knowledge of language, and (4) perfect knowledge of courageous eloquence. They are the means of maintaining the vast and profound teachings.

The four stages of aspirational practice: The level of aspirational practice corresponds to the practice on the first two of the five paths. It is so-called because there is not yet a direct realization of emptiness, and so practice is done on an aspirational level. There are four stages that are successively attained: (1) realization that all things are appearances; (2) increase in realization of appearances; (3) abiding by a partial recognition of suchness; and (4) unimpeded concentration.

The four ways of attracting students: These are the qualities of teachers that enable them to gather fortunate students. Namely, that (1) they should be generous; (2) their language should be pleasant; (3) they should teach each individual according to that person's needs; and (4) they should act in conformity with what they teach.

The four wisdoms: The four wisdoms of a buddha are: (1) the mirror-like wisdom; (2) the wisdom of discernment; (3) the wisdom of equality; and (4) the all-accomplishing wisdom.

Front-visualization: The deities are visualized in front of oneself, as opposed to a self-visualization, where we visualize ourselves as the deities.

Gandhola: This means "temple" in Sanskrit. It is also the name of the main temple in Samyé.

Gemang tradition: The Gemang tradition is the tradition followed at Gemang Monastery, which is a branch of Dzogchen Monastery in the Trama Valley, Dzachukha, Kham (eastern Tibet). The Longchen Nyingtik cycle has been one of the monastery's main practices. The monastery is currently headed by Dongni Rinpoche, and populated by three hundred monks and nuns.

Ging (gingkara): These are minor deities who attend to the main deities in some wrathful mandalas. They appear as skeletons who beat a drum, wear a triangular pennant pinned in the middle of their hair, and ear ornaments that look like colorful fans.

Gyalse Shenpen Taye (1800–1869/70): Also known as Kushok Gemang, was an incarnation of Minling Terchen Gyurmé Dorje (1646–1714). He followed many great Sarma and Nyingma masters of the Rimé movement, especially the first Dodrupchen Rinpoche Jigme Trinlé Özer and Jigme Gyalwe Nyugu. He is responsible for completely rebuilding Dzogchen Monastery and establishing its famous shedra, Shri Singha. His personal students included Jigme Gyalwe Nyugu and all three incarnations of Jigme Lingpa—Patrul Rinpoche, Do Khyentse Yeshe Dorje, and Jamyang Khyentse Wangpo.

Heruka: This is another name for a wrathful deity. In the Nyingma tradition, the term is often used to refer specifically to Chemchok Heruka or Yangdak. In the Sarma schools of Tibetan Buddhism—Kagyü, Sakya, and Geluk—heruka generally refers to Chakrasamvara and other chief deities of the mandalas of the Mother Tantras. The term heruka can also be used to denote a realized tantric practitioner. In the Zindri, Khenpo Ngakchung says that according to Patrul Rinpoche, heruka means "one in whom absolute space (*he*) and primordial wisdom (*ka*) are united (*ru*)."[2]

Highest Yoga Tantra: In the Nyingma tradition, Highest Yoga Tantra corresponds to the three inner tantras: Mahayoga, Anuyoga, and Atiyoga. The Sarma school distinguishes between father tantras, Mother Tantras, and nondual tantras. See also "four or six classes of tantra" in this glossary.

The investiture thread: This is a Hindu ritual string given during an initiation ceremony, which is essential to the members of the three higher castes (Brahmins, Kshatriyas, and Vaishyas). It marks a boy's official acceptance into his caste. At this point he becomes "twice-born." Everyone has a first, biological birth, but when a young man seeks his spiritual identity he symbolically accepts a spiritual teacher as father and the Vedas as mother. He may also receive a new, spiritual name. At the ceremony, he receives the sacred thread, which he will wear for his entire life. It is replaced at intervals, but never removed until the new one has been put on.

Lungtok Tenpe Nyima (1829–1901): was Patrul Rinpoche's greatest disciple. During the twenty-eight years that he followed Patrul Rinpoche, he acted as his attendant and heard every teaching he gave. He was regarded as an emanation of Shantarakshita.

Mount Malaya: The Blazing Meteoritic Mount Malaya is the most important sacred place associated with Secret Mantra Vajrayana and Vajrasattva. It is the place where these teachings originated in our world when the Lord of Secrets taught them to the Five Excellent Ones of Sublime Nobility. It is also the place where the Buddha descended from heaven and taught the *Descent to Lanka Sutra*. Situated in present day Sri Lanka, it is known as Adam's Peak or Shripada.

Nada: A nasal sound represented by a semicircle on top of letters in Sanskrit and Tibetan scripts. When the syllable HUNG, which is topped by a nada, dissolves, it dissolves from bottom to top so the last part of the syllable to dissolve is the nada.

Ngari Panchen Pema Wangyal (1487–1542): an important Nyingma scholar and tertön, is counted among the previous incarnations of Jigme Lingpa.

Nine yanas: Within the Nyingma tradition, the nine yanas or nine successive vehicles represent the full spectrum of spiritual paths divided into nine vehicles, a system of practice bringing together all the approaches of the Buddha's teaching into a single comprehensive path to enlightenment. The nine yanas are referred to in the *Kulayaraja Tantra* (*Kunje Gyalpo*) and in the *General Sutra of the Gathering of All Intentions* (*Düpa Do*). The yanas are the sutra vehicles of the shravakas, pratyekabuddhas, and bodhisattvas, the three outer tantra vehicles (Kriyayoga, Charyayoga, and Yoga Tantra), and the the three inner tantra vehicles (Mahayoga, Anuyoga, and Atiyoga or Great Perfection).

The Palace of Lotus Light: The abode of Guru Rinpoche on the summit of the "Glorious Copper-Colored Mountain."

The path of no more learning: The fifth of the five paths and another name for buddhahood in the Mahayana. It is so-called because at this stage there is nothing more to learn or train in.

The practice mandala: The mandala on the shrine or in the mandala house.

Sang offering: A practice of offering fragrant incense smoke.

Self-visualization: Visualizing oneself as the deity. Also see "front-visualization" above.

The seven attributes of the three kayas: There are three attributes of the nirmanakaya, one of the dharmakaya, and three of the sambhogakaya. Specifically, for the nirmanakaya: (1) the ultimate unceasing compassion for all sentient beings; (2) the mindstream is thoroughly imbued with compassion; and (3) it is unobstructed; for the dharmakaya: (4) the union of emptiness and compassion, beyond true existence or elaboration; and for the sambhogakaya: (5) the unending enjoyment of the prayer wheel of the deep and profound mantra; (6) the union achieved through uniting the wisdom kaya with the consort who is one's own radiance; and (7) uninterrupted, untainted great bliss.

The seven inherent aspects of a sambhogakaya buddha: (1) Complete enjoyment, (2) union, (3) great bliss, (4) absence of a self-nature, (5) presence of compassion, (6) being uninterrupted, and (7) being unceasing.

The seven precious emblems of royalty: (1) The precious golden wheel, (2) the precious wish-fulfilling jewel, (3) the precious queen, (4) the precious minister, (5) the precious elephant, (6) the precious horse, and (7) the precious general.

The seven regular or outer offerings: (1) Drinking and cleansing water, (2) flower, (3) incense, (4) light, (5) perfume, (6) food, and (7) music.

The seven qualities of the vajra: (1) Uncuttable, (2) indestructible, (3) true, (4) solid, (5) stable, (6) completely unobstructable, and (7) completely invincible.

The seventeen Dzogchen tantras: These are the seventeen tantras of the Great Perfection of the category of pith-instructions, the root and most fundamental of all other teachings of the Pith-Instruction Category (*mengak dé*) of Dzogchen teachings. These tantras were brought to Tibet by Vimalamitra and Guru Padmasambhava. Each tantra is not dependent upon the others, but is complete in itself.

The six extraordinary features of Samantabhadra's liberation:

1. Appearing to one's own awareness (*rang ngor nangwa*): this liberation arises in your own awareness as the display of this awareness. There are no deluded perceptions that come from clinging to this display as outer phenomena.

2. Transcending the ground (*shyi le pakpa*): this liberation transcends the aspects of primordial ground (*shyi*) and of the manifestation that arises from the primordial ground (*shyi nang*). If it did not, there would be the

possibility of falling into delusion as phenomena arise from the primordial ground.

3. Discernment (*chedrak chepa*): if you recognize the primordial wisdom that is free from all obscuration, at that very instant all the qualities that naturally dwell within the expanse of that wisdom spontaneously appear. You realize that the obscurations related to the various karmic tendencies accumulated upon the basic consciousness have been pure since the beginning. The ground of samsara is utterly transcended, just like a bright sun emerging from behind the clouds.

4. Instant liberation (*che toktu drolwa*): at the same instant, the transcendent insight matures as the dharmakaya itself; you capture the citadel of primordial purity and dwell in it immutably.

5. Not produced by other (*shyen lé majungwa*): the actualization of your own awareness is not born from outer circumstances provided by something other than awareness itself, and is independent of all conditions. Buddhahood is attained when awareness recognizes its own nature, through its own strength.

6. Dwelling in itself (*rang sar nepa*): the ground of liberation dwells primordially in the continuum of its own nature and cannot be penetrated by the causes of delusion.

The six munis: The supreme nirmanakaya buddhas for each of the six classes of beings. They are: (1) Indra Kaushika for the god realms; (2) Vemachitra for the demigods, or asura realms; (3) Shakyamuni for the human realm; (4) Shravasingha or Dhruvasimha for the animal realm; (5) Jvalamukhadeva for the preta realms; and (6) Dharmaraja for the hell realms.

Supreme siddhi: Enlightenment.

Sur: A burnt offering. The actual offering is the smoke that comes from burning a mixture of roasted barley flour (*tsampa*), the "three whites" (milk, butter, and yogurt), the "three sweets" (sugar, molasses, and honey), and blessed substances. Combined with meditation upon the Buddha of Compassion, Avalokiteshvara in the form of Kasarpani, and the recitation of his mantra, this smoke relieves the unending pangs of hunger and thirst of the hungry ghosts.

The ten misdeeds of objects of annihilation: These are described in the *Glorious Heruka Root Tantra* as: "(1) destroying the Buddhadharma; (2) debasing the Three Jewels; (3) robbing the Sangha of its wealth; (4) defaming the Mahayana teachings; (5) creating a schism in the Sangha; (6) creating obstacles to sadhana practice; (7) harboring wrong views; (8) being a merciless monster; (9) falling into the mistaken ways of the tirthikas; and (10) being antagonistic toward a practitioner."[3]

The ten strengths: The ten strengths of the realization of a buddha correspond to their unobstructed knowledge of all things. They are: (1) knowing what is correct and incorrect; (2) knowing the results of actions; (3) knowing the aspirations of beings; (4) knowing all the elements; (5) knowing the different capacities of beings; (6) knowing all the paths; (7) knowing all the different ways to establish meditative concentration; (8) knowing previous lives of oneself and others; (9) the knowledge of transference, death, and future rebirth; and (10) knowing that the defilements are exhausted or knowing the path and result.

The thirty-seven factors of enlightenment: See Appendix 1 pages 191–96.

The three bases for grasping at the self: are the body, possessions, and merit.

The three Dharma robes: These three robes are part of the thirteen items of livelihood for monks as prescribed by the Buddha in the Vinaya: (1) *sangati*, a large patched shawl made of thirty-two patches, usually yellow in the Tibetan tradition, worn only by fully ordained monks; (2) *uttarasanga*, a large patched shawl, usually yellow in the Tibetan tradition, which can be worn by both fully ordained monks and novice monks, now often called a *chögö*; and (3) *antarvasas*, the lower robe of a fully ordained monk, sewn in pieces.

The three fears: These three, also known as dangers, are, according to Jigme Lingpa: (1) in general, sentient beings fear the sufferings of samsara; (2) less generally, bodhisattvas dread the attitude of selfishness; and; (3) most particularly, practitioners of Secret Mantra fear deluded clinging to phenomena, experienced as ordinary.[4]

The three kindnesses of a master: (1) To bestow empowerments; (2) to explain the tantras; and (3) to offer the pith-instructions.

The three types of ignorance: (1) Belief in the self, (2) coemergent ignorance, and (3) conceptual ignorance.

The three types of suffering: (1) The suffering of suffering, (2) the suffering of change, and (3) the suffering of all conditioned phenomena (or all-pervasive suffering).

Tsakli cards: Miniature paintings of deities, mandalas, auspicious symbols, and so on that are used in rituals, such as empowerments or the setting up of a mandala, as a substitute for ritual implements, or to represent a particular deity or mandala.

The twelve links of interdependent origination: (1) Ignorance, (2) formation, (3) consciousness, (4) name and form, (5) the six *ayatanas*, (6) contact, (7) sensation, (8) craving, (9) grasping, (10) becoming, (11) rebirth, and (12) old age and death.

The (higher) two truths: The two truths according to the Vajrayana. Mipham Rinpoche explains: "In short, basic space adorned with the bodies and wisdoms is emptiness endowed with all supreme aspects at the time of the fruition. This is the higher absolute truth. As manifestations of this state, the appearances of the world and its inhabitants are by nature bodies and wisdoms that lack true establishment. This illusory wisdom is the higher relative truth. Thus, appearance and emptiness are beyond meeting and parting in the context of both truths. Furthermore, as the two truths include the purity of the bodies and wisdoms, they are higher than or superior to the common two truths," *Luminous Essence*, 21.

Universal Monarch: A universal monarch, a *chakravartin*, someone who has the power to overcome, conquer, and rule all inhabitants of a four continent world system. In the Buddhist teachings this is considered an example of the most powerful rebirth possible within samsara. Rebirth as a universal monarch can occur only when the lifespan of the human beings of the four continent world system ranges from eighty thousand to a countless number of years.[5]

The vajra seat: The very place where the Buddha reached enlightenment under the bodhi tree, by the river Nairanjana in today's Bodhgaya, India. In Buddhist cosmology, it is considered to be the center of the universe and the place where the 1002 buddhas of this fortunate kalpa reach enlightenment.

Vidyadhara with power over life: See the "four levels of a vidyadhara."

The view of the transitory collection: The belief in "I" and "mine" based on the five transitory aggregates.

Water torma (*chutor*): An offering of water and grain to deities of wealth and starving spirits.

Yerpa: Drak Yerpa is especially sacred because it was visited by Guru Padmasambhava. In this setting of great scenic beauty, there are over eighty caves, where many great beings from all lineages have meditated. Above are the caves of Guru Padmasambhava and of Yeshe Tsogyal (Sang Puk). Below is Drubtop Puk, the great cave where the eighty siddhas of Yerpa (Guru Padmasambhava's disciples) meditated together. There is also a cave where Lord Atisha practiced.

NOTES

FOREWORD

1. See Tulku Thondup Rinpoche, *Hidden Teachings of Tibet*.
2. Jigme Lingpa, *Rig 'dzin bsnyen yig dngos grub gyi za ma tog*, 1985b, f. 4a4.
3. Khenpo Chemchok, *Rig 'dzin 'dus pa'i zin bris rig 'dzin zhal lung bde chen dpal ster* (unpublished manuscript).
4. Khangsar Tenpe Wangchuk, *Rig 'dzin 'dus pa'i zin bris bskyed rdzogs nyi zla'i 'od snang*, 2005.
5. See Jigme Lingpa 1985b, f. 4b3, and Khenpo Chemchok, f. 38a2. *Nyenpa* means the way of making oneself intimate with the deity and the deity with oneself.
6. Jigme Lingpa, *Rig 'dzin gyi gab byang gnad kyi mig tshags*, f. 1b1.
7. Khenpo Chemchok, f. 54a2.
8. Jigme Lingpa 1985b, f. 3a2.
9. Khangsar Chemchok Wangchuk 2005, 27.8.
10. Könchok Drönme (Lushul Khenpo), *Yum ka'i zin bris kyi kha skong rig 'dzin zhal lung*, 104–16.
11. Könchok Drönme, f. 18b1.
12. Pema Ledreltsal, *Rtogs brjod sgyu ma'i rol gar*, f. 48a4. See also Heidi Nevin and J. Jakob Leschly, *Wondrous Dance of Illusion*.
13. Pema Ledreltsal, f. 62b1.
14. Ibid., f. 52b2.
15. Khenpo Chemchok, f. 6b3.
16. See Tulku Thondup, *The Heart of Unconditional Love*.
17. Pema Ledreltsal, f. 33b2.
18. Ibid., f. 68a3.

INTRODUCTION

1. There are four lama practices in the Longchen Nyingtik, the outer practice of guru yoga, the inner practice of Rigdzin Düpa, the secret practice of Duk-ngal Rangdrol, and the innermost practice of Tiklé Gyachen. The yidam is the Palchen Düpa, and the dakini practices are Yumka Dechen Gyalmo and Sengé Dongma.
2. The three inner tantras are Mahayoga, which emphasizes kyerim practice; Anuyoga, which emphasizes *tsalung* practices; and Dzogchen. There can be purely Mahayoga approaches (called Maha-Maha) or Mahayoga practices that also involve aspects

of Anuyoga (called Maha-Anu), and Mahayoga practices that are also Dzogchen practices (called Maha-Ati). Most of the Nyingma practices, and particularly the sadhanas revealed in terma cycles, are Maha-Ati.

3. Jamgön Mipham, *Luminous Essence*, 5.
4. Patrul Rinpoche's text has also been translated by the Dharmachakra Translation Committee: "The Melody of Brahma Reveling in the Three Realms: Key Points for Meditating on the Four Stakes that Bind the Life-Force," in Jigme Lingpa, Patrul Rinpoche, and Getse Mahāpaṇḍita, *Deity, Mantra, and Wisdom*, 81–95.
5. Tulku Thondup, *Masters of Meditation and Miracles*, 32–33.
6. Dilgo Khyentse Rinpoche, *Brilliant Moon*, 141.
7. For a presentation and translation of some of these texts, see Sam van Schaik, *Approaching the Great Perfection*.
8. Dilgo Khyentse, *The Wish-Fulfilling Jewel*, 52.
9. From Dilgo Khyentse Rinpoche's foreword to Yeshe Tsogyal's *The Lotus-Born*, 1.
10. Tulku Thondup, *Masters of Meditation and Miracles*, 122–23.
11. Tulku Thondup Rinpoche, *Hidden Teachings of Tibet*, 89–90.
12. For the lineages of the Khandro Nyingtik and Vima Nyingtik, see Tulku Thondup, *Masters of Meditation and Miracles*.
13. Dodrupchen Jigme Tenpe Nyima, "Wonder Ocean," translated by Tulku Thondup in *Hidden Teachings of Tibet*, 162–63.
14. Refer to the list of Jigme Lingpa's chief disciples in Tulku Thondup, *Masters of Meditation and Miracles*, 334–35.
15. Jigme Lingpa wrote similar texts for Yumka Dechen Gyalmo, Sengé Dongma, Palchen Düpa, Takyung Barwa, Tiklé Gyachen, Zhitro Ngensong Jangwa, and Duk-ngal Rangdrol.
16. For a translation see Padmasambhava and Jamgön Mipham, *A Garland of Views*.
17. Jamgön Mipham, *Luminous Essence*, 5.
18. This is a summary of the more detailed account by Tulku Thondup in *Masters of Meditation and Miracles*, 283–91.

PRAYER TO RIGDZIN JIGME LINGPA INVOKING HIS PREVIOUS INCARNATIONS

1. Buddha Shakyamuni.
2. Mandarava's father, the king of Zahor.
3. Gampopa.
4. "Samyépa," which literally means "the man from Samyé," is an epithet of Longchenpa. His teacher Lama Dampa gave him this name as Longchenpa continued the work to revive Samyé Monastery that Lama Dampa had initiated.
5. Probably a disciple of Jigme Lingpa called Yeshe (Alak Zenkar Ringpoche, interview, July 2007).

THE CASKET OF SIDDHIS

1. This refers to the representation of the mandala. There are three types that could be used: the best is made of colored sand, the medium is painted cloth, and the lesser alternative consists of heaps of grain.

2. The crossed vajra symbolizes unchanging primordial wisdom, and it might therefore be considered disrespectful to sit on it.

3. Dzongsar Khyentse Rinpoche: "You make a cross with the kusha grass and put it underneath your bed to represent the unchanging, indestructible samaya of this retreat." Dzongsar Khyentse Rinpoche, *Rigdzin Düpa Manual*, 20.

4. In other words, all phenomena are generated spontaneously out of the space of emptiness.

5. Longchenpa's famous autocommentary on *Finding Comfort and Ease in the Nature of Mind*. Longchenpa, *Shing rta chen po*, in *The Great Chariot: A Treatise on the Great Perfection*, translated by C. Ives Waldo III, forthcoming, www.sacred-texts.com/bud/tib/chariot.htm.

6. See also Jigme Lingpa, Patrul Rinpoche, and Getse Mahāpandita, *Deity, Mantra, and Wisdom*, 184–85.

7. Jigme Lingpa, *Bskyed rim gyi rnam gzhag 'og min bgrod pa'i them skas*. See Jigme Lingpa and Patrul Rinpoche, "Ladder to Akaniṣṭha," in *Deity, Mantra, and Wisdom*, 21–79.

8. In other words, the eight herukas (*kagyé*).

9. From the prayer for auspiciousness at the end of the Rigdzin Düpa.

10. The five types are similar to the six classes, but the demigods are included within the categories of gods and animals.

11. Jigme Lingpa, *Gab byang gnad kyi mig tshag*, translated in *Gabjang—the Inner Mantra Practice: Dazzling Key Points—The Vidhyādhara's Manual of Concealed Instructions, from the Heart Essence of the Vast Expanse*, n.d.

12. Tulku Thondup Rinpoche says this is probably Jigme Kündol of Bhutan, one of the four main students of Jigme Lingpa known as the "four Jigmes" (e-mail to translator, October 12, 2006).

THE CRUCIAL POINTS OF VISUALIZATION FOR RIGDZIN DÜPA LONG-LIFE PRACTICE

1. "HRIH tsewang pema jung..."

2. Jigme Lingpa's text literally reads "During the breaks in-between sessions." Tulku Thondup explains that here this means "at the time of ending the meditation session" (e-mail to translator, October 22, 2007).

The Words of the Vidyadhara That Bestow the Majesty of Great Bliss

1. According to Tulku Thondup, this refers to Khenpo Chemchok's root teacher, Lushul Khenpo Könchok Drönme (1859–1936). For a biography, see Tulku Thondup, *Masters of Meditation and Miracles*, 230–36.

2. "The swastika design symbolizes changelessness. You put a few blades of kusha grass on this swastika with the tops pointing toward the front of the mat, as did Lord Buddha when he attained enlightenment under the bodhi tree: he was sitting on an armful of kusha grass offered by a grass cutter. In Tibetan texts, her name is Rtsa tshong bkra shis ldan, 'Swastika the grass cutter'" (Tulku Thondup, e-mail to translator, October 22, 2007).

3. In other words, the Three Jewels never deceive us (Tulku Thondup, e-mail to translator, October 22, 2007).

4. Dorsem Ngön Ga is a short guru yoga practice based on Vajrasattva. Jigme Lingpa, *Rdo rje sems dpa' la brten pa'i bla ma'i rnal 'byor mngon dga'i zhing sbyong*. The empowerment text is in Jigme Lingpa, *Rdo rje sems dpa' la brten pa'i bla ma mchod pa'i cho ga gzhan phan gyi phrin las dang bcas pa bde chen lam bzang*.

5. Also known as chöd practice. See Patrul Rinpoche, *Words of My Perfect Teacher*, 297–308, for more information.

6. Translation in Herbert Guenther, *Kindly Bent to Ease Us: Part 1: Mind*.

7. The *Royal Anointment Empowerment* (*Rtsa dbang rgyal thabs spyi blugs*) is the root empowerment text of the Rigdzin Düpa, by Jigme Lingpa. What is being said here is that we need to have received a Rigdzin Düpa empowerment in order to practice the guru yoga accumulation (Alak Zenkar Rinpoche, interview, July 19, 2007). On the Rigdzin Düpa empowerment, see Tulku Thondup, *Hidden Teachings of Tibet*, Appendix 2, 177–81. The Royal Anointment Empowerment is the basis that Jamgön Kongtrul expands on in the empowerment text presented in this book. See also pp. 177–90 of this publication for the empowerment text by Jamgön Kongtrul that is based on the Royal Anointment Empowerment, the root Rigdzin Düpa empowerment. The meaning of the expression "Royal Anointment Empowerment" is as follows: When the universal monarch (*chakravartin*) appointed his successor, he would gather his five hundred sons and give his empowering vase to the royal elephant. The elephant would go and place it on the head of the prince who had been chosen. At that precise moment, the prince became the heir to the throne. The Royal Anointment Empowerment is also an essential form of bestowing the four empowerments, condensed into one, given through the vase (*bumpa*) blessing. Like completely emptying the contents of one vase into another, the entire blessing is transferred and the corresponding six wisdoms are received, liberating the beings of the six realms from suffering.

8. In the days leading up to the practice, practitioners should recite sutras ideally in each of the four directions around the practice place. If one does not have much time, he or she could recite, for example, short sutras such as Samantabhadra's *Aspi-*

ration to Good Actions—the King of Aspiration Prayers, the *Heart Sutra*, *Confession of the Bodhisattvas*, and *The Sutra of the Three Heaps*.

9. Here the mantras of the four great kings, who were the first to pledge to protect the gateways of the mandala, are written as lists and placed in the four directions around the practice area to prevent negativity from entering. You can also put up images of the four great kings, as long as the mantras are included. The four great kings are Dhritarashta in the east, Virudhaka in the south, Virupaksha in the west, and Vaishravana in the north. An image of Hayagriva, or Amritakundali if the recitation is of a wrathful practice, is usually put on the back of the post, facing inward, to prevent the siddhis from leaking out (Dudjom Rinpoche, audio recording held in Sogyal Rinpoche's private collection, n.d.).

10. This refers to the usual offering of the seven offering bowls and the light offering.

11. Traditionally, before establishing the altar of the four great kings and their retinues, the practitioner thinks of all the people from outside he might meet during his retreat—such as his lama, his doctor—and for each person he might meet, he places a stone that is mentally associated with that particular person in front of the shrine of the great king by the main entrance to the retreat place (Gonpo Tulku Rinpoche, daily interviews, May 2006).

12. The text means that we should take in whatever we are going to use or eat during the retreat before it starts. Nowadays, however, this is quite unrealistic (Gonpo Tulku Rinpoche, daily interviews, May 2006).

13. Ideally, you would have brought in everything you need before the start. However, since they are needed at the end of the retreat, you could bring the siddhi substances in—food and other items—toward the end of the retreat, so that they are still fresh when you use them (Gonpo Tulku Rinpoche, daily interviews, May 2006).

14. Tulku Thondup says that although the text mentions Bhurkumkuta practices and Vajrasattva, he has seen that in actual practice practitioners do Bhurkumkuta and Hayagriva practices.

15. This prayer composed by Jigme Lingpa appears, for example, in *A Great Treasure of Blessings*, 437–56. See Jigme Lingpa, *Zangs mdog dpal ri'i smon lam dpal ri'i gsang lam*.

16. This prayer is the final four lines of the "Dissolution" section of the Longchen Nyingtik guru yoga. See Jigme Lingpa, Jamyang Khyentse Wangpo, Patrul Rinpoche, and Chokyi Drakpa, *A Guide to the Practice of Ngöndro*, 96.

17. Khenpo Chemchok was a great holder of the Dodrupchen tradition during the first half of the twentieth century. Although this text clearly states that after seven days of guru yoga practice we should perform these preliminaries a second time, Gonpo Tulku tells us that this is not how it is done at Dodrupchen Monastery nowadays. They are only completed once, at the beginning of the retreat (daily interviews, May 2006).

18. The sadhanas that are part of the Lama Rigdzin cycle that are not mentioned here are: Yamantaka, Hayagriva, Yangdak, and Vajrakilaya practices, which are connected with Palchen Düpa, as well as Tara practice. Tara practice is in turn

connected with Rigdzin Yumka Dechen Gyalmo. The sadhanas of the Longchen Nyingtik that are not part of the Lama Rigdzin cycle are Shyitro Ngensong Jongwa and Purba Gyülug, which are combined *terma* and *kama* (Tulku Thondup, e-mail to translator, January 11, 2008).

19. This means practicing the approach and accomplishment, but not getting signs of realization (Khenpo Namdrol, personal communication).

20. Sangye Lingpa. *Bla ma dgongs pa 'dus pa las ma 'ongs lung bstan bka' rgya ma'i skor.*

21. Khyentse Özer is one of the names of Jigme Lingpa.

22. Jigme Lingpa, *Rig 'dzin thugs sgrub dpal chen 'dus pa*, 1.

23. A terma revealed by Ngari Panchen Pema Wangyal (1487–1542). Ngari Panchen Pema Wangyal, *Bla ma bka' brgyad rig 'dzin yongs 'dus*, in *Rin chen gter mdzod chen mo*, vol. 10: 353–521.

24. A terma revealed by Drodül Lingpa (1518–1584), also known as Sherab Özer and Trengpo Tertön. This cycle of teachings is also known as the Gongpa Rangdrol cycle. See Trengpo Tertön Sherab Özer, *Grol tig dgongs pa rang grol bla ma rig 'dzin kun 'dus sogs*, in *Rin chen gter mdzod chen mo*, vol. 11: 187–354.

25. "The king, the subject, and the friend" refers to Trisong Detsen, Vairochana, and Yeshe Tsogyal.

26. Quoted from Jigme Lingpa et al., *Gnad byang thugs sgrom bu*, in *Klong chen snying thig rtsa pod*, 72.1–2. *Gnad byang* is the text in the Longchen Nyingtik that contains the various prophecies concerning its revelation, and the individuals who will have a special connection with this cycle.

27. "The Dharma king and his son" are King Trisong Detsen and Prince Murup Tsenpo. Jigme Lingpa, the revealer of the Longchen Nyingtik, was an incarnation of King Trisong Detsen, while his main disciple and custodian of this terma, the first Dodrupchen Jigme Trinlé Özer, was an emanation of his son, Prince Murup Tsenpo (Gonpo Tulku Rinpoche, daily interviews, May 2006).

28. This refers to the fact that Jamyang Khyentse Wangpo was the incarnation of Jigme Lingpa, the revealer of the Longchen Nyingtik cycle, and had a recollection of the Longchen Nyingtik. See p. 34.

29. Rigdzin Düpa sadhana. See *Nang sgrub rig 'dzin 'dus pa*, in *Klong chen snying thig rtsa pod*, 226.

30. For a more detailed presentation, see the first part of Patrul Rinpoche's "A Clearly Reflecting Mirror: Chöpön Activities for the Inner Sadhana Rigdzin Düpa," p. 69 of this publication.

31. Vajradhara is blue and holds a vajra and bell. Datvishvari is white and holds a hooked knife and skull (Tulku Thondup, e-mail to translator, October 25, 2007).

32. When the words of the root text of Rigdzin Düpa appear in the commentaries, they are identified by bold font. A similar distinction between the original text and its commentary was made in the Tibetan original, and it also helps the reader connect the commentary to the original text.

33. "At my heart is a letter HUNG that sends out rays of light. As a result, from the natural abode arise the lama and the ocean-vast assembly of vidyadharas indivisible

from him. All the deities of the Mahaguru's mandala, surrounded by all sources of refuge from all ten directions and four times without any missing, appear in the space in front of me—VAJRA SAMADZA!" In Jigme Lingpa et al., *Gsal gdab*, in *Klong chen snying thig gi 'don cha*, 91.

34. As usual, when we take refuge we visualize ourselves in our ordinary form (Tulku Thondup, e-mail to translator, January 25, 2008).

35. Quoted from Asanga's *Ornament of Clear Realization*, I, 18. For an English translation, see Karl Brunnhölzl, *Groundless Paths*.

36. See pp. 3–9 for the translation.

37. The *sobhawa*, or emptiness mantra is OM SOBHAWA SHUDDHA SARWA DHARMA SOBHAWA SHUDDHO HANG.

38. The reason to do this mudra is that garudas have the capacity to transform the poison of the nagas into nectar. Likewise, all impurities and pollution in the offerings are blessed and transformed into nectar (Tulku Rigdzin Pema, teaching given at Lerab Ling, September 5, 2015).

39. OM SARWA BHUTA AKARSHAYA DZA.

40. SARWA BIGHANEN NAMA SARWA TATHAGATÉ BAYO BISHÉ MUKHÉ BÉ SARWA THAKHAM UTGATÉ SAPARANA IMAM GAGANA KHAM GRIHANA EDAM BALINGTA YE SOHA.

41. The mantra of the four HUNGs or *sumbhani* mantra is: OM SUMBHANI SUMBHANI HUNG GRIHANA GRIHANA HUNG GRIHANAPAYA GRIHANAPAYA HUNG ANAYA HO BHAGAWAN BIDYA RADZA KRODHA HUNG PHET.

42. As the Abhidharma explains, the fire at the end of a kalpa is much hotter than a normal fire. For example, it can incinerate the hot hells (see Khenpo Ngawang Pelzang in *A Guide to Words of My Perfect Teacher*, 57–58). It is the hottest kind of fire.

43. See pp. 197–99.

44. A king lives in a palace. Therefore, this is the place he comes from. This is the nature of the association being made here (Gonpo Tulku Rinpoche, daily interviews, May 2006).

45. To describe dharmakaya Samantabhadra and the five families of victorious ones from the perspective of those to be trained: In the tradition of the New Translation school, the dharmakaya buddha Samantabhadra, the primordial buddha who is perfectly enlightened from the very beginning, is called Vajradhara or Vajradhara the sixth. As the lord of all the families, he is the lord of the five families, and so he is known as the sixth, Vajradhara, which refers to the dharmakaya. The nature of the dharmakaya can be understood in terms of the five wisdoms, which are connected with the five buddha families. The five victorious ones associated with those families are Akshobhya, Ratnasambhava, Amitabha, Amoghasiddhi, and Vairochana. Though there is this fivefold classification, there are essentially no differences of high and low or greater or lesser compassion between Samantabhadra and the five victorious ones. They are all buddhas. They can be compared to many forms reflecting in a crystal ball. See Dilgo Khyentse Rinpoche, *Primordial Purity*, 7.

46. Jamyang Khyentse Wangpo was an incarnation of Jigme Lingpa. His "recollection

from a past life" refers to his recalling the Longchen Nyingtik terma, which is what authenticates these two lines (Gonpo Tulku Rinpoche, daily interviews, May 2006).

47. This is a reference to the offering goddesses. There can be five, six, or eight of them, and sometimes as many as sixteen (Tulku Thondup, e-mail to translator, April 24, 2008).

48. The visible form is symbolized by a mirror, sound by a lute, odor by incense, taste by a torma, and touch by white silk.

49. Probably Lushul Khenpo (Tulku Thondup, e-mail to translator, October 25, 2007).

50. An advanced meditator (Tulku Thondup, e-mail to translator, May 13, 2008).

51. Dodrupchen Jigme Tenpe Nyima, *Yum ka bde chen rgyal mo'i sgrub zhung gi zin bris bde chen lam bzang gsal ba'i sgron me*, 11b–12a.

52. This means "if the deities, mantras, and wisdom can be recognized as rigpa" (Gonpo Tulku Rinpoche, daily interviews, May 2006).

53. Often the color of the main deity (Guru Rinpoche is the main deity here and he is white) is the color of the inside layer of the palace. Alternatively, as is the case here, the color of the outside layer is the same color as the main deity.

54. A *chatren* is a relative measure, not a measure of fixed length. Four *chatren* make up one *chachen*. When drawing a mandala, for example, the space where the mandala will be set is first divided into a grid of sixteen or eighteen *chachen*.

55. This layer is a net that supports a covering that is usually made of earth in Tibetan temples. The net prevents the covering from falling through.

56. The roof has a flat central area and slopes at the edges. The sloping part is called a pagoda roof.

57. For the thirty-seven aspects of enlightenment, see Appendix 1, pp. 191–96.

58. This means that whatever you perceive or appears before you does not fall into the four extremes: you do not see appearance as either existent or nonexistent, good or bad, this or that, and so on (Tulku Thondup, personal communication, May 13, 2008).

59. This sentence appears in many sources; for example, see chapter 32 of the Pema Kathang in one of the main biographies of Guru Rinpoche, revealed as a terma by Orgyen Lingpa (b. 1323), (Tulku Thondup, personal communication, May 25, 2008).

60. For example, see the Rigdzin Düpa "Tseguk–The Summoning of Long Life" in the Rigdzin Düpa long-life practice (*tsedrup*), called *Elixir from the Amrita Vase* (Jigme Lingpa, *Rig 'dzin tshe sgrub bdud rtsi bum bcud*).

61. Usually the colors are white in the east, yellow in the south, red in the west, and green in the north, as depicted in the different images of the mandala. However, Khangsar Tenpe Wangchuk says that the south is dark-blue, rather than yellow (see p. 123).

62. Jigme Lingpa, *Dbang gi spyi don snying po rab gsal*, in *Jigs med gling pa'i bka' 'bum*, vol. 7, 85–120.

63. The ear ornaments of the ging look like colorful fans.

64. Female deities do not wear the Brahmin's bone thread. They wear the thread of hair from a slain thief. Usually the bone belt is counted as the fifth bone ornament, as the Brahmin's bone thread is worn only by the males (Gonpo Tulku Rinpoche, daily interviews, May 2006).

65. Dodrupchen Jigme Tenpe Nyima, *Rta khyung bsnyel tho rin chen sgron med*, 280, explains: "When it says the face of the mantra-mala at the heart should be turned inside, 'face' refers to the point where we start to read and not the surface of the letter."

66. The six periods of day and night are dawn, morning, midday, afternoon, dusk, and midnight.

67. *Gi wang*: a very effective medicine, therefore highly prized, it is one of the eight auspicious substances. It is a yellow paste made from the bile stones formed in the gall bladder of men, animals, or elephants, the latter of which is considered the best one.

68. *Thug sog* refers to the seed syllable at the heart of the main deity. It is like the core, vital essence, or heart (*nying po sog*); in other words, what is central or main (*thug sog shing*).

69. See pp. 3–9.

70. When practicing sadhanas, we usually bless the mala before beginning the mantra recitation. In the Rigdzin Düpa, we do this before the recitation of the vajra guru mantra, after the words: "Until this is actualized, I shall not let go of the practice!" Recite the vowel and consonant mantras and the mantra of the essence of interdependent origination three times, then OM RUTSI PRAMARTANA YE ATNA MANI DHARA JÑANA DEWA ABHI KHINTSA HUNG SOHA three times, and OM SUPRATITTA BENZA YE SOHA" once, while blessing your mala with blessed grains. Then recite the approach mantra. When practicing on retreat, this is usually only done in the first session, although it can be done each time. During a drupchö or a drupchen it is done every day in the first session (Gonpo Tulku Rinpoche, daily interviews, May 2006).

71. This is because Guru Rinpoche is part of the Lotus family, whose color is red.

72. In Tibetan texts, practice advices are woven into the text of a sadhana practice in smaller fonts. These notations generally appear in English translations in italics. The Rigdzin Düpa notations are part of the original terma as put down in writing by the omniscient Jigme Lingpa.

73. For Rigdzin Düpa, the "required approach recitation" is 1,300,000 mantras. This is the number of approach mantra recitations required before you can practice a sadhana in a drupchen, a drupchö, on the tenth day, or can perform the fire offering (*jinsek*). Nowadays, however, this is quite a difficult requirement to fulfill (Gonpo Tulku Rinpoche, daily interviews, May 2006).

74. Most probably Lushul Khenpo (Tulku Thondup, e-mail to translator, June 11, 2008).

75. The *do-li*, or palanquin recitation, is the rosary of the mantra of great bliss. It starts at the heart of the jnanasattva, comes out of his mouth, enters the mouth of the consort, circles the syllable BAM at her heart, passes through her lotus, enters his

jewel and merges back into the heart. The palanquin recitation is the continuous whirling of the great cycle of bliss (Tulku Thondup, e-mail to translator, June 11, 2008).

76. In relation to mantra recitation, deficiencies are such things as omitting or mispronouncing syllables, while excesses are such things as adding syllables.

77. "Bless the offering with LHA DZE DANG TING NGE DZIN LÉ DRUB PE CHI NANG SANG WÉ CHÉ TRIN NGOWO YESHE KYI DUDTSI LA NAMPA DÖ YÖN GYI TRIN PUNG ZÉ MI SHE PA KUNTUZANGPÖ CHÖ PE NAM ROL TU GYÉ PAR GYUR CHIK. May the outer, inner, and secret cloud of offerings, accomplished with divine substances and meditation, be transformed in essence into the nectar of wisdom, and in form into inexhaustible clouds of objects of enjoyment, magnified by Samantabhadra's way of offering. NAMA SARWA TATAGATE BAYO BISHO MUGEBE SARWA TAKAM UTGATE SAPARANA IMAM GA GA NA KAM SOHA. At the same time, sprinkle water from the lebum" (Tulku Thondup, e-mail to translator, June 24, 2008).

78. See note 15, p. 227.

79. This is the mahaguru mantra.

80. The three awarenesses are the awareness of all appearance as the mandala of the deities, all sound as the mantra, and all thought as wisdom.

81. Here, "clear and stable" (sel ten) is not a particular technical term. It means you must train, or gain experience, in having clear and stable images of the deities (Tulku Thondup, e-mail to translator, November 3, 2008).

82. Jigme Lingpa, Rig 'dzin thugs sgrub dpal chen 'dus pa, 10b6–11a1.

83. So far Khenpo Chemchok has been commenting on the Gabjang. But at this point the "notations" of this text gives a presentation of the path and bhumis, and our author chooses not to comment.

84. The Scroll of the Oral Lineage contains the tsalung instructions for the Longchen Nyingtik. Jigme Lingpa, Bde stong rlung gi rdzogs rim snyan rgyud shog dril yid bzhin nor bu. See "The Scroll of the Aural Lineage of Empty Exaltation and Wind in the Stage of Completion, the Wish-Fulfilling Jewel," in Jigme Lingpa, From the Heart Essence of the Great Expanse, 17–30.

85. Though widely used, "confession" might not be the most appropriate name for this practice. I also used to translate the Tibetan shakpa as confession. But actually, the meaning of confession is the admission of our misconduct, followed by regret for the faults that one has committed. This is only one of the four powers necessary for this practice. The four powers are the power of support, the power of regret, the power of resolution or pledge, and the power of the action, the antidote (the actual meditation of purification). The second power, the power of regret, is, I think, the confession. Therefore "purification" might be better for this shakpa practice, as both purification and shakpa cover all the four powers that include the cleaning of all impurities through the stream of nectar in Vajrasattva practice. In common terms, outside of Dharma language, shakpa can mean cleaning dirt or sweeping away dust (Tulku Thondup, e-mail to translator, November 27, 2008). We chose

nevertheless to use "confession," fearing that some readers may not recognize the meaning of "purification" in this context.

86. "Yeshe kyi khorlo tamché kha kyap tu separ gyur" is a preliminary verse often appended to the *Inexpressible Ultimate Confession* (*Yeshe Kuchok*).

87. *Glang chen rab 'bogs kyi rgyud.*

88. The three inner liquids are tsok chang, amrita, and amrita from the lama's *nangchö* (generally, a small receptacle that looks similar to a kapala).

89. Only during a drupchen or a drupchö (Gonpo Tulku Rinpoche, daily interviews, May 2006).

90. These are the first lines of the remaining fragment in Tibetan of the root *Vajrakilaya Tantra*, the *Fragment of the Root Vajrakilaya Tantra*. For a translation see M. Boord, *A Bolt of Lightening from the Blue*, 80.

91. Explained by Khangsar Tenpe Wangchuk on page 154 of this publication.

92. This is the name of a tantra in the *Nyingma Gyubum* (Tulku Thondup, e-mail to translator, October 25, 2007).

93. Shantideva, *Way of the Bodhisattva*, Chapter 8, verse 134. 1–3.

94. Dodrupchen Jigme Tenpe Nyima, *Sgrub chen zin bris.*

95. Khangsar Tenpe Wangchuk also explains them briefly. See page 153.

96. Jigme Lingpa, *Skong bshags rdo rje'i thol glu.*

97. The remainder offering can be blessed by a lama spitting on it, providing he has attained a very high level of realization (Gonpo Tulku Rinpoche, daily interviews, May 2006).

98. The *akaro* mantra is: OM AKARO MUKHAM SARWA DHARMANAM ADYANUT-PANNATOTA OM AH HUNG PHAT SOHA.

99. At Dodrupchen Monastery we put a portion of the impure remainder into the pure remainder, and pour the pure into the rest of the impure remainder. Also, we do not offer the "magnificent remainder offering" (Gonpo Tulku Rinpoche, daily interviews, May 2006).

100. TSOK CHÖ PULWÉ DÖNAM KYI   Through this offering of desirable objects,
MIZÉ TER LA YONG CHÖ CHING   Completely enjoy the inexhaustible treasure and
YESHE NANGWA RAB DZOK NÉ   In the utter perfection of appearances
KADAK CHENPÖ SA TOP SHOK   May we attain the level of great primordial purity!

101. Chögyam Trungpa writes: "In Tibetan 'authentic presence' is wangthang, which literally means a 'field of power.' However, since this term refers to a human quality, we have loosely translated it here as 'authentic presence.' The basic idea of authentic presence is that, because you achieve some merit or virtue, therefore that virtue begins to be reflected in your being, your presence. So authentic presence is based on cause and effect. The cause of authentic presence is the merit you accumulate, and the effect is the authentic presence itself.

There is an outer or ordinary sense of authentic presence that anyone can experience. If a person is modest and decent and exertive, then he will begin to manifest some sense of good and wholesome being to those around him. The inner meaning of authentic presence, however, is connected more specifically to the path of Shambhala warriorship. Inner authentic presence comes, not just from being a decent, good person in the ordinary sense, but it is connected to the realization of primordial space, or egolessness. The cause or the virtue that brings inner authentic presence is emptying out and letting go. You have to be without clinging. Inner authentic presence comes from exchanging yourself with others, from being able to regard other people as yourself, generously and without fixation. So the inner merit that brings inner authentic presence is the experience of nonfixed mind, mind without fixation.

When you meet a person who has inner authentic presence, you find he has an overwhelming genuineness, which might be somewhat frightening because it is so true and honest and real. You experience a sense of command radiating from the person of inner authentic presence. Although that person might be a garbage collector or a taxi driver, still he or she has an uplifted quality, which magnetizes you and commands your attention. This is not just charisma. The person with inner authentic presence has worked on himself and made a thorough and proper journey. He has earned authentic presence by letting go, and by giving up personal comfort and fixed mind." From *Shambhala: The Sacred Path of the Warrior*, 129–130.

102. Cheto means the "signs" or "offering" (*to*) that fulfills the "obligation" or "agreement" (*che*). In ancient times, the dharmapalas made an agreement in front of Guru Rinpoche, that if followers make such offerings in the future, then they will protect them. So this offering is the gesture (*to*), which fulfills that promise (Tulku Thondup, e-mail to translator, November 26, 2008).

103. This quotation is not from Jigme Lingpa's secret autobiography, *Dancer Like the Moon in Water, Gsang ba chen po nyams snang gi rtogs brjod chu zla'i gar mkhan*. Khenpo Chemchok is actually quoting from the beginning of Jigme Lingpa's secret account of the revelation of the Longchen Nyingtik cycle as he experienced it, *The Expression of Realization Called "The Great Secret Words of the Dakinis," Rtogs pa brjod pa dakki'i gsang gtam chen mo*. In *Klong chen snying thig rtsa pod*.

104. Rigdzin Pema Trinlé (1641–1717) of Dorje Drak Monastery was the reincarnation of Rigdzin Ngakgi Wangpo. The second throne holder of Dorje Drak Monastery, he was also a student of the Fifth Dalai Lama. Like Lochen Dharmashri, he was killed during the Dzungar war of 1717–18.

105. Khangsar Tenpe Wangchuk offers an explanation of the Tenma sisters below on pp. 159–60.

106. The "glorious lama" means Rigdzin Düpa (Tulku Thondup, e-mail to translator, July 3, 2008).

107. The twelve Tenmas protect all of us like a mother protects her child, or like sisters protect their siblings (Alak Zenkar Rinpoche, interview, August 18, 2007).

108. The mantra for receiving the siddhis is: OM AH HUNG VAJRA GURU PEMA TÖTRENG TSAL VAJRA SAMAYA DZA KAYA WAKKA TSITTA A LA LA SID-DHI PALA HUNG.

109. There are specific texts for expelling the obstructing forces (*gek*) from the siddhi

substances. Alternatively, the expelling negative forces section in the Rigdzin Düpa text can also be done at this point.

110. This prayer is from chapter three of "The Prayer in Seven Chapters to Padmakara, the Second Buddha" in *Nyingma Monlam Prayer Book-Bilingual Edition*, 120–21.

111. The accomplishment torma is the lama torma at the center of the mandala.

112. Jigme Lingpa, *Ri chos zhal gdams ngo mtshar rgya mtsho*, 591.

113. The prayer to depart is part of the gyalto practice that contains words requesting the four great kings to stay for the duration of the retreat, and words requesting them to leave when the practice is completed. See p. 199.

114. Dudjom Rinpoche explains: "Just as you protect your house so that it doesn't fall into someone else's hands, you protect your place for about three days after the retreat by not going out too much, and by not allowing just anyone to enter" (audio recording held in Sogyal Rinpoche's private collection, n.d.).

115. They represent the eight fears: doubt, lust, avarice, envy, wrong views, hatred, delusion, and pride.

THE LIGHT OF THE SUN AND THE MOON—GENERATION AND PERFECTION STAGES

1. Jigme Lingpa, *Bskyed rim gyi rnam gzhag 'og min bgrod pa'i them skas*, translated by Dharmachakra: "Ladder to Akaniṣṭha," in *Deity, Mantra, and Wisdom*, 21–80.

2. Khangsar Tenpe Wangchuk, in this commentary, reproduces Patrul Rinpoche's text almost entirely, which is inserted in different places. For an alternative translation, see Patrul Rinpoche, "Melody of Brahma Reveling in the Three Realms," 2006, 81–95.

3. See page 3.

4. See page 13.

5. These are the teachings of the Kama lineage, as opposed to the short lineage of the terma teachings.

6. Chapter 11, 2.

7. The Tibetan text says that the Tibetan letter ༀ (OM) unfolds on the basis of the coming together of three elements, a (ཨ), o (◌ོ), and m (◌ྃ).

8. This expression means they mutually cover each other, that they are mutually present in each other. The seal here is to be understood as the mark left by the seal in wax (Alak Zenkar Rinpoche).

9. See "Ladder to Akanishtha" in Jigme Lingpa, Patrul Rinpoche, and Getse Mahāpaṇḍita, *Deity, Mantra, and Wisdom*, 26–27. This whole section of the four types of kyerim practice follows Jigme Lingpa's presentation closely.

10. *Two Segment Hevajra Root Tantra.*

11. Longchenpa, *Shing rta chen po*, 36. Translated in H.V. Guenther, *Kindly Bent to Ease Us, Part 1: Mind*, 160. See also chapter 9 in Longchen Rabjampa, *The Great Chariot*.

12. The Tibetan text, which is a transcription of Khangsar Tenpe Wangchuk's oral teaching, by mistake has "*med las rim bzhin...*" at the beginning of the second

line, when Longchenpa wrote, "*ming* las rim bzhin," which is what Khangsar Tenpe Wangchuk seems to have said on the recording. We have translated "*ming* las rim bzhin..."

13. Meaning having received many transmissions (Alak Zenkar Rinpoche, interview, August 14, 2007).

14. "*ma bcos rig pa stong gsal nang*," Rigdzin Düpa, deity generation section.

15. In the Anuyoga approach, we use words to ignite the view and so on, whereas in the Atiyoga approach the view is already there before the words. The first line of the visualization section evokes the view and the second line evokes the unfolding of the appearance aspect (Alak Zenkar Rinpoche, interview, August 14, 2007).

16. *rang gi snying ga'i hung gi 'od zer gyis rang bzhin gyi gnas nas bla ma dang gnyis su med pa rigs 'dus ma h'a gu ru'i dkyil 'khor gyi lha tshogs rnams la phyogs bcu dus bzhi'i skyabs yul ma tshang ba med pas bskor ba thams cad mdun gyi nam mkhar ba dzra sa ma dzah* (*Gsal gdab*, in *Klong chen snying thig 'don cha*, 591.2–4).

17. Indrabhuthi, *ye shes grub pa.*

18. Jigme Lingpa, "gcod yul mkha' 'gro'i gad rgyangs," in *Klong chen snying thig rtsa pod*, vol.3 p. 61/l.2–3.

19. This terminology is particular to the Nyingma teachings. When we use a vacuum cleaner we suck up every particle without thinking about whether each one is good or bad. In the same way, absolutely all phenomena of samsara or nirvana are gathered back and dissolved within emptiness (Alak Zenkar Rinpoche, interview, August 14, 2007).

20. The expression "signs of the treasury of space of dharmata" here is a reference to the Longchen Nyingtik terma that arose as a sign, or mere indication of the true meaning, out of the treasury of space of dharmata. To understand what this means, consider the life of Rigdzin Jigme Lingpa. He didn't have to study extensively and apply the three wisdom tools in the earlier part of his life. His qualities of realization burst forth out of the expanse of space so that all appearances were simply the appearances of dharmata. Since he saw perfectly, based on indicative signs, the self-arising, self-appearing enlightened body, speech, and mind of the treasury of space (treasury of space has the sense of being inexhaustible), he is a lama of the sign-transmission lineage (Alak Zenkar Rinpoche, interview, August 14, 2007).

21. Hayagriva.

22. Patrul Rinpoche, *Melody of Brahma Reveling in the Three Realms.*

23. In other words, the four nails that bind the life-force of the practice.

24. In *Rigdzin Düpa*, prayer for auspiciousness.

25. Probably a reference to a very similar passage that Khangsar Tenpe Wangchuk Rinpoche must have quoted from memory in the "Four Stakes that Bind the Life-Force of the Practice." See Jigme Lingpa, Patrul Rinpoche, and Getse Mahapandita, *Deity, Mantra and Wisdom,* 84–85.

26. The other three nails will be explained in the section on the mantra recitation. See page 139 and following.

27. See page 5.

28. See *Words of My Perfect Teacher*, page 314.

29. See Khenpo Chemchok's notation, page 48.
30. In *The Casket of Siddhis.* See page 5.
31. The five kinds of sensual stimulants are: (1) the mirror for form, (2) the vina for sound, (3) incense for smell, (4) torma for taste, and (5) white silk for touch.
32. The three "spheres" are the three aspects we grasp at: subject, object, and the act itself. Grasping at the three spheres corresponds to cognitive obscurations.
33. i.e., Dzogchen.
34. See page 120 and following.
35. These lines are not part of the Rigdzin Düpa sadhana, but the secret instruction for mantra recitation that is recited whenever doing the practice in gathering practices or on retreat, called *Gabjang—the Inner Mantra Practice: Dazzling Key Points— The Vidhyādhara's Manual of Concealed Instructions, from the Heart Essence of the Vast Expanse,* Rigpa Translations, unpublished.
36. So in this case we should accumulate 1,200,000 vajra guru mantras, plus 100,000 to make up for any deficiencies.
37. i.e., the Longchen Nyingtik cycle. See Jigme Lingpa, *The Queen of Great Bliss,* the introductory practice instruction to the tsok, 68.
38. The sambhogakaya is known as the Great Lord because he has mastery over all things that can be experienced (sambhoga).
39. The word *la* means "above" or "higher" and is sometimes translated as "spirit." The *la* is what remains behind when a person dies, while the life-force is what ends, and the consciousness is what proceeds to take rebirth. From Khenpo Karthar Rinpoche, *Karma Chakme Mountain Dharma, vol. 2,* 88.
40. Palchen Heruka here refers to Chemchok Heruka Vajra Tötrengtsal, the central deity of the Palchen Düpa (Alak Zenkar Rinpoche, interview, August 19, 2007).
41. i.e., Dzogchen.
42. Longchen Nyingtik.
43. See note 103, page 234.
44. See page 83.
45. Drekpa Kundul is the chief figure in the mandala of Jikten Chötö in the Kagyé.
46. Jigme Lingpa, "dpal chen 'dus pa," in the Tenma section, 673.
47. For the eight fears, see note 115, page 235. The six wealths are long life, power, auspiciousness, majesty and attractiveness, a large retinue, and wealth.
48. We practice on an aspirational level when we are not able to practice fully all the instructions that can be managed by great beings; so instead we practice in an aspirational way, trying to emulate the practice of these great beings in the best way we can. See glossary for the four stages of aspirational practice.

A Clearly Reflecting Mirror

1. These instructions are for a drupchö as well as drupchen since the main difference is that during a drupchen there are night practices that do not take place during a drupchö (Khenpo Yeshe Dorje, personal communication, 2004).
2. The offerings are the seven bowls, placed around the mandala. If done elaborately,

four sets of seven bowls are placed in the four directions; otherwise just place the set of bowls around or in front of the mandala (Khenpo Yeshe Dorje, personal communication, 2004).

3. The torma for *The Spontaneous Vajra Song of Fulfillment and Confession*, the fulfillment practice of Rigdzin Düpa. Jigme Lingpa, "skong bshags rdo rje'i thol glu."

4. The "red glorious torma."

5. The lama and confession tormas, and to the left and right of the three tormas, if using the Emptying the Lower Realms from Their Very Depths tormas (Khenpo Yeshe Dorje, personal communication, 2004).

6. A turning triangular torma in the center and eight smaller identical tormas around it (Khenpo Yeshe Dorje, personal communication, 2004).

7. The "corpses with flesh" and the "mountains of fire" are made of torma substances. Powdered meat can be added for the "flesh" (Khenpo Yeshe Dorje, personal communication, 2004).

8. There are many different kinds of tormas. Some stay in place for the whole time of the practice (*tak tor*, "permanent torma")—e.g., the tormas on the three levels of shelves—or some are renewed every day (chö tor, "offering torma"), e.g., the ones in front of the three levels of shelves (Khenpo Yeshe Dorje, personal communication, 2004).

9. Usually it is to the left and the cheto torma is to the right, but here Patrul Rinpoche says something different (Khenpo Yeshe Dorje, personal communication, 2004).

10. At Chokling Monastery, we offer black tea with some *tsokdzé* in the bowls for each offering (Khenpo Yeshe Dorje, personal communcation).

11. i.e., on the roof (Khenpo Yeshe Dorje, personal communication, 2004).

12. In the form of specific dough pellets. Tepkyus could do also (Khenpo Yeshe Dorje, personal communication, 2004).

13. i.e., RAM YAM KHAM (Khenpo Yeshe Dorje, personal communication, 2004).

14. This means when there are two sessions in one day when the mantra is accumulated.

15. Human skin, tiger skin, the drawing of a human skin, or at least a black cloth (Khenpo Yeshe Dorje, personal communication, 2004).

16. Khenpo Yeshe is not sure of the meaning of this phrase (personal communication, 2004).

17. Do not rush around with the offerings like during empowerments when lamas present the empowerments substance in the assembly; instead take your time, and present the tsok offerings elegantly (Khenpo Yeshe Dorje, personal communication, 2004).

18. At Chokling Monastery we place the clean remainder on a tripod and the impure remainder offerings next to it on the table. We don't have the mandala that Patrul Rinpoche mentions (Khenpo Yeshe Dorje, personal communication, 2004).

19. Khenpo Chemchok explains how to mix them. See page 80.

20. A candle, for example.

21. "Sol lo chö to bul lo."

22. When you offer them together you need to hold the cheto and Tenma tormas

together. So it is not easy to use the cheto rinsing water to bless the Tenma! The timing also makes it difficult. So in that case you can sprinkle the Tenma torma with clean water (Khenpo Yeshe Dorje, personal communication, 2004).

23. "tub ten rinchen barwé nö...": entrusting with activity liturgy. Jigme Lingpa, "'phrin bcol," in *Klong chen snying thig rtsa pod*, Shechen (Kathmandu, Nepal: Shechen publications, 1994), 5:57–8.

THE LOTUS GARLAND ADORNMENT

1. Draw five tiklés or circles on the sindhura.
2. *Bla ma dgongs pa 'dus pa las ma 'ongs lung bstan bka' rgya ma'i skor.*
3. The additions in parentheses are based upon Mipham Rinpoche's *Luminous Essence.*
4. Rāhulabhadra, *Praise to Prajñāpāramitā* (*sher phyin bstod pa, Prajñāpāramitās- totra,* Toh. 1127).
5. Jigme Lingpa, "dbang gi spyi don snying po rab gsal."

APPENDIX 1: THE THIRTY-SEVEN FACTORS OF ENLIGHTENMENT

1. Khenpo Namdrol, in an oral commentary on Chandrakirti's *Introduction to the Middle Way* recorded on tape (Mysore, India: Nagagyur Nyingma Institute, 1990s). All quotations in this appendix are from the same teachings.

GLOSSARY

1. Khenpo Ngawang Pelzang, *A Guide to the Words of My Perfect Teacher* (Boston: Shambhala, 2004), 118–119
2. Ibid., 275.
3. Padmasambhava and Jamgön Kongtrul, *The Light of Wisdom, Volume 2,* 202.
4. See Jigme Lingpa, and Longchen Yeshe Dorje, *Treasury of Precious Qualities: Book One,* 123.
5. See Jamgön Kongtrul, *Myriad Worlds,* 134–38. See also Robert Beer, *The Handbook of Tibetan Buddhist Symbols,* 36–48.

Bibliography

Texts Translated

Jamgön Kongtrul Lodrö Tayé. *Rig 'dzin 'dus pa'i rtsa dbang rgyal thabs spyi blugs kyi mthsams sbyor khyer bdes brgyan pa padma'i do shal*. In *Rin chen gter mdzod chen mo*, vol. 14. Stod lung mtshur phu'i par khang edition. Paro, Bhutan: Ngodrup and Sherab Drimay, 1976–1980.

Jamyang Khyentse Wangpo. *Rgyal tho bsgrub pa*. No publication data.

Jigme Lingpa. *Nang sgrub rig 'dzin 'dus pa*. In *Klong chen snying thig rtsa pod*, vol. 1, 225–48. Kathmandu: Shechen Publications, 1994.

———. *Rig 'dzin bsnyen yig dngos grub kyi za ma tog*. In *Klong chen snying thig rtsa pod*, vol. 1, 249–60. Kathmandu: Shechen Publications, 1994.

———. *Rig 'dzin 'jigs med gling pa'i 'khrungs rabs gsol 'debs*. In *Klong chen snying thig rtsa pod*, vol. 4, 11–12. Kathmandu: Shechen Publications, 1994.

———. *Rig 'dzin tshe sgrub dmigs gnad gal mdo*. In *Klong chen snying thig rtsa pod*, vol. 1, 271–73. Kathmandu: Shechen Publications, 1994.

Kenpo Chemchok. *Rig 'dzin 'dus pa'i zin bris rig 'dzin zhal lung bde chen dpal ster*. In *Klong chen snying thig rtsa pod*, vol. 5, 97–238. Kathmandu: Shechen Publications, 1994. Also in *Klong chen snying gi thig le las rtsa gsum bsnyen yig dang bskyed rdzogs zin bris bcas*, 1–130. Kathmandu: Swayambhunath, 1999. Corrections to the original text were made by Tulku Thondup, who owns the original hand-written text.

Khangsar Tenpe Wangchuk. *Klong chen snying thig le las nang bsgrub rig 'dzin 'dus pa'i 'bru 'grel gyi zin bris bskyed rdzogs nyi zla'i 'od snang*. In *Skyabs rje khang sar rin po che dbon sprul bstan pa'i dbang phyug gi gsung 'bum*, vol. 3, 231–90. Beijing, China: Mi rigs dpe skrun khang, 2005.

Patrul Rinpoche. *Nang bsgrubs rig 'dzin 'dus pa'i phyag len mthong gsal me long*. In *O rgyan 'jigs med chos kyi dbang po'i gsung 'bum*, vol. 4, 348–55. Chengdu, China: Si khron mi rigs dpe skrun khang, 2003.

Texts Quoted in the Primary Texts

Asanga. *Ornament of Clear Realization. Abhisamayalankara. Shes rab kyi pha rol du phyin pa'i man ngag gi bstan bcos mngon par rtogs pa'i rgyan zhes bya ba'i tshig le'ur byas pa*. In *Dergé Tengyur*, mdo grel *ka*, ff.1a–13b.

Dodrupchen Jigme Tenpe Nyima. *Rig 'dzin 'dus pa'i brgyud 'debs dngos grub char* 'bebs. In *Klong chen snying thig rtsa pod*, vol. 4, 75–76. Kathmandu: Shechen Publications, 1994.

———. *Rta khyung bsnyel tho rin chen sgron med*. In *Rdo grub chen 'jigs med bstan pa'i nyi ma gsung 'bum*, vol. 4, 273–90. Chengdu, China: Si khron mi rigs dpe skrun khang, 2003.

———. *Sgrub chen zin bris rig pa 'dzin pa dga' ba'i skyed mos tshal*. In *rdo grub chen 'jigs med bstan pa'i nyi ma gsung*, vol. 5, 140–92. Chengdu, China: Si khron mi rigs dpe skrun khang, 2003.

———. *Yum ka bde chen rgyal mo'i sgrub zhung gi zin bris bde chen lam bzang gsal ba'i sgron me*. In *Klong chen snying thig rtsa pod*, vol. 5, 415–82. Kathmandu: Shechen Publications, 1994.

Glang chen rab 'bogs kyi rgyud. In *Nyingma Gyubum*, vol. *tsha*, 250.3–357.1. Mtshams brag edition. Thimpu, Bhutan: National Library, Royal Government of Bhutan, 1982.

Gsal gdab. In *Klong chen snying thig gi 'don cha*. Rdo grub dgon gyi lugs, 59. Gangtok, Sikkim, India: Pema Thinley for Dodrupchen Rinpoche, 1985.

Guhyagarbha Tantra. *Dpal gsang ba'i snying po de kho na nyid rnam par nges pa*. In *Dergé Kangyur*, rnying rgyud *kha*, ff. 110b–132a. Translation: Gyurme Dorje. "The Guhyagarbhatantra and Its XIVth Century Commentary Phyogs-Bcu Mun-Sel." PhD diss., SOAS, University of London, 1987. www.trans-himalaya. com/tibet-bhutan-buddhist-publications1.php. See also: Kloṅ-chen-pa Dri-med-'od-zer, Sangye Khandro, and Lama Chonam. *The Guhyagarbha Tantra: Secret Essence Definitive Nature Just as It Is*. Ithaca, NY: Snow Lion Publications, 2011.

Indrabhuti. *Jnanasiddhinamasadhanopayika*. *Ye shes grub pa zhes bya ba'i sgrub pa'i thabs*. In *Dergé Tengyur*, rgyud *wi*, ff. 36b–60b.

Jamgön Kongtrul Lodrö Tayé. *Dpal rdo rje phur pa rtsa ba'i rgyud kyi dum bu'i 'grel pa snying po bsdus pa dpal chen dgyes pa'i zhal lung*. In *Rgya chen bka' mdzod*, vol. 3, 15–155. Lhasa: Bod ljongs bod yig dpe rnying dpe skrun khang, 2012.

Jigme Lingpa. *The Queen of Great Bliss of Long-Chen Nying-Thig*. Translated by Tulku Thondup. Gangtok, Sikkim: Do-drup-chen Rinboche, Sikkhim National Press, 1982.

———. *Bcod yul mkha' 'gro'i gad rgyangs*. In *Klong chen snying thig rtsa pod*, vol. 3, 55–69. Kathmandu: Shechen Publications, 1994.

———. *Bde stong rlung gi rdzogs rim snyan rgyud shog dril yid bzhin nor bu*. In *Klong chen snying thig rtsa pod*, vol. 3, 13–22. Kathmandu: Shechen Publications, 1994.

———. *Bskyed rim gyi rnam gzhag 'og min bgrod pa'i them skas*. In *Jigs med gling pa'i bka' 'bum*, vol. 11, 143–96. Paro, Bhutan: Lama Ngodrup and Sherab Demy, 1985. Translation: "Ladder to Akaniṣṭha." In *Deity, Mantra, and Wisdom: Development Stage Meditation in Tibetan Buddhist Tantra*. 21–79. Translated by Dharmachakra. Ithaca, NY: Snow Lion, 2007.

———. *Dbang gi spyi don snying po rab gsal*. In *Jigs med gling pa'i bka' 'bum*, vol. 7, 85–120. Paro, Bhutan: Lama Ngodrup and Sherab Demy, 1985.

———. *Gab byang gnad kyi mig tshag.* In *Klong chen snying thig rtsa pod*, vol. 1, 243–48. Kathmandu: Shechen Publications, 1994. Translation: "Gabjang: the Inner Mantra Practice: Dazzling Key Points: The Vidhyādhara's Manual of Concealed Instructions, from the Heart Essence of the Vast Expanse." Translated by Rigpa Translations. Unpublished.

———. *Gnad byang thugs sgrom bu.* In *Klong chen snying thig rtsa pod*, vol. 1, 71–80. Kathmandu: Shechen Publications, 1994.

———. *Gsang ba chen po nyams snang gi rtogs brjod chu zla'i gar mkhan.* In *Klong chen snying thig rtsa pod*, vol. 1, 19–70. Kathmandu: Shechen Publications, 1994.

———. *Nang sgrub rig 'dzin 'dus pa.* In *Klong chen snying thig rtsa pod*, vol. 1, 225–48. Kathmandu: Shechen Publications, 1994.

———. *Phrin bcol.* In *Klong chen snying thig rtsa pod*, vol. 5, 57–58. Kathmandu: Shechen Publications, 1994.

———. *Rdo rje sems dpa' la brten pa'i bla ma'i rnal 'byor mngon dga'i zhing sbyong.* In *Klong chen snying thig rtsa pod*, vol. 4, 205–207. Kathmandu: Shechen Publications, 1994.

———. *Rdo rje sems dpa' la brten pa'i bla ma mchod pa'i cho ga gzhan phan gyi phrin las dang bcas pa bde chen lam bzang.* In *Klong chen snying thig rtsa pod*, vol. 4, 211–58. Kathmandu: Shechen Publications, 1994.

———. *Ri chos zhal gdams ngo mtshar rgya mtsho.* In *Klong chen snying thig rtsa pod*, vol. 3, 585–600. Kathmandu: Shechen Publications, 1994.

———. *Rig 'dzin 'jigs med gling pa'i 'khrungs rabs gsol 'debs.* In *Klong chen snying thig rtsa pod*, vol. 4, 11–12. Kathmandu: Shechen Publications, 1994.

———. *Rig 'dzin thugs sgrub dpal chen 'dus pa.* In *Klong chen snying thig rtsa pod*, vol. 1, 641–76. Kathmandu: Shechen Publications, 1994.

———. *Rig 'dzin tshe sgrub bdud rtsi bum bcud.* In *Klong chen snying thig rtsa pod*, vol. 1, 261–70. Kathmandu: Shechen Publications, 1994.

———. *Rtogs pa brjod pa dakki'i gsang gtam chen mo.* In *Klong chen snying thig rtsa pod*, vol. 1, 5–17. Kathmandu: Shechen Publications, 1994.

———. *Rtsa dbang rgyal thabs spyi blugs.* In *Jigs med gling pa'i bka' 'bum*, vol. 7, 79–84. Paro, Bhutan: Lama Ngodrup and Sherab Demy, 1985.

———. *Skong bshags rdo rje'i thol glu.* In *Klong chen snying thig rtsa pod*, vol. 2, 339–54. Kathmandu: Shechen Publications, 1994.

———. *Yum ka mtsho rgyal bde chen rgyal mo'i rtsa ba'i sgrub pa bde chen dpal phreng.* In *Klong chen snying thig rtsa pod*, vol. 1, 293–312. Kathmandu: Shechen Publications, 1994.

———. *Zangs mdog dpal ri'i smon lam dpal ri'i gsang lam.* In *Klong chen snying thig rtsa pod*, vol. 1, 213–20. Kathmandu: Shechen Publications, 1994.

———. *'Jigs-med-gling-pa'i rnam thar.* Chengdu, China: Si khron mi rigs dpe skrun khang, 1998.

Khenpo Chemchok. *Dpal chen 'dus pa'i zin bris.* No publication data.

Khenpo Ngawang Palzang. *Wondrous Dance of Illusion: The Autobiography of Khenpo Ngawang Palzang.* Translated by Heidi L. Nevin and J. Jakob Leschly. Boulder: Shambhala Publications, 2013.

Könchok Drönme (Lushul Khenpo). *Yum ka'i zin bris kyi kha skong rig 'dzin zhal lung*. Golok, China: Sanglung Gon.

Longchenpa. *Rdzogs pa chen po ngal gso skor gsum dang rang grol skor gsum bcas pod gsum*. 3 vols. Adzom, P.R.C.: A-'dzom 'brug-pa chos-sgar, n.d.

———. *Rdzogs pa chen po sems nyid ngal gso*. In *Rdzogs pa chen po ngal gso skor gsum dang rang grol skor gsum bcas pod gsum*, vol. 1, 5–116. Adzom, P.R.C.: A-'dzom 'brug-pa chos-sgar, 1999. Translation: Dri-med-'od-zer, Klon-chen-pa, and Herbert V. Guenther. *Kindly Bent to Ease Us: Mind*. Berkeley, CA: Dharma Publishing, 1975.

———. *Rdzogs pa chen po sems nyid ngal gso'i 'grel pa shing rta chen po*. In *Rdzogs pa chen po ngal gso skor gsum dang rang grol skor gsum bcas pod gsum*, vol. 1–2. Adzom, P.R.C.: A-'dzom 'brug-pa chos-sgar, 1999.

———. *Rdzogs pa chen po sems nyid ngal gso'i 'grel pa shing rta chen po (glegs bam phyi ma)*. In *Rdzogs pa chen po ngal gso skor gsum dang rang grol skor gsum bcas pod gsum*, vol. 2, 1–380. Adzom, P.R.C.: A-'dzom 'brug-pa chos-sgar, 1999.

Ngari Panchen Pema Wangyal. *Bla ma bka' brgyad rig 'dzin yongs 'dus*. In *Rin chen gter mdzod chen mo*, vol. 10, 353–521. Stod lung mtshur phu'i par khang edition. Paro, Bhutan: Ngodrup and Sherab Drimay, 1976.

Patrul Rinpoche. *Srog sdom gzer bzhi'i dmigs pa'i gnad 'gags khams gsum rol pa'i tshangs pa'i sgra dbyangs*. In *O rgyan 'jigs med chos kyi dbang po'i gsung 'bum*. Lhasa blockprints, vol. 4, 485–502. Gangtok, Sikkim: Sonam Topgay Kazi, 1970–1971. Translation: "The Melody of Brahma Reveling in the Three Realms: Key Points for Meditating on the Four Stakes that Bind the Life-Force." In *Deity, Mantra, and Wisdom: Development Stage Meditation in Tibetan Buddhist Tantra*. Translated by Dharmachakra Translation Committee, 81–95. Ithaca, NY: Snow Lion, 2007.

Rdo rje phur pa rtsa ba'i rgyud kyi dum bu, Fragment of the Root Tantra. In Martin Boord, *A Bolt of Lightning from the Blue: The Vast Commentary on Vajrakila That Clearly Defines the Essential Points*, Episode II, 79–92. Berlin: Khordong, 2002.

Sangye Lingpa. *Ma 'ongs lungs bstan gsang ba'i dkar chag bkod pa*. In *Bla ma dgongs 'dus*, vol. 6, 65–605. Gangtok, Sikkim: Sonam Topge Kazi, 1972.

Shantideva. *The Way of the Bodhisattva*. Translated by the Padmakara Translation Group. Boston: Shambhala Publications, 2011.

———. *Shiksasamuchaya. Bslab pa kun las btus pa'i tshig le'ur byas pa*. In *Dergé Tengyur*, dbu ma khi, ff. 1b–3a. Translation: Śāntideva, Cecil Bendall, and W. H. D. Rouse. *Śikśā Samuccaya: A Compendium of Buddhist Doctrine*. Delhi, India: Motilal Banarsidass Publisher, 2006.

Tantra of Self-Arising Rigpa. Rig pa rang shar chen po'i rgyud. In *Nyingma Gyubum*, vol. da, 323–693. Mtshams brag edition. Thimpu, Bhutan: National Library, Royal Government of Bhutan, 1982.

Trengpo Tertön Sherab Özer. *Grol tig dgongs pa rang grol bla ma rig 'dzin kun 'dus*. In *Rin chen gter mdzod chen mo*, vol. 11, 187–354. Stod lung mtshur phu'i par khang edition. Paro, Bhutan: Ngodrup and Sherab Drimay, 1976.

Two Segment Hevajra Root Tantra. Dgyes pa rdo rje rtsa ba'i rgyud brtag pa nyis pa. No publication data.

Zangpo Drakpa. "The Prayer in Seven Chapters to Padmakara, the Second Buddha." In *Nyingma Monlam Prayer Book–Bilingual Edition*, 106–64. Bylakuppe, India: Nyingma Monlam Chenmo International Foundation, 2016.

REFERENCES

A Great Treasure of Blessings. London: The Tertön Sogyal Trust, 2004.

Beer, Robert. *The Handbook of Tibetan Buddhist Symbols.* Boston: Shambhala Publications, 2003.

Boord, Martin. *A Bolt of Lightning from the Blue: The Vast Commentary on Vajrakīla That Clearly Defines the Essential Points.* Berlin: Khordong, 2002.

Brunnhölzl, Karl, trans. *Groundless Paths: The Prajnaparamita Sutras, The Ornament of Clear Realization, and Its Commentaries in the Tibetan Nyingma Tradition.* Ithaca: Snow Lion, 2012.

Chögyam Trungpa. *Shambhala: The Sacred Path of the Warrior.* In *The Collected Works of Chögyam Trungpa*, vol. 8. Boston: Shambhala Publications, 2004.

Dilgo Khyentse Rinpoche. *Brilliant Moon: The Autobiography of Dilgo Khyentse.* Boston: Shambhala Publications, 2009.

———. *Primordial Purity: Oral Instructions on the Three Words That Strike the Vital Point.* Translated by Ane Jinba Palmo. Restricted title. Halifax: Vajravairochana Translation Committee, 1999.

———. *The Wish-Fulfilling Jewel: The Practice of Guru Yoga According to the Longchen Nyingthig Tradition.* Boston: Shambhala Publications, 1999.

Dodrupchen Jigme Tenpe Nyima. *Mkhas shing grub pa'i dbang phyug chen po rdo grub chen 'jigs med bstan pa'i nyi ma dpal bzang po'i gsung 'bum legs bshad nor bu'i bang mdzod.* 7 vols. Chengdu, China: Si khron mi rigs dpe skrun khang, 2003.

———. *Rta khyung bsnyel tho rin chen sgron med.* In *Rdo grub chen 'jigs med bstan pa'i nyi ma gsung 'bum*, vol. 4, 273–90. Chengdu, China: Si khron mi rigs dpe skrun khang, 2003.

Dodrupchen Rinpoche the Fourth, Thupten Trinlé Pal Zangpo. *Klong snying rig 'dzin thugs sgrub dang 'brel ba'i dkyil 'khor sgrub mchod kyi khog dbub dngos grub gter mdzod.* Gangtok, Sikkim: Soman Topgay Kazi, 1970–1971.

Dzongsar Khyentse Rinpoche. *Rigdzin Düpa Manual.* 5th edition. Lodeve, France: Rigpa, 2005.

Jamgön Kongtrul Lodrö Tayé. *Rin chen gter mdzod chen mo.* 111 vols. Stod lung mtshur phu'i par khang edition. Paro, Bhutan: Ngodrup and Sherab Drimay, 1976.

———. *Zab mo'i gter dang gter ston grub thob ji ltar byon pa'i lo rgyus mdor bsdus bkod pa rin chen bai durya'i phreng ba.* In *Rin chen gter mdzod chen mo*, vol. 1, 357–782. New Delhi: Shechen Publications, 2007.

Jigme Lingpa. *Gsang ba chen po nyams snang gi rtogs brjod chu zla'i gar mkhan.* In

Klong chen snying thig rtsa pod, vol. 1, 19–70. Kathmandu: Shechen Publications, 1994.

———. *Rdo rje sems dpa' la brten pa'i bla ma'i rnal 'byor mngon dga'i zhing sbyong.* In *Klong chen snying thig rtsa pod*, vol. 4: 205–207. Kathmandu: Shechen Publications, 1994.

———. *Rtogs pa brjod pa dakki'i gsang gtam chen mo.* In *Klong chen snying thig rtsa pod*, vol. 1, 5–17. Kathmandu: Shechen Publications, 1994.

———. *Bskyed rim gyi rnam gzhag 'og min bgrod pa'i them skas.* In *Jigs med gling pa'i bka' 'bum*, vol. 11, 143–96. Paro, Bhutan: Lama Ngodrup and Sherab Demy, 1985.

Jigme Lingpa et al. *Klong chen snying thig rtsa pod.* 5 vols. Kathmandu: Shechen Publications, 1994.

———. *Klong chen snying thig gi 'don cha.* Rdo grub dgon gyi lugs. Gangtok, Sikkim, India: Pema Thinley for Dodrupchen Rinpoche, 1985a.

———. *Rig 'dzin bsnyen yig dngos grub gyi za ma tog.* Sikkim, India: Choten Gonpa, 1985b.

———. *Rig 'dzin gyi gab byang gnad kyi mig tshags.* Sikkim, India: Choten Gonpa, n.d.

Jigme Lingpa, Jamyang Khyentse Wangpo, Patrul Rinpoche, and Chokyi Drakpa. *A Guide to the Practice of Ngöndro.* Lodeve, France: Rigpa, 2006.

Jigme Lingpa and Longchen Yeshe Dorje. *Treasury of Precious Qualities: Book One.* Translated by Padmakara Translation Group. Boston: Shambhala Publications, 2001.

Jigme Lingpa, Patrul Rinpoche, and Getse Mahapandita. *Deity, Mantra, and Wisdom: Development Stage Meditation in Tibetan Buddhist Tantra.* Translated by Dharmachakra Translation Committee. Ithaca, NY: Snow Lion, 2007.

Khangsar Tenpe Wangchuk. *Skyabs rje khang sar rin po che dbon sprul bstan pa'i dbang phyug gi gsung 'bum.* 5 vols. Beijing, China: Mi rigs dpe skrun khang, 2005.

Khenpo Karthar Rinpoche. *Karma Chakme's Mountain Dharma, vol. 2.* Woodstock, NY: KTD Publications, 2006.

Khenpo Ngawang Pelzang. *Rtogs brjod sgyu ma'i rol gar (The Autobiography of Pema Ledreltsal [Khenpo Ngawang Palzang]).* India: Jatral Rinpoche. Translation: *Wondrous Dance of Illusion: The Autobiography of Khenpo Ngawang Palzang.* Translated by Heidi L. Nevin and J. Jakob Leschly. Boulder: Shambhala Publications, 2013.

———. *A Guide to the Words of My Perfect Teacher.* Boston: Shambhala Publications, 2004.

Klong chen snying thig gi gtor dpe 'di nyid mdo mkhyen brtse ye shes rdo rje'i phyag bzhed ltar bkod pa. In *Klong chen snying thig gi bla ma rig 'dzin 'dus pa'i gdang rol nyung ngu blo gsal mgul rgyan gtor ma'i dpe'u ris bcas dang pad gling gi dbyangs yig*, vol. 1. Thimphu, Bhutan: Pema Kunkhyab, 1985.

Longchen Rabjampa. *The Great Chariot: A Treatise on the Great Perfection.* Translated by C. Ives Waldo III. Edited by Connie Miller. www.sacred-texts.com/bud/tib/chariot.htm.

"Meaningful to Behold" the Official Bilingual Prayer Book of the Nyingma Monlam Chenmo Great Prayer Ceremony for World Peace, Bodhgaya. Bylakuppe, India: Nyingma Monlam Chenmo International Foundation, 2016.

Mipham Rinpoche. *Gateway to Knowledge.* 4 vols. Hong Kong: Rangjung Yeshe Publications, 2004.

Jamgön Mipham. *Luminous Essence: A Guide to the Guhyagarbha Tantra.* Translated by Dharmachakra Translation Committee. Ithaca, NY: Snow Lion, 2009.

Mtshams brag rnying ma rgyud 'bum. Thimpu, Bhutan: National Library, Royal Government of Bhutan, 1982.

Orgyen Lingpa. *Pad ma bka' thang.* Beijing: Mi rigs dpe skrun khang, 1996. Translation: Yeshe Tsogyal. *The Life and Liberation of Padmasambhava (Padma bKa'i Thang).* 2 vols. Berkeley: Dharma Publishing, 1978.

Padmasambhava and Jamgön Kongtrul. *The Light of Wisdom, Volume 2: A Collection of Padmasambhava's Advice to the Dakini Yeshe Tsogyal and Other Close Disciples.* Translated by Erik Pema Kunsang. Hong Kong: Rangjung Yeshe Publications, 1998.

Padmasambhava and Jamgön Mipham. *A Garland of Views: A Guide to View, Meditation, and Result in the Nine Vehicles.* Translated by Padmakara Translation Group. Boulder: Shambhala Publications, 2016.

Patrul Rinpoche. *O rgyan 'jigs med chos kyi dbang po'i gsung 'bum*, vol. 8. Chengdu, China: Si khron mi rigs dpe skrun khang, 2003.

———. *The Words of My Perfect Teacher.* Revised. New Haven, CT: Yale University Press, 2010.

Sangye Lingpa. *Bla ma dgongs 'dus.* 13 vols. Gangtok, Sikkim: Sonam Topge Kazi, 1972.

———. *Bla ma dgongs pa 'dus pa las ma 'ongs lung bstan bka' rgya ma'i skor.* Gangtok, Sikkim: Sherab Gyaltsen Lama, 1983.

Shantideva. *The Way of the Bodhisattva.* Translated by Padmakara Translation Group. Boston: Shambhala Publications, 2011.

Sutra of the Ten Bhumis. Dashabhūmikasūtra. Sa bcu pa'i mdo. Toh. 44:31. Translation: M. Honda. "An Annotated Translation of the 'Daśabhūmika.'" In *Studies in South, East and Central Asia*, Śatapitaka Series 74, ed. D. Sinor, 115–276. New Delhi: International Academy of Indian Culture, 1968.

Tulku Thondup. *The Heart of Unconditional Love: A Powerful New Approach to Loving-Kindness Meditation.* Boulder: Shambhala Publications, 2015.

———. *Masters of Meditation and Miracles: Lives of the Great Buddhist Masters of India and Tibet.* Boston: Shambhala Publications, 2002.

Tulku Thondup Rinpoche. *Hidden Teachings of Tibet: An Explanation of the Terma Tradition of Tibetan Buddhism.* Edited by Harold Talbott. Boston: Wisdom Publications, 1999.

van Schaik, Sam. *Approaching the Great Perfection: Simultaneous and Gradual Methods of Dzogchen Practice in the Longchen Nyingtig.* Boston: Wisdom Publications, 2004.

Yeshe Tsogyal. *The Lotus-Born: The Life Story of Padmasambhava.* Translated by Erik Pema Kunsang. Boston: Shambhala Publications, 1993.

INDEX

Akanishtha, 48, 55, 61, 75, 82, 115, 150, 157
all-pervading space, 71, 75, 149, 164
  of great simplicity, 32
  of phenomena, 130
  of primordial purity, 40
  resting in, 88
  wisdom and, 22, 27, 57–58, 98, 103, 121,
    123
Amitabha, 131
Amitayus, 11–12
amrita (medicinal nectar), 59–60, 135
  in annihilation, 79
  in blessing offerings, 36, 37
  in cheto, 82, 84
  offering, 3, 73, 170, 171–72
annihilation, 77–79, 81–82, 153–55,
  154–55
Anuttarayoga Tantra. See Highest Yoga
  Tantra
Anuyoga, 5, 39–40, 102, 104, 119, 121,
  223n2, 236n15
appearances
  controlling, 166
  as deity, 39, 41–42, 98, 109, 139–40,
    147, 153
  emptiness and, 4, 121–22, 128, 129–30,
    135–36, 162
  existence and, 70, 112, 125, 144
  impure, 27, 30, 79, 92, 97–99, 110
  nature of, 32, 41, 108, 113
  purifying attachment to, 23–24, 119–
    20, 185
  setting the boundary of, 32, 112
  See also clear appearance
approach and accomplishment
  accomplishment, 9, 69–70
  approach, 7–9, 63–68, 141, 237n36
  confidence in, 21–23
  key points of practice, 70–72
  postmediation and, 88–89
  prayers and blessings in, 23–25

preparation for, 3–7
seven preliminary sections, 24–33
aspirational level, 4, 8, 166, 237n48
Atiyoga, 40, 103–5, 118–20, 126, 236n15.
  See also Dzogchen
authentic presence (wang tang), 82, 156–
  57, 233n101
awareness, pure. See rigpa

bardo, 40–41, 102
bells, blessing of, 23–24, 228n31
Bhurkumkuta, 18
birth, four modes of, 5, 40, 41, 46,
  99–104, 119, 121, 140
blessings, descent of, 5, 33–35, 86, 113–16,
  171, 183–84
bliss, great
  in accomplishment, 69–70
  in blessings, 115–16, 177
  and deity, uniting, 71
  in empowerments, 179, 187
  and emptiness, unity of, 6, 24, 47, 51,
    60, 102, 125, 148
  experiences of, 35, 63–64, 66, 75, 80,
    136–37
  of mantra, 7, 92, 120, 140–41, 166–67
  in offerings, 36, 76, 79, 108, 134–35, 144
  palace as, 46, 83, 158–59
  tiklé of, 101
blue yogini, 54, 140–41
bodhichitta, 72
  absolute, 4, 25, 106–7
  in empowerments, 181
  in four thoughts, 14
  generating, 3–4, 15, 25, 89–90
  red and white, 185
  relative, 25, 107
bodhisattvas, eight, 6, 49, 127, 128
bone ornaments, 49, 52–54, 127, 140,
  231n64
Buddha Kashyapa, 1, 2

of equality, 60, 116, 123
gathering accumulation of, 8
innate, views on, 38, 39
paramita of, 4
and space, indivisibility of, 98, 103
symbols of, 6, 24, 46
See also five wisdoms
wisdom dakinis, 83, 158–59, 179–80, 184, 185
wisdom nectar, 48, 74, 75, 79–81, 82–84, 116, 150, 156
Words of the Vidyadhara That Bestow the

Majesty of Great Bliss, The (Khenpo Chemchok), 95, 158
wrathful activity, 81–82, 92, 156
wrathful deities, nine dance expressions of, 129

Yeshe Tsogyal, 35, 188, 228n25
yoga of prana and bindu, 38–39. *See also* tsalung
Yoga Tantra, 7, 50, 101
Yumka Dechen Gyalmo, 20, 40, 104, 227–28n18